The Web Architect's Handbook

• • • •

The
Web Architect's
Handbook

Charles Stross

ADDISON WESLEY

Harlow, England · Reading, Massachusetts · Menlo Park, California

New York · Don Mills, Ontario · Amsterdam · Bonn · Sydney · Singapore

Tokyo · Madrid · San Juan · Milan · Mexico City · Seoul · Taipei

© Addison Wesley Longman 1996

Addison Wesley Longman Limited
Edinburgh Way
Harlow
Essex
CM20 2JE

The programs in this book have been included for their instructional value, They have been tested with care but are not guaranteed for any particular purpose. The publisher does not offer any warranties or representation, nor does it accept any liabilities with respect to the programs.

Many of the designations used by manufacturers and sellers to distinguish their products are claimed as trademarks. Addison-Wesley has made every attempt to supply trademark information about manufacturers and their products mentioned in this book. A list of the trademark designations and their owners appears on p.viii.

Cover designed by op den Brouw, Design & Illustration, Reading
and printed by The Riverside Printing Co. (Reading) Ltd.
Typeset by Pantek Arts, Maidstone, Kent.
Printed in Great Britain at the University Press, Cambridge.

First printed 1996

ISBN 0-201-87735-X

British Library Cataloguing in Publication Data
A catalogue record for this book is available from the British Library.

Library of Congress Cataloging in Publication Data applied for.

Contents

Contents

Typographical conventions

It is hoped that the context in which sections of HTML and program source code appear in the text should be fairly obvious. However, as a general rule the following typographical conventions have been observed:

Filenames   In running text, the names of files and directories are formatted in italics.

Source code   Program source code (in Perl) appears in monospaced courier.

HTML   HTML (hypertext markup language) appears in monospaced courier.

Program names   The names of executable programs (run under UNIX by typing the program name) appear in boldface where they are embedded in running text.

Trademark notice

Acrobat™, PhotoShop™, Display Postscript™, SiteMill™ and Postscript™ are trademarks of Adobe Systems, Inc.
Cray™ is a trademark of Cray Research, Inc.
Delphi™ is a trademark of Borland International, Inc.
Director™ is a trademark of Macromedia, Inc.
Frontier™ and ClayBasket™ are trademarks of Userland
HoTMetal Pro™ is a trademark of Softquad
Iced Java™ is a trademark of Dimension X
Informix™ is a trademark of Informix Software Inc.
Java™, SparcServer™, SunOS™ and Solaris™ are trademarks of Sun Microsystems, Inc.
Lycos™ is a trademark of Lycos, Inc.
Macintosh® is a registered trademark and Appletalk™, Applesearch™, AppleEvents™, Quadra™, Newton™, Messagepad™, MacOS™, Applescript™, MPW™, Macintosh Classic II™, Power Macintosh™, MacTCP™ are trademarks of Apple Computer, Inc.
Microsoft® is a registered trademark and DOS™, Windows™, Windows/NT™, Microsoft Word™, Microsoft Internet Explorer™, Windows 95™, Microsoft HTML Assistant™, Microsoft SGML Explorer™, Microsoft Network™, Excell™ and FoxPro™ are trademarks of Microsoft Corporation
Mosaic™ is a trademark of National Center for Supercomputing Applications
Motif™ is a trademark of Software Foundation
MVS™ is a trademark of International Business Machines Corporation
NetBSB™ is a trademark of Berkley Software Design
Netscape™, WebForce™, Netscape Navigator Gold™ and Netsite Commerce Server™ are trademarks of Netscape Communications Corporation
Oracle™ is a trademark of Oracle Corporation UK Limited
Pentium® is a registered trademark of Intel Corporation
Saturn® is a registered trademark of Dega International
UNIX™ and SCO UNIX™ are trademarks of SCO, Inc.
VAX™, VMS™ and PDP-11™ are trademarks of Digital Equipment Corporation
WAIS™ is a trademark of AOL Productions, Inc.
WebStar™ and MacHTTP™ are trademarks of Star NINE
X™ is a trademark of MIT X Windows Consortium
Yahoo™ is a trademark of Yahoo, Inc.

Acknowledgements

No book is written in a vacuum, this one least of all. Many people contributed to this project in various ways. I owe a lot to Gavin Bell, Jon Crowcroft, Jonathon Fletcher, Matthias Neerarcher, Dave and Jenny Raggett, Lincoln Stein, Bill Thompson and George Weir for their invaluable guidance and expertise during the gestation of the project. Thanks are also due to Fearghas, Libby and the other staff at fma Ltd for putting up with my eccentric sabbatical requirements; to my parents and sister for general moral support; and to Feorag, who has now discovered why authors' partners usually get mentioned in the acknowledgements. Last but not least, this book wouldn't have come to term with the enthusiastic and excellent help of Addison-Wesley's editors, namely Nicky Jaeger (commissioning and editing) and Sheila Chatten (production and subbing).

Charlie Stross
Edinburgh, March 1996

INTRODUCTION

• • • •

The World Wide Web (WWW) is less than five years old, but growing very fast. As a result, standards and file formats proliferate; there is confusion in the streets and despondency in the palaces; and nobody is quite sure what it all means. In the rush to get on the web, everybody is going through the same painful learning process. It usually starts with the first sight of a web browser – typically Mosaic (in one of its many incarnations) or Netscape – and the introduction to the dizzy idea of globe-spanning hypertext. The next stage is the formation of the idea 'Why can't I write some of this stuff?' This is followed by endless confusion as the basic ideas of the HyperText Markup Language (HTML) and hyperlinks (URLs) are absorbed. And then ... more confusion. 'Why don't my pages work? How do I add interactive pages or forms? Why does the logo in my web page have a different coloured background from the page? How do I ensure that my web is still readable in ten years' time?'

This book aims to clarify some of the issues by describing the fundamental principles underlying the web. Along the way, it explains how to plan, design, write and maintain webs. In this context, a web is a collection of hypertext documents stored on a web server and accessible over the Internet. The documents may be simple files containing text and hyperlinks, or they may be complex 'virtual pages' – generated by software running on the computer. It is relatively easy to write a simple personal information web, but large publications, such as a book or sales catalogue, are much harder to organize. Complex webs typically consist of hundreds or even thousands of files; virtual libraries that can rapidly deteriorate into chaos if they are not adequately planned and maintained. In this book I will describe some techniques for designing (and maintaining) medium-to-large hypertext webs, and give a concise overview of the standards and tools available to the professional web author.

What this book contains

No book on the web is complete without an introduction to HTML, but HTML is not the only constituent of the web. This book starts with a brief introduction and tutorial on HTML, and discusses some of the different sub-types of HTML that have sprung up in its short history.

No discussion of HTML is complete without an explanation of HTTP, the HyperText Transport Protocol. If HTML is the cargo, HTTP is the truck that delivers it to your door; without at least some understanding of HTTP, it is not possible to understand how hyperlinks work, how best to structure webs, or indeed how to write programs that run over webs.

HTML is an application of a much more general markup language called SGML; few web browsers use SGML yet (or its multimedia extensions, HyTime), but HTML is a development of SGML so a brief look at this burgeoning field is essential in order to put the state of HTML today in the context of its likely future. Other web document formats and style sheet systems are touched upon, including setext, Adobe Acrobat, and DSSSL-Lite, but as these are not yet central to the web they are not described in detail: the web is still primarily HTML based, and the move to a three-level open document system (consisting of authoring/storage language, style sheet/markup language and page layout language) is some way off.

The Perl programming language has become particularly popular among web architects because its design goal – quickly and conveniently churning through huge volumes of text and making changes – makes it ideal for web tools. It is also the language of choice for writing 'dynamic pages' – programs that run on web servers and *generate* HTML, in response to user requests. These are essential components of any web with pretensions towards interactivity. Therefore this book contains a brief introduction to the basics of Perl (in case you haven't met 'the UNIX Swiss Army chainsaw' before), and several example programs written in that language. It also contains a discussion of some of the commonly available tools for maintaining and checking webs (many of which are written in Perl), and of the Perl software library for handling the world wide web.

Big collections of documents need automatic tools to keep them updated and in step with each other. There are few web maintenance tools on the market at present, although some are now beginning to appear. Consequently, it's handy to be able to structure and maintain your own webs. A discussion of one of the commonest HTTP servers, the NCSA httpd program, is included along with some comments about server security and portability of webs between servers.

One of the problems of maintaining large webs is to provide access to all the information stored in them. Although most world wide web information is stored as HTML files, it may not be possible to massage your data into this format. Therefore it is useful to know how to handle foreign file formats and to search huge archives rapidly (using search engines such as WAIS or glimpse). It is also handy to be aware of the advantages and limitations of servers running on different platforms. Web servers exist for UNIX, VAX/VMS, MS-DOS, Microsoft Windows, the Macintosh system and almost every other computer system that has been connected to the Internet. However, some servers are more useful than others – and this is quite important when planning dynamic webs because, unlike HTML documents, the scripts that generate web pages on a server may not run under different environments. (Versions of Perl exist for VMS, DOS, Macintosh and the UNIX family, and are generally available free of charge; another reason for using Perl as a toolbox.)

One of the main reasons the Internet is growing at present is its unparalleled potential for commerce in information. It should be no surprise that the net (which started life as an academic/military research project) is rapidly turning into a marketplace. The world wide web predates the overt commercialization of the net, and does not (in its original form) contain mechanisms that permit billing and electronic fund transfer. However, such mechanisms are coming. Technologies for selling information and services include: the use of encryption (to protect network traffic from snoopers), a 'next generation' hypertext transport protocol (HTTP-NG) with support for billing, verification and copyright protection, the SSL protocol for secure HTTP transactions, and the use of out-of-band communications to permit orders to be made against accounts established through other (trusted) channels. All these techniques are discussed, although it should be stressed that commerce on the web is evolving so fast that anything written today may be edging towards obsolescence in twelve months.

Moving beyond the local web, how do you go about handing really huge collections of hypertext? An automated search of the world wide web as a whole discovered over 800 000 documents in November 1994. As of mid-1995, no accurate figure for the size of the web was available, except that it is known to be in excess of four million documents (the number indexed by the Lycos search engine). Such a vast body of knowledge may be extremely valuable, if it can be catalogued and indexed. Furthermore, if you maintain a web you probably want to use pointers to other web resources, where they're available, to reduce the storage requirements on your own server. But the web is like the sea: it's never still, and what is rock solid one week may be gone by the next. Automatic search engines (spiders) fill a valuable niche by providing the capability to check for the existence of documents on the web, and to check the web for non-local consistency. However, their use is fraught with numerous pitfalls and hazards (some of which are not immediately obvious), and should be undertaken only with caution. This book describes the use and abuse of spiders, and explains how to use them safely (and when not to use them).

Finally, some words on hypertext in general. The concept of hypertext is not new; over twenty-five years have passed since Ted Nelson first saw a PDP-8 and had a radically innovative vision of his personal Xanadu. Hypertext is still a long way from fulfilling its true potential; constraints of bandwidth, and the very philosophy underpinning most commercial attempts to use it, frustrate its current success. This is primarily a book about the theory of the web, but I couldn't resist the temptation to finish with a look at what the future may hold for us.

What this book doesn't contain

This isn't a book about learning to use Mosaic, Netscape, or any other web browser. It isn't an introduction to connecting yourself to the Internet. It isn't a book about writing HTML, either, although it covers some of the same ground at high speed. Nor is it a full-blown tutorial guide to programming in Perl; if you don't already know Perl it will be useful to have such a book to hand when you are reading this one.

I've been unable to cover adequately some very recent developments in the web, notably VRML and Java. Both of these will in due course revolutionize the Internet, but it is somewhat difficult to write a book about them when no mainstream applications of these languages are yet out of beta-test, only the programmers who invented them can boast more than twelve months' experience in the field, and even the developer documentation is patchy.

In writing this book, my goal has been to provide a comprehensive understanding of the principles, standards and architecture of the web, along with some specific insight into how each area of the web works. Any chapter of this book could easily be expanded into a book in its own right; that is both a strength and a weakness of this approach. (I didn't want to write a 'doorstop'; nor did I want to concentrate on one field to the exclusion of others – for example, by writing a monograph about inline images and all there is to know about them.)

Wherever possible I have tried to provide references to external web resources which contain material supplementing or supporting this book. Your best aid when using this book will be a web browser and a live Internet connection. You can find additional supplementary information, pointers, source code to programs and updates on the web site I maintain:

```
http://www.fma.com/webbook/
```

Before the WWW: a potted history of the Internet

The world wide web is the most sophisticated expression of the Internet to date. The Internet was born in the early 1970s, a bastard child of academia and the US government's Advanced Research Projects Agency (ARPA). ARPAnet was a government-run network, established to tie ARPA sites and defence contractors together. A backbone of leased lines stretched between sites where modified DEC minicomputers kept track of data packets and acted as gateways to the local mainframes. Researchers at one or another site could log onto mainframes at other sites via the ARPAnet, send and receive electronic mail and move files around the net – all without needing to set up a modem connection or post a tape.

During the 1970s, the ARPAnet was seen to be a good thing; it improved productivity among the computer scientists with access to it, and greatly enhanced their ability to communicate. Universities got in on the act, initially tentatively, then with more and more complex networks of their own. In the late 1970s and early 1980s, as UNIX became an academic standard, UUnet (the UNIX network based on the UUCP protocol) began to expand and finally interfaced with ARPAnet directly.

The 1980s saw continued growth, which became explosive around 1987 as virtually every university in the United States came online. In the late 1980s the ARPAnet was slowly replaced as a backbone carrier by NSFnet, the National Science Foundation's network. At the same time, UNIX workstations running the TCP/IP protocols used to carry Internet communications became standard in academia, and the Internet Protocols (the IP in TCP/IP) began to leak out into the commercial universe.

TCP/IP is a flexible networking protocol, an alternative to the OSI reference model for networking. TCP/IP can run on top of just about any kind of hardware, from a pair of Crays communicating over a T3 link to a pair of Babbage engines connected by two tin cans and a length of string. It relies on splitting data up into packets for transmission via any available route; these packets are reassembled at the receiving end and transformed back into the original data. TCP/IP stacks (the software interfaces that permit communications using the protocol) are available for all flavours of UNIX, for most mainframe systems, for the PC and Macintosh, and can run on top of a variety of networks (including Ethernet, token ring, Appletalk and modems).

The Internet is the name now given to the collection of computers that are linked together via TCP/IP (and more primitive protocols, such as UUCP). Many are connected by permanent leased lines, while others dial in over modems. TCP/IP hosts have a unique numerical IP address, which is mapped to a more easily memorable name. By using the name in conjunction with lookup tables, it is possible to read from or write to files on any other computer on the Internet that you have permission to access.

Until about 1991, the Internet was mainly used by academics and governments, but this pattern changed rapidly through the early 1990s, until by 1994 the majority of traffic on the net was commercial in origin.

The one thing that impeded the acceptance of the Internet in the commercial sector, if anything, was the lack of a single application that was so obviously necessary that people would go out and get themselves connected just so they could run that single application. Getting an Internet connection isn't free; even a cheap home connection via modem costs a noticeable amount, and a full-scale leased line connection costs even more. These prices will not move significantly until commercial cable providers begin providing low-cost bandwidth to the kerb, a process which is expected later in the decade.

While academics, students and UNIX industry workers became used to the convenience of email and FTP, there was until recently little or no commercial pressure to make use of the net. After all, email more or less duplicates the existing media of fax and telephone, while FTP presents potential security holes – if files can come in, what's to stop them going out? Ignorance of the Internet has been a major factor in slowing its uptake in the commercial arena. Ignorance has also been a major factor in making people who want email go to commercial services that offer only a mailbox, rather than the full TCP/IP connectivity that would allow them to run network applications across the Internet.

However, there's one thing the Internet is really good at that no commercial service can provide, and that's access to information distributed across servers. The Internet has spawned a myriad of client–server applications, starting with the email servers that use SMTP to route messages to their destinations, and working up to the NNTP servers that transport Network News, a vast distributed bulletin board. Postings made to a discussion area or 'newsgroup' are transported across the Internet from server to server, so that the contents of a group propagate worldwide; each server stores an image of the entire news system, and you can access it by using a client application or 'newsreader'. While it sounds more complex than a Bulletin Board messaging System (BBS), it looks and feels very similar – except that no simple BBS will let you talk to a forum read by a quarter of a million people worldwide.

The distributed client–server model is important. If you want to read news or collect your mail, you run a client application that makes a network connection to a server, which might easily be on another continent; your client invisibly (to you) asks for the information you need, and the server punts it at you. In the background, the servers talk to each other, making sure that anything you send to one server is forwarded to all the other servers that need to know about it. In this way, the Internet stores vast amounts of information in a distributed manner.

But how do you get at it?

An historical detour

A long time ago, in a land far away, there lived a wise man who had never seen a computer. One day, he met his first minicomputer, and saw that it was good: only his idea for what you could do with it was so utterly at odds with the Way Things Were that it took two decades for them to bear fruit. In the meantime, the wise man wrote books, kicked ass and generally raised everybody's consciousness about his wonderful new use for a computer or computer network. He even attempted to bring his idea to market, but was defeated by circumstance on several occasions.

His name is Ted Nelson. His commercial project was called Xanadu. And his new use for a computer was called hypertext.

Admittedly, the idea of linking references in a document to the actual text they refer to was not Nelson's idea; the earliest technical description of such a device was produced by the early computing pioneer Vannevar Bush, in a seminal paper entitled 'The way we think'. Bush described a hypothetical machine (which he called a Memex) that enabled a scientist or engineer or scholar to cross-reference their library of files in such a way that they could easily browse the interrelation of facts and opinions. Nelson, however, took the idea much, much further. Xanadu was to be a computer-based distributed hypertext – and a multi-user one at that. Any text you entered into Xanadu would be able to reference, or actually contain, any other text in the system. Anyone to whom you granted permission could browse it. In time, Xanadu would come to be a commercial marketplace for information; documents containing pointers to original papers would be as valuable as, or more valuable than, the originals. Hypertext is the ultimate answer to the indexer's dilemma of making information accessible. Ted Nelson saw this in the 1960s, and set out to bring it to the people.

Still, Project Xanadu foundered. It is hard to convince any corporation to invest in an open-ended project of a speculative nature. It is harder still to keep promoting an idea for years in the wilderness. Demonstrations of Xanadu notwithstanding, it has still not come to market; development continues, but in the meantime the idea of hypertext has come of age.

In 1992, a new client–server protocol, with new browser tools and new servers, made its tentative appearance on the Internet. No other utility has caused such excitement, or grown in popularity as fast, as the world wide web. The web is a distributed hypertext system à la Xanadu. It is not as sophisticated as Ted Nelson's dream – but it is here today, and it works.

CERN and the WWW project

The world wide web started out as an attempt to control an information explosion. For many years, the CERN research institute in Switzerland has been one of the world's leading centres for research into particle physics. Like many academic sites, CERN has a large computer network linked to the Internet. The job of the computer support department at CERN is to support the work of the institution; and like many IS departments in the late 1980s and early 1990s, CERN had been experiencing difficulties in getting information where it was needed.

The problem was simple. A large scientific research institute generates a flood of information; not confidential documents that need to be kept secret, but stuff that should actually be disseminated. Existing information servers running over the networks were just not good enough; WAIS (Wide Area Information Server) databases could provide free-text retrieval on keywords, and Gopher servers could serve up documents accessed via hierarchical menus, but there was nothing even approaching the flexibility of Vannevar Bush's Memex, outlined forty-five years earlier, let alone Ted Nelson's Xanadu. And these were the networked tools; the proprietary systems were even worse, limited to running on a single operating system or type of computer.

Growing frustration with the existing tools prompted Tim Berners-Lee to write a proposal in late 1989 for a new information system; a hypertext system that, rather than being a program, defined a protocol. In principle, any client program (viewer) could use the protocol to talk over a network to any server program (file store) and request documents. So any computer capable of connecting to the global Internet could, in principle, make use of the hypertext web. Moreover, the protocol was not limited solely to text; it could recognize other file types, such as graphics images, sounds and multimedia. Text could be transferred either as raw ASCII, or formatted in a relatively simple language called HTML – hypertext markup language.

HTML files are straightforward text files with tags (formatting commands) enclosed in greater-than and less-than signs; for example text that needs to print in boldface is marked `<b>like this</b>`. For cross-references to other files, a tag called HREF (Hyper REFerence) is used, along with a URL (Universal Resource Locator).

A URL consists of the Internet protocol to use in retrieving a file, followed by the name of the server to retrieve it from and the pathname of the file being retrieved. Taken together these three bits of information tell a client application how to lay its hands on a file anywhere on the Internet. So an HTML file containing a HREF pointing to

```
http://info.cern.ch/CERN/computing.html
```

is telling the client application to create a link via HyperText Transport Protocol (HTTP) to the server `info.cern.ch` and retrieve the file *CERN/computing.html*.

The advantage of such a scheme is that any computer attached to the Internet and able to run a world wide web client can, in principle, retrieve any file stored on a server. All the server has to do is to run a server program that listens for a request for a file coming in over the network, and sends the file back out to the client.

The world wide web was such an obvious boon to the academic community that the initial development work at CERN was funded rapidly. The web was announced on the Internet in August 1990, and web software development groups started up at other institutions – notably the USA's National Center for Supercomputing Applications (NCSA).

The initial tools used for browsing the web were primitive. NCSA set up a development group which began to write code for an application that has taken on a life of its own – Mosaic. Mosaic was the acme of world wide web clients (until late 1994); a brilliantly usable hypertext reader that runs on UNIX workstations, Macintoshes and PCs (under Windows 3.1). You took a Macintosh with MacTCP and MacMosaic, or a PC with a winsock DLL and WinMosaic, plugged them into the Internet – even via a modem and a dialup line – and you suddenly had a hugely powerful information-gathering tool.

As of early December 1993, there were more than 600 000 HTML-formatted documents accessible on the web, and more than 650 servers; a total of more than two million files were available for browsing via the older, less flexible protocols that Mosaic also supports. By November 1994, the web had grown beyond comprehension; there were over 1.3 million known URLs, on tens of thousands of servers.

During mid-1994, the web began to attract commercial attention. Marc Andreesen and the other developers of Mosaic left NCSA to found a new company, Netscape Communications Corporation. During autumn 1994, the first specialist web consultancies began to appear, helping companies develop a presence on the web for marketing and sales purposes. The consultancy I work in, fma ltd, was founded in October 1994; as of December 1995, it employed twelve people and was growing rapidly.

Today – meaning 'by the earliest possible time you can have bought this book' – the web has swallowed the Internet. Commercial transactions are beginning to make it a business-friendly marketing tool, but it is a strange kind of business, because rather than broadcasting adverts at a passive audience it is necessary to entice active readers. Indexes and robots have begun to tame the web, bringing its myriad of information resources into view by organizing its content. Multimedia and dynamic documents (prepared on the fly) are beginning to mutate the nature of text, turning the written word into a much less passive kind of medium. And the resources of a thousand libraries are laid out at your fingertips, in a rich abundance of information never before so accessible to non-specialists.

The world wide web is to the Internet as the first spreadsheets were to the personal computer industry – the 'killer app' that sells it. But the Internet is potentially far greater than the PC revolution. This is the future of computing, of publishing, and of a whole new industry that has not yet learned to say its own name. In the next chapters we will look at the fundamentals on which the edifice is built.

2

UNDERSTANDING HYPERTEXT MARKUP LANGUAGE

● ● ● ●

If you've used the world wide web, you've seen documents written in HTML (HyperText Markup Language). This chapter contains an accelerated overview of standard HTML, and how to create it.

There's nothing particularly mysterious about hypertext files written in HTML. Like any word processor input document, the language consists of text interspersed with special formatting commands. Unlike a word processor document, an HTML file is not intended to be printed on paper; it is intended to be formatted (rendered) on a computer screen by a piece of software called a browser. The text is rendered in accordance with the formatting commands (tags) embedded in it.

Most word processing or typesetting packages don't show you their embedded formatting commands; they hide them in arcane storage formats, preferring to show you instead an approximation of the way the page will appear when it is printed. HTML, however, is naked. You can compose HTML using virtually any word processor or text editor; its markup tags are readable characters. There exist some specialized, syntax-directed HTML editors, and WYSIWYG HTML authoring systems such as Netscape Navigator Gold, but the fact remains that you don't have to use one to edit HTML, wheras you must use a copy of Microsoft Word to edit a Word file.

HTML is a simple application of a complex document description language called SGML (Standard Generalized Markup Language, described in the standards document ISO 8879/1, issued by the International Standards

Organization). However, it's not necessary to understand SGML to use HTML, so I'll describe SGML and its place in the scheme of things later.

When you view an HTML file using a world wide web browser, you are doing one of two things:

1 You tell the browser to open a file stored locally. The browser loads the file and shows you what it looks like.

2 You click on a hot-spot in a document (or tell your browser to load a file stored remotely). The web browser works out where the file is stored from the URL associated with the hot-spot text. It opens an HTTP connection to the server that the file is stored on and requests the file. The server sends the file (if it exists), and the browser loads the file and shows you what it looks like.

The last step – the browser loads the file and shows you what it looks like – is the one that concerns us here. The file contains HTML markup tags that tell the browser how to display it. But HTML files have to be viewed by a multitude of different browsers running on different computers, with different display capabilities. So HTML does not describe how the information is to be presented; it merely indicates the type of information that is being displayed.

A second point needs to be made at this time. You can click on a hot-spot in a document, and your web browser will load the target document associated with that hot-spot. But there is *no permanent connection* between the two files; they are not part of some overarching structure. Files can go away, either by being renamed or moved. Thus, hyperlinks in HTML are *unreliable*.

HTML tags tell the browser how to render text components of a document (entities) by declaring the entities in the document to be of a certain type; the browser is presumed to know how to deal with different types of entity. For example, graphical browsers usually display top-level headings in a larger point size than subordinate headings. However, how the browser treats entities is ultimately the browser's decision. For example, the CERN line-mode browser (which runs on dumb terminals) can only print the text in an HTML file; it does not apply any special highlighting to tags that direct it to underline or emphasize text, even though it detects them.

This is diametrically opposed to the philosophy of document presentation formats such as Adobe's Postscript, which rigidly enforces a description of the appearance of a page in such detail that the only things the display device has control of are its resolution, and whether to display the file in colour or in black and white. This is an important feature of HTML, and we'll revisit it later. HTML is not a page description language (like Postscript) that describes the layout of information on a page – rather, it describes the relationship between entities in a document, and leaves the browser to take care of displaying it.

Introducing tags

HTML actually contains two kinds of tags: those that describe attributes of text in the document, and those that define meta-information about the document itself. These don't show up when you view a document in a browser, although you can see them if you examine the HTML source of the file. They provide the browser with information about the document and its relationship to other documents in the world wide web, hence the prefix 'meta-'; the tags provide information about the information in the document. (In SGML, as opposed to HTML, you can define your own tags using a special file called a DTD – Document Type Definition. This effectively defines the structure of a document and the relationship between its components. In HTML, the tag definitions are fixed, making it a lot simpler to deal with. HTML 2.0 is, in fact, defined by an SGML DTD.)

Tags generally follow a simple format:

```
<TAG_NAME [tag attributes ...] > </TAG_NAME>
```

or

```
<TAG_NAME [tag attributes ...] > ... tagged text ...
```

The first format is used to delimit a block of text: `<TAG_NAME>` indicates that text following the tag has some attribute, while `</TAG_NAME>` ends the application of that attribute to the text. For example:

```
<B>This text is tagged in the B (boldface) tag.</B>
```

For some types of tag, the 'end' tag `</TAG_NAME>` is optional; this is usually the case where text tagged by a 'start' tag can be implicitly closed by the presence of some other 'start' tag. For example:

```
<P>
This is a new paragraph, as indicated by the preceding P tag.
Paragraphs are implicitly closed by another 'start' paragraph
tag, or by some other type of text block (such as a list, table
or form).
<P>
This second paragraph implicitly closes the previous paragraph.
```

The second format is used for some commands. Rather than applying an attribute to the text following it, it embeds some kind of object in the text or indicates some kind of markpoint. The tag parameters are simply additional commands within the tag; they vary and we'll discuss them in due course. For example:

```
<!-- this is a comment; it will not be displayed by
  the browser -->
<IMG SRC= "photograph.gif" ALT="A photograph of myself">
```

Tags sometimes have attributes that modify the way in which they are applied; these are usually optional (as denoted by their enclosure in square brackets).

Note that HTML tags are case-insensitive, that is, <B> is equivalent to <b>.

HTML document structure

A word of warning. HTML is evolving through a process in which bits are being added to the language. Wherever possible, this section takes a pragmatic approach, but sometimes it is necessary to describe two alternative syntaxes for different levels of HTML.

The general structure of an HTML 1 document is as follows:

```
<TITLE>The title of the document</TITLE>
<!-- some text goes here -->
```

The only mandatory tag that *must* be present in a basic HTML document is the TITLE tag. This indicates what the document is; most web browsers display it as a label on the window containing the document.

The more recent HTML 3 document specification has a more complex structure:

```
<HTML>
<HEAD>
<TITLE>The title of the document</TITLE>
<!-- Any other 'head' information goes here -->
</HEAD>
<BODY>
<!-- Body of document goes here -->
</BODY>
</HTML>
```

The document is enclosed in <HTML> ... </HTML> tags, which tell the browser what it's reading; that is, that it's an HTML document and not something else.

Internally, the document consists of two sections – the head and its body. The head section contains various tags that provide meta-information about the file – its title, and its relationship to other documents on the Web. (These, and other entities that refer to interdocument links, are described in 'Entering the WWW', p. 38.)

Document HEAD sections describe the document; the BODY section *is* the document. Under some circumstances, you can retrieve and examine the HEAD of a file without looking at the BODY.

Note the comment text. The tag `<!-- -->` is a comment (containing a single space); text inside it, `<!-- like this,-->` will not be displayed. It's often useful to scatter your documents with explanatory comments – notes about the document that you don't want your users to see. (Be aware, however, that the comments are downloaded across the net when someone reads your document, so don't place confidential information in them.)

The `<HEAD>` and `<BODY>` sections are, technically, optional. Your HTML documents can safely exist without them, but it's good practice to use them, for reasons which will be discussed in subsequent chapters.

The main text of the document – known as the body text – is pretty similar to any other word-processed document. It consists of text in the ISO Latin-1 codeset, also known as ISO 8859/1; this is an 8-bit superset of ASCII (originally a 7-bit codeset), the characters above 127 being reserved for various accented glyphs. Latin-1 was chosen by CERN because it can be used to represent English, and also all the main Western European languages. It is possible that future versions of HTML will support other codesets defined by the ISO 8859 committee, or possibly multibyte codesets such as Unicode, but at the time of writing support for non-European languages is not part of any accepted standard for HTML.

If this business about character sets worries you, relax. Latin-1 is virtually identical to ASCII; any text editor capable of outputting ASCII files can write acceptable HTML.

Some characters (notably < and >) have special meanings within HTML. In addition, not all keyboards can produce all the characters in Latin-1. Consequently, HTML provides two ways of referring to characters (in addition to interpreting them literally). You can enter a character by number position in the Latin-1 codeset; for example, you can specify a < symbol by typing `&#60`, and it will be interpreted as a < in the text, rather than as the beginning of a tag. You can also specify a character by its symbolic name. Because character index numbers are hard to remember, many characters are assigned a name; the < (less-than) symbol's name is 'lt' (and you can insert a literal less-than symbol in your HTML by typing `&lt;`).

HTML entities (as opposed to tags) are started by an ampersand & character, and terminated by a semi-colon ; . If an entity name begins with a # and is followed by a decimal number in the range 32–126 or 161–255, it is replaced with the character at that numerical position in the Latin-1 character set; otherwise it is replaced by the character associated with the named symbol.

Basic text formatting in HTML

HTML is the product of a collision between two schools of thought about how to create a generic text formatting language.

First let's look at the uncontroversial stuff. The basic elements of an HTML document are chunks of text, aggregated into paragraphs. Because HTML is rendered to fit different-sized windows on different systems, all HTML browsers do their own word-wrapping to fit the width of the line to the width of the window. A space character or carriage return in an HTML document is basically interpreted by a browser as an opportunity to insert a space or a line break at its own discretion. If you just type text in and separate your paragraphs with blank lines, the browsers will happily ignore the blanks and concatenate your text into one monster paragraph.

HTML gives us a tag, <P>, to indicate a new paragraph. A paragraph consists of text enclosed in the tag <P> ... </P>. However, in practice, the </P> is not necessary; the paragraph is implicitly closed by the start of the next paragraph or heading element. For example:

```
<BODY>
<TITLE>My first document</TITLE>
This is my first paragraph in an HTML document. As you can
see, there isn't much to it.
<P>
And this is a separate paragraph.
</BODY>
```

A browser will display that text like this:

```
This is my first paragraph in an HTML document. As you can
see there isn't much to it.
And this is a separate paragraph.
```

It's worth noting that most browsers render paragraphs by leaving a gap between them. If you want simply to end a line at a given point, but not start a new paragraph, there's a line break tag, <BR>, which just breaks the line but doesn't add any vertical space.

Of course, paragraphs of text are all very well, but how do we highlight topic headings and titles?

HTML provides six levels of headings. Heading tags go in pairs:

```
<H1>This is a level one heading</H1>
<H2>This is a level two heading</H2>
<H6>This is a level six (very small!) heading</H6>
```

It's a good idea to use heading levels sparingly, and to start with an H1 and work down from there. For example, a simple monograph might look a bit like this:

15

```
<HTML>
<HEAD>
<TITLE>Some appropriate title</TITLE>
</HEAD>
<BODY>
<H1>Diagnosis of familial hypobetalipoproteinaemia in
neonates</H1>
<!-- abstract-->
This disease is an extremely rare inborn error of
metabolism. Less than fifty cases have been diagnosed
world-wide. It was first characterised in the 1950's by
Bassen and Kornzweig (qv) and is sometimes referred to as
the Bassen-Kornzweig syndrome.
<P>
This article discusses the differential diagnosis of FHBP
in neonates, with particular reference to ...
<!-- end of abstract-->
<HR>
<H2>Signs and Symptoms</H2>
<!-- what it looks like at first -->
The abetalipoproteinaemic infant typically presents with a
generalized failure to thrive.
Atypical retinitis pigmentosa is not an initial presenting
condition in most cases ...
<!-- end of symptoms-->
</BODY>
</HTML>
```

The structure of this document is explicit; you can get away without the <HTML>, <HEAD> and <BODY> tags in real life, and many documents do in practice omit them.

Separate blocks of text are distinguished by heading tags or paragraph tags; because the text following a heading 'close' tag is not part of the heading itself, an implicit new paragraph follows each heading.

The <HR> tag after the introduction inserts a horizontal rule in the document – a line that splits the first section off from those following it.

When you view this file using a web browser (for example, Netscape 1.1), it looks something like Figure 2.1.

There should be nothing particularly confusing about the system so far; the HTML simply consists of text containing formatting directives. The controversy sets in when we try to emphasize text. Because different browsers have different fonts and radically different appearences, there is no guarantee that this document will look the same when viewed on different computers. How, then, do we go about emphasizing text?

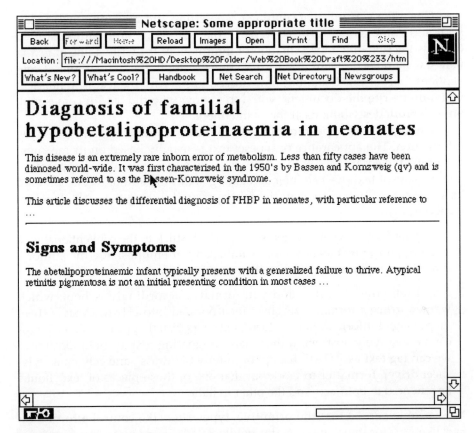

Figure 2.1

Typography and HTML

Old-fashioned word processors inherited a model from the golf-ball electric typewriter. When you wanted to emphasize some text, you'd take out the print ball and drop in a new one with italic characters on it. When you finished with the emphasis, you'd put the old (roman) font ball back in the typewriter and carry on working. By adding underlined, bold and a few other attributes, the word processors could achieve a variety of effects in a way that was easy to understand.

However, typeset text isn't like that. The font may come in a variety of sizes, and a number of weights, with a wide range of slant attributes. And you can change its colour. Although such fine control over appearance only appeared on high-end or specialized computers at first, it rapidly spread during the 1980s. Today, just about any PC or Macintosh with the right software can surpass the typesetting capability of an expensive linotronic from the beginning of the 1980s.

Given the versatility of computer typesetting and rendering tools today, it should come as no surprise to learn that the focus of attention shifted towards the semantic representation of information. If I write a line of text in italics, what does it mean? You can, of course, refer to the 'typographical conventions' part of this book. But how do you know why the text is in italics, if you didn't write the document, you don't know who did, and it comes with no such blurb describing its author's intentions?

We rely on the appearance of text, as much as on its content, to convey information. The appearance of typeset text is usually based on its meaning, determined in accordance with a style sheet. By noticing the visual appearance of a passage of text, we can infer something about the author's conception of its significance. Two schools of thought appeared during the early development of HTML:

1 The 'what I say is what you get' school, which stuck to the conventional idea of highlighting text as boldface or italic, and of emphasizing the author's direct typographical control over the visual presentation of their data.

2 The 'I tell you what it is and you format it accordingly' school, which wanted to see a formal style sheet incorporated into HTML. A style sheet maps tagged information in a document to its visual appearance. Such tags can be relatively abstract: rather than designating text as 'bold' or 'italic', we can tag text as 'HTML listing' or 'internet address', and rely on a style-sheet driven formatter to work out that one of those pieces of text should be rendered in boldface, and the other in italic.

Most people agreed that the primitive, typewriter-like control afforded by tags like <I> (for italic) and <B> (for boldface) was inadequate. But as soon as the developers tried codifying a set of built-in style tags for HTML, they ran into huge problems. Simply put, there is no such thing as a universal style sheet that can cover all contingencies. A novel requires different text styles from a car maintenance manual, which in turn does not resemble a poem, a letter, or a paper submitted to a refereed academic journal. If tags to cover all contingencies were incorporated into HTML, HTML would cease to be simple; however, if tags to cover all contingencies were *not* incorporated into HTML, it would fail in its goal of providing a useful way of delivering a wide variety of documents over the net.

Consequently, we're stuck with a hybrid compromise; a tag set that contains both primitive formatting commands and a few (common) style elements. The style elements are interpreted arbitrarily by the browsers; the primitive formatting commands are a bit more coercive insofar as they specify a specific attribute of a typeface, but they're still open to interpretation.

Later on, we'll see that there are several solutions to this problem: one of them, which most clearly represents the typographic-control school, is a commercial system, Adobe's Acrobat while the markup school proffer the powerful but not yet commonly available (or understood) DSSSL (Document Style Sheet Specification Language).

Basic formatting tags

Here are the basic formatting tags:

`<B>Boldface</B>`	Text is enclosed in the `<B>` ... `</B>` tags.
`<I>Italic</I>`	Text is enclosed in the `<I>` ... `</I>` tags. According to the HTML 2.0 specification, if a browser doesn't understand italics it should try to render this as a slanted font.
`<TT>Typewriter</TT>`	Text is enclosed in the `<TT>` ... `</TT>` tags; it should be rendered in monospaced font.

And here are the style tags:

`<ADDRESS>A mail address</ADDRESS>`	This is rendered in italics, and is separated by a paragraph break from the text above and below it. This is typically used for indicating where the author of a file can be found.
`<CITE>The HTML 2.0 specification</CITE>`	This defines a citation style, for referring to the titles of other documents. It is typically rendered in italic.
`<CODE>Example source code</CODE>`	Reserved for bits of software source code used in examples. It is usually rendered in a monospaced font.
`<EM>Emphasis</EM>`	Provides typographic emphasis; unlike the `<B>` or `<I>` tags, it leaves the precise form of emphasis up to the browser. It is typically rendered in italics, but might come out in flashing pink neon if the browser feels like it.
`<KBD>Keyboard</KBD>`	Tags are used to identify text typed by a user, and are usually rendered in a monospaced font. (You would use this tag to indicate text typed by a user in an example – such as showing a login session via FTP or telnet.)
`<SAMP>Samples</SAMP>`	Samples of literal characters are usually rendered in a monospaced font. This is another example style, like `<SAMP>` and `<CODE>`.
`<STRONG>Strong</STRONG>`	Strong typographic emphasis is provided as an alternative to `<EM>` emphasis; it is typically rendered in bold, but again the final decision on presentation belongs to the browser.
`<VAR>Variable</VAR>`	Variable names are typically rendered in italics.

Sometimes it is necessary to present raw text, preformatted with spaces, knowing exactly where the lines will break. The `<PRE>` ... `</PRE>` tags effectively switch off word-wrapping and pagination within the designated body of text. If you separate two words by five space characters, five space characters will appear between the words when you view them in a preformatted block; normally, a web browser will eat all but one of the spaces.

Now we can have a look at an example of a formatted file. This one is a manual page for a short program (part of the UNIX system):

```
<HTML>
<HEAD>
<TITLE>cat - catenate and print</TITLE>
</HEAD>
<BODY>
<H1>NAME</H1>
cat - catenate and print
<H2>SYNOPSIS</H2>
<CODE>cat [ -benstuv ]</CODE> <VAR>file ...</VAR>
<H2>DESCRIPTION</H2>
Cat reads each file in sequence and displays it on the
standard output. Thus
<P>
<KBD>cat file</KBD>
<P>
displays the file on the standard output, and
<P>
<KBD>cat file1 file2 &gt;file3</KBD>
<P>
concatenates the first two files and places the result on the
third.
<P>
If no input file is given, or if the argument '-' is
encountered, cat reads from the standard input file. Output
is buffered in the block size recommended by
<CITE>stat(2)</CITE>
unless the standard output is a terminal, when it is
line buffered. The -u option makes the output completely
unbuffered.
<H2>SEE ALSO</H2>
<UL>
<LI>cp(1)
<LI>ex(1)
<LI>more(1)
<LI>pr(1)
<LI>tail(1)
</UL>
```

```
<H2>BUGS</H2>
Beware of <CODE>cat a b &gt; a</CODE> and <CODE>cat a
b &gt;b</CODE>, which destroy the input files before
reading them.
</BODY>
</HTML>
```

A few points need to be made about this example:

- The `<CODE> ... </CODE>` tags are used here to denote commands executed by the UNIX shell. However, the `<KBD> ... </KBD>` tags are also used to denote commands typed by the user. Any of the commands tagged as `<CODE>` could equally well be typed by a user. Furthermore, the tag `<VAR>` is used to denote filenames (which are variable parameters to the program). But are these really variables? Or would they be better represented using some other tag? This highlights one of the problems of style tags; how do you determine the correct context in which to use a given tag?

- The entity `&gt;` is an alternative to the greater-than sign (>). A naked greater-than encountered in an HTML document may be mistaken for part of a tag. So when entering literal greater-than (or less-than, `&lt;`) symbols, it is essential to use the appropriate character entity.

- The `<UL> ... </UL>` section is an unnumbered list; this is explained in the next section.

It should be obvious that once you begin using complex markup or character entities in text, the text becomes hard to read with the naked eye. So Figure 2.2 shows what it looks like in Netscape.

Lists and structured documents

The basic tags introduced above can be used to give us basic structured documents. But many documents don't simply contain paragraphs of text that flow from one to another. It's pretty important to be able to list items, using bulleted or numbered lists. HTML provides a number of lists.

The unordered list

An unordered list is simply a list of items, preceded by bullets. It looks like this:

```
<UL>
<LI>First item
<LI>Second item
<LI>Third item
</UL>
```

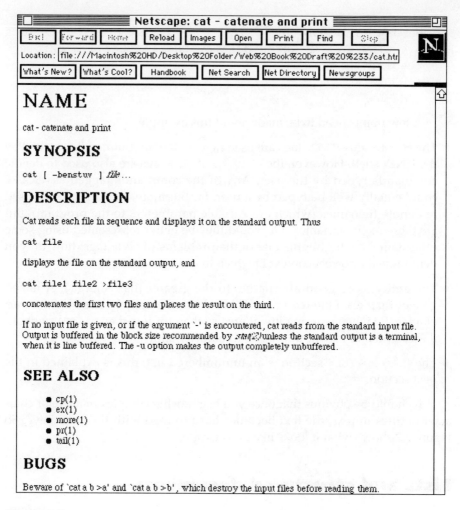

Figure 2.2

The `<LI>` tag introduces a new list item. Each new item starts on a new line, and is usually preceded by a bullet (generated by the browser), as in the example above.

The menu list

A menu list is like an unordered list, but displayed more compactly. Use `<MENU> ... </MENU>` instead of `<UL> ... </UL>` when you want to reduce the amount of white space above and below the list. For example:

```
<MENU>
<LI>Apples
<LI>Bananas
<LI>Oranges
/MENU>
```

(Note that the menu list isn't commonly used. Indeed, some browsers treat menu lists identically to unnumbered lists.)

The ordered list

An ordered list is like an unordered list, except that instead of a preceding bullet each item is numbered. For example:

```
<TITLE>An idiot's guide to cooking beans on toast</TITLE>
<H1>An idiot's guide to cooking beans on toast</H1>
<OL>
<LI>Get at the beans
<OL>
<LI>take the tin can out of the cupboard
<LI>close the jaws of the can-opener around one edge of the lid
<LI>rotate the handle until the lid comes off
</OL>
<LI>Make some toast
<OL>
<LI>take the bread out of the cupboard
<LI>remove a slice of bread from the loaf and put it in the
toaster
<LI>ensure toaster is plugged in
<LI>remove bread from toaster before it burns, not ·using
fingers, thumbs, or metal implements
<LI>put toast on a plate
</OL>
<LI>Pour beans onto toast
<LI>Put plate in microwave oven
<LI>Turn oven on and cook for sixty seconds
</OL>
```

Note that you don't have to specify the numbering of items in the list, the web browser does it for you. You can also have nested sublists; these are each numbered starting from 1. This example comes out as Figure 2.3.

According to the HTML specification, you can use the optional COMPACT parameter to an ordered list (that is, <OL COMPACT>); this causes some browsers to pack it into a smaller space.

```
          An idiot's guide to cooking beans on toast
  1. Get at the beans
          1. take the tin can out of the cupboard
          2. close the jaws of the can-opener around one edge of the lid
          3. rotate the handle until the lid comes off
  2. Make some toast
          1. take the bread out of the cupboard
          2. remove a slice of bread from the loaf and put it in the toaster
          3. ensure toaster is plugged in
          4. remove bread from toaster before it burns, not using fingers, thumbs, or
             metal implements
          5. put toast on a plate
  3. Pour beans onto toast
  4. Put plate in microwave oven
  5. Turn oven on and cook for sixty seconds
```

Figure 2.3

The definition list

The lists just described are designed to contain entries denoted by a small tag in the left margin – a bullet or a number. A definition list, in contrast, is designed to present more complex tags, for example, a glossary of terms. In such a list, the tag is printed flush with the left margin, while the associated definition is indented below it. For example:

```
<DL>
<DT>HTML<DD>HyperText Markup Language
<DT>HTTP<DD>HyperText Transport Protocol
<DT>MIME<DD>MultiMedia Mail Extensions
</DL>
```

is rendered like this:

```
HTML
     HyperText Markup Language
HTTP
     HyperText Transport Protocol
MIME
     MultiMedia Mail Extensions
```

The <DT> tag introduces a definition term. The <DD> tag introduces the associated definition for the preceding term. You can have two or more definition terms in a row, for example for synonyms:

```
<DL>
<DT>Red
<DT>Blue
<DT>Green
<DD>These are all primary colours
</DL>
```

A definition list usually leaves a fair amount of white space around items. If you want to close everything up, use the COMPACT attribute:

```
<DL COMPACT>
```

This reduces the space for definition terms and closes up white space generally. For example:

Definition list

```
HTML
      HyperText Markup Language
HTTP
      HyperText Transport Protocol
MIME
      MultiMedia Mail Extensions
```

Compact Definition list

```
HTML HyperText Markup Language
HTTP HyperText Transport Protocol
MIME MultiMedia Mail Extensions
```

The directory list

Directory lists are unordered, highly compact lists, typically used for listing large numbers of items up to 20 characters long (such as filenames). A directory list is enclosed in the <DIR> ... </DIR> tags, and items can be arranged in columns (typically 24 characters wide). Some web browsers can balance column widths, so that the columns are left-justified and packed to an appropriate left margin. For example:

```
<DIR>
<LI>file1.html
<LI>file2.html
<LI>file3.html
<LI>file4.html
</DIR>
```

Note, however, that some browsers render this as a standard unnumbered list (for example, Netscape). This mechanism for arranging data in columnar order is also arguably obsolescent, given the availability of tables (see 'Tables', p. 41).

Using these formatting tags it is possible to write moderately complex structured documents that have a moderately rich visual appearance. But if you've used the web for any length of time, by now you'll be scratching your head; where are the embedded graphics and the hyperlinks to other documents or other places within the same document?

We'll deal with references next.

Links and anchors

An anchor is a special tag that does not determine the appearance of text; instead, it indicates a connection between the current document and some other entity (which might be another anchor in the same document, or an entirely different document on another server).

There are several types of anchor, but all of them use the <A> ... </A> tag (with optional parameters). Notably, there are anchor tags that define a target for a hypertext jump, and tags that define a hypertext reference.

In general, to create a link between two places in a document or web, you need to use two anchors: one to name a cross-reference target, and one to insert a hypertext reference into the text. The hypertext reference appears in the text as a highlighted hot-spot word or phrase, often coloured, and usually underlined. When you click on the hot-spot, the browser uses the information in the anchor tag to locate and load the target entity.

From another angle: when you insert a cross-reference target anchor into a document, you give it a name. Thereafter, you can use cross-reference pointers that refer to that name (Figure 2.4).

The simplest kind of anchor is used to navigate within a long document. For example, suppose we have an academic paper structured like this:

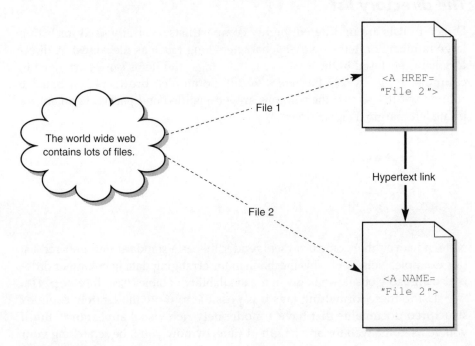

Figure 2.4

```
<HTML>
<HEAD>
<!-- header info -->
</HEAD>
<BODY>
<!-- body text -->
<H1>Title</H1>
<!-- preamble -->
<H2>Introduction</H2>
<!-- intro text -->
<H2>A subsection</H2>
<!-- lots of text -->
<H2>Another subsection</H2>
<!-- some more text -->
<H2>Yet another ...</H2>
<!-- a chunk of bumph -->
<H2>Conclusions</H2>
<!-- more of the same, in a nutshell -->
<H2>References</H2>
<!-- all the footnotes -->
</BODY>
</HTML>
```

It is reasonable for the Conclusions section to refer back to text in the first three sections. It is also useful in the first three sections to be able to refer forward to the references. Therefore we need to provide a target anchor with each reference, which can be jumped to from the body of the text. We also need to provide target anchors under each <H2> heading, for use in the Conclusions.

The format for a target is:

```
<A NAME="target_name">hot spot text</A>
```

target_name is a symbolic name that can be referenced by other anchors; the hot-spot text is displayed by a web browser in some highlighted format. (It is usually omitted from NAME anchors, because clicking on it doesn't take you anywhere.)

The format for a pointer, within the same document, is:

```
<A HREF="#target_name">hot spot text</A>
```

The HREF attribute means 'hypertext reference'; the hash sign (#) means that it is an internal reference to an anchor placed within the current document. The text hot spot text is displayed in the document. Clicking on it takes you to the target identified by target_name.

We can take the paper described in Figure 2.5 and add internal target anchors to the HTML copy:

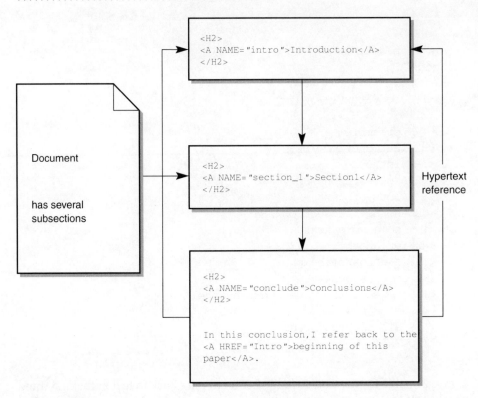

Figure 2.5

```
<HTML>
<HEAD>
<!-- header info -->
</HEAD>
<BODY>
<!-- body text -->
<H1>Title</H1>
<A NAME="title">
<!-- preamble -->
<H2>Introduction</H2>
<A NAME="intro">
<!-- intro text -->
<H2>A subsection</H2>
<A NAME="sect1">
<!-- lots of text -->
<H2>Another subsection</H2>
<A NAME="sect2">
```

```
<!-- some more text -->
<H2>Yet another ...</H2>
<A NAME="sectn">
<!-- a chunk of bumph -->
<H2>Conclusions</H2>
<A NAME="conclusions">
<!-- more of the same, in a nutshell -->
Well, you've read the article. As
<A HREF="#sect1">Section 1</A>
shows, there is a crying need for further research
into this field. As
<A HREF="#sect2">Section 2</A>
shows, all previously used methodologies are suspect. And as
<A HREF="#sectn">Section N</A>
shows, we weren't any more successful.
<P>
Draw your own conclusions.
<HR>
<H2>References</H2>
<A NAME="refs">
<!-- all the footnotes -->
</BODY>
</HTML>
```

The Conclusions section contains three pointers to the targets specified by $sect_1$, $sect_2$ and $sect_n$. The text between the `<A>` and `</A>` tags is presented as a hypertext link that takes the reader to the appropriate section if they click on it.

The construct:

```
<H2>Another subsection</H2>
<A NAME="sect2"></A>
```

is a little clumsy. You can nest some tags; an equally valid construct is:

```
<H2><A NAME="sect2">Another subsection</A></H2>
```

which makes the association between the anchor and the heading a little bit more explicit.

You can also apply the usual text highlighting tags to text in an anchor, although it's probably not sensible to do so without good reason. Note, however, that you should not enclose header tags in an anchor, or mess around with the order in which you start and end tags: the following is illegal, and guaranteed to screw up some badly behaved browsers:

```
<A NAME="sect2"><H2>Another subsection</A></H2>
```

Links between files

Now we've seen the basics of anchors, we can consider how to create hotlinks between separate files. For the time being, we're going to deal with files in the same web – in fact, in the same directory (or folder, for Macintosh users).

Let's look again at the academic paper we've been writing. Structurally, it's going to look something like this:

```
<HEAD>
<TITLE>My dissertation</TITLE>
</HEAD>
<BODY>
<H1>Introduction</H1>
[pointers to sect1 .. sectn, conclusion, refs]
Sect1.html
<H2>Section 1</H2>
Sect2.html
<H2>Section 2</H2>
Sectn.html
<H2>Section N</H2>
Concl.html
<H2>Conclusions</H2>
refs.html
<H2>References and Bibliography</H2>
</BODY>
```

It has obviously grown so huge, cumbersome and complex that it needs to be broken down; instead of having separate headers in one big file, we need several separate files.

Note: Pathnames on an HTTP server do not work in exactly the same way as pathnames on a normal UNIX system. See 'Understanding directories' for details.

Figure 2.6 shows only the headers in each file; the other document structure information is omitted. Note also that this view assumes that the operating system can handle long filenames with mixed-case characters. This isn't available under MS-DOS (which is limited to uppercase only, eight characters, a period, then three characters), but most modern operating systems are sufficiently flexible to allow filenames like the above. (Naming constraints and portability to DOS-based servers will be discussed later.)

We need to point to other files, rather than to markers in the same file. The same HREF notation is used, but instead of #target_name we use filename as a parameter. For example:

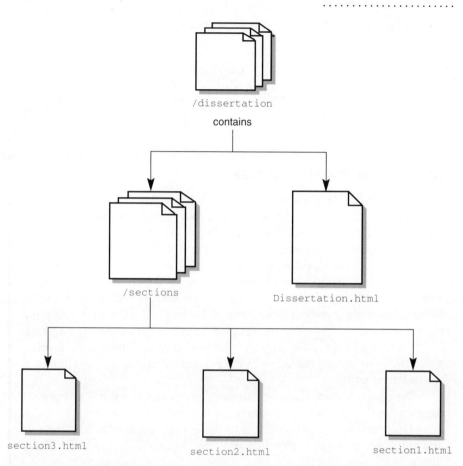

/dissertation

contains

/sections

Dissertation.html

section3.html

section2.html

section1.html

Figure 2.6 The dissertation web.

```
for a full discussion of this, see
<A HREF="section3.html">my conclusions</A>.
```

The leading hash symbol, #, in front of an anchor indicates a local target, embedded in the current file; in the absence of the #, the browser assumes that the target is a filename and searches the current directory for it.

You can also play mix and match. For example, if you have target anchors for each subheading in a document, you can reference specific sections of that file by using an HREF of the form:

```
<A HREF="filename.html#target">go here</A>
```

The file designated by *filename.html* is loaded, and the named anchor 'target' is jumped to.

Nor are you limited to your current directory. Suppose you keep the sub-sections in a subdirectory, so that the structure is as shown in Figure 2.6.

You can place a reference in *dissertation.html* like this:

```
<A HREF="sections/section1.html">Section 1</A>
```

or

```
<A HREF="sections/section1.html#part1">Part 1 of Section
1</A>
```

Understanding directories

Pathnames in HTML are specified in UNIX format.

A *path* consists of a list of directories that must be entered in order to reach a file. (Directories contain other directories, and/or files.)

A *pathname* is the name of a file, appended to the path necessary to reach it through the directory structure of the filesystem.

In a path, directories and files are separated by a forward slash, /. The '..' operator means 'go up a directory level'. For example, *foo/bar/../quux* is equivalent to *foo/quux*. A leading / in front of a pathname means that the path is to be constructed from the very top of the accessible directory hierarchy (that is, an 'absolute' path); if there is no leading slash, the path is constructed from the current default directory (that is, it is a 'relative' path).

On a web server, the root directory, /, is not the same as the root directory of the server. See Chapter 6 for details.

These semantics are identical to those used by MS-DOS, Windows and OS/2, except for the substitution of the / character in place of \. They differ from the Macintosh programming pathname semantics; the Macintosh directory separator is the colon, :. Two colons, ::, are equivalent to .., three colons, :::, are equivalent to ../.., and so on. Also, confusingly, a relative path on a Macintosh begins with a directory separator character, while an absolute pathname does not. So *Macintosh HD:MacHTTP:public_html:hello.html* is an absolute pathname, but *:public_html:examples:something.html* is a relative pathname. VAX/VMS is even stranger, and IBM mainframe operating system semantics worse. Luckily there is little sign of the web being modified to conform to VM/CMS file naming conventions ...

Pictures

It is possible to include references to graphics in HTML files. Images do not come as part of the HTML language, but you can link external graphics files into HTML using a specialized tag resembling an anchor.

Pictures should ideally be saved as Graphics Interchange Format files; virtually all graphical browsers can handle this format, which incorporates a degree of data compression.

Graphics file formats

The web was originally designed to link text documents. It rapidly became apparent to the developers at CERN that scientific papers needed illustrations; so they initially created a mechanism for including XBM files (X Window System Bitmaps).

However, the XBM file format is extremely large and wasteful; it doesn't incorporate any compression mechanism. Although it is easy to work with, it is grossly inefficient to transport over slow, low-band-width networks.

The next graphics file format to be supported was the CompuServe GIF. This comes in two flavours, GIF87a and GIF89a; generally, browsers support both varieties. GIF was designed for encoding graphics that would be transmitted over slow links, and incorporates the fairly efficient, loss-free LZW and LZH compression algorithms. In addition, GIFs can be interlaced so that alternate scan-lines are encoded; while this does not speed the process of decompression, it does trick the eye by beginning to fill in the whole area of an image rapidly, rather than working down it from top to bottom.

GIF files are subject to two problems: they are intended only to store images containing up to 8 bits of colour information per pixel, and the compression algorithm they use turns out to have been patented under an obscure filing by Unisys in the mid-1980s. In addition, more efficient compression algorithms are available if some loss of picture quality is acceptable.

JPEG files implement a more sophisticated, but computationally expensive, compression mechanism. They can contain greater numbers of bits per pixel, but tend to lose (or obscure) some information during the compression process – an expanded bitmap derived from a JPEG image is not identical to the bitmap that was compressed to produce that image.

To insert a graphics file at the current location in an HTML document, use the IMG tag:

```
<IMG SRC="picture.gif">
```

This causes the source file *picture.gif* to be inserted at that point in the text. For example:

```
<P>
This is a paragraph of text before one with an inline image.
<P>
This paragraph contains <IMG SRC="test.gif"> an image.
<P>
The previous paragraph contained an image.
```

displays as shown in Figure 2.7.

Not all browsers can display graphics. For example, the Lynx browser (used on UNIX terminal systems) cannot display any images at all. Some browsers support a restricted range of image file types; Netscape Navigator, unlike other browsers, permits the use of inlined JPEG images (a more efficient compressed format than GIF), but these will not show up under NCSA Mosaic. And there is always a possibility that your images will not be delivered to the browser for some reason or other. Therefore, when including inline images in text, you should provide an alternative textual representation:

```
<IMG SRC="test.gif" ALT="floppy disk icon">
```

The ALT parameter specifies that if "test.gif" cannot be displayed, the browser should display the text "floppy disk icon" instead (Figure 2.8).

When you insert a graphic into text, it breaks the flow of the page – the browser inserts it with its baseline aligned with the text to either side of it, and shifts the line it is on down to make space. However, you can align it relative to the browser's window using the ALIGN parameter:

```
<IMG SRC="test.gif" ALT="floppy disk icon" ALIGN="MIDDLE">
```

In this case, the ALIGN="MIDDLE" option ensures that the middle of the image is aligned with the baseline of the text line it is inserted in (Figure 2.9). (You can also specify "ALIGN=TOP" and "ALIGN=BOTTOM", which behave as you might expect.)

Note, however, that ALIGN directives in HTML 2.0 do not not cause text to flow round the graphic – only the first line after the graphic is affected, so an ALIGN=TOP directive will look rather odd next to a large graphic. The ALIGN directives are extended considerably by Netscape and HTML 3.0.

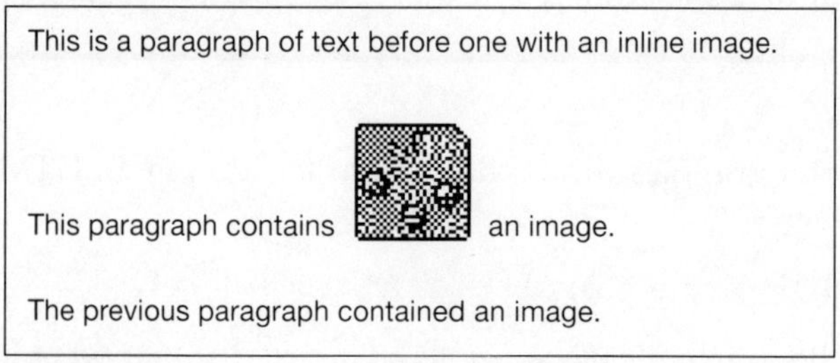

This is a paragraph of text before one with an inline image.

This paragraph contains ▓ an image.

The previous paragraph contained an image.

Figure 2.7

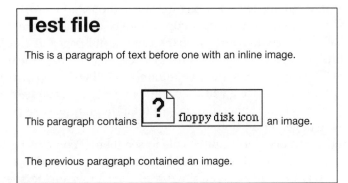

Figure 2.8

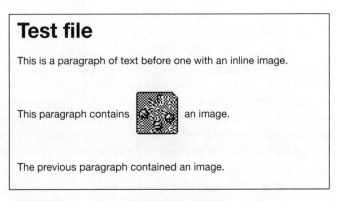

Figure 2.9

Finally, you can put an inline image wherever you would expect to put body text in an HTML document. You can't put them in the <HEAD> section, but it is perfectly valid to do something like:

```
<A HREF="sections/sect1.html#part1">
<IMG SRC="button.gif" ALT="Press me">
</A>
```

This inserts *button.gif* into the flow of the text, as a clickable link to the anchor Part 1 in the file *sect1.html*. If the button cannot be displayed, the alternative text Press me is rendered in its place.

Some comments about graphics

Without doubt, graphics can enhance the appearance of any page. However, there are some major issues to be aware of.

Firstly, the old adage that 'a picture says a thousand words' is no longer true in HTML. A thousand words occupy about 6 kb of disk space. In contrast, quite a small graphic will overflow that space – a full-page GIF in 256 colours (using 8 bits to represent the colours of each pixel) will typically occupy 250–300 kb. Thus, graphics should be minimized – they're expensive in terms of bandwidth. If you place a 750 kb graphic in a page that someone accesses over a dialup modem connection, it will take them at least five minutes to download the page. If they bother.

Secondly, not everyone will be able to see them. People using line-mode browsers won't get the full effect. People working over a dialup modem line frequently switch image auto-loading off in their browsers, to speed access. And an 8-bit graphic can look poor when viewed on a high-performance graphics workstation capable of displaying 24-bit colour images.

Thirdly, it's dangerous to go image-happy. Images are secondary files, linked into your core HTML document. A document that depends heavily on images for effect is going to look poor to a user who cannot download or view images, or who has switched image loading off. And in some extreme cases, images can severely damage the usability of a web page.

In general, inline images are best used to emphasize the appearance of text (for example, as coloured icons to replace the bullets in a list), and as 'thumbnails' for larger files. For example, suppose you wish to put a 300 kb self-portrait of yourself in your personal 'who-am-I' web page. The sensible way to do this is to embed a 20 kb icon of the self-portrait, within an anchor pointing to the real thing – and to add a warning to the effect that 'this is a big picture!'.

Big pictures are probably best presented as JPEG files. JPEG is a 'lossy' compression technique that potentially provides much better compression than GIF; it is most suitable for extremely big images, or for those with a large number of colours, such as photographs of natural objects. However, few web browsers (other than Netscape) can render inlined JPEG images. Thus, it is common practice to use a small thumbnail GIF as the hot-spot for a hyperlink to the JPEG image; the browser loads the image file and passes it to an external 'helper application' which then displays it.

As a first principle, never include any graphics in the top page of a web. The top page – the usual point of entry for those users who discover a reference to your web somewhere else – performs the same function as the flyleaf of a book. It's not there to look pretty or to convey huge numbers of facts; it's simply there to inform readers of the nature of the document they are looking at, and to orient them. If you need to include large graphics in pages below that one, all well and good – but make sure you warn your readers beforehand. As a general rule of thumb, a page that takes more than 30 seconds to load over a slow line (without warning) may make your audience reluctant to continue; and if they are using an ancient V22. bis modem, as little as 2 kb of text might clog up their system for that long.

There is a tendency among some designers to use inline graphics to get around the typographical limitations of the HTML medium. By building complex images of control panels and widgets in the form of graphics with clickable maps, an HTML document can be made to look quite similar to a glossy printed magazine page, or to a multimedia presentation system. However, this is in opposition to the original design purpose of the web, which is to provide a simple, universal means of transferring textual information. By choosing to make their pages graphically complex, these designers ensure that their documents cannot be downloaded rapidly, are not readable by all browsers and are not searchable.

In extreme cases, I've seen cases of design-trained authors using one pixel wide transparent GIF images to control leading (the space between words) in their text on screen. While that kind of control is normal in typesetting systems, HTML makes no provision for it. This technique works, after a fashion, but has some problematic consequences: users who have turned image loading off are going to see a horrible mess on screen, and users who are trying to search the document for a string of words (using a search tool) are probably not going to find what they're looking for.

These problems are discussed in more detail in Chapters 4 and 7.

To get the best out of the compression built into the GIF format, use drawings in preference to scanned photographs, and minimize the number of colours in the images. Big blocks of a uniform colour occupy far less space in an image file than graduated washes of colour. The LZH data compression algorithm used in GIF compressors works by locating sequences of bits in an image raster, and replacing them with pointers into a table containing a list of identified (repeating) sequences. As more patterns are added to the table, the size of the pointers required to index them grows. Thus, images consisting mainly of runs of uniform colours are represented by relatively short pointers into the index table. Gradual colour changes act to defeat this compression scheme; the number of bit patterns to be encoded in the compressed file rises and the file grows larger. The upshot of this is that it is possible to create small, fast GIF images for web pages, *if* you:

- minimize the number of colours in the images, ideally by sticking to less than four, or less than sixteen, primary colours;

- use drawings prepared on-line, rather than scanned images or photographs.

Of course, if you know your audience will only ever see your web on a local system, or over a high-speed network, you don't need to pay any attention to this advice. But if you have any doubt at all – or if your pages are destined for public access – it is best not to ignore those slow, old modems. They're out there, there are millions of them, and their owners are unlikely to invest in an expensive upgrade in order to make life easier for you.

Finally, note well: there is no direct equivalent of the <IMG SRC> tag for text. You cannot insert a tag that says: <TXT SRC="somefile.html"> and have the contents of *somefile.html* magically appear in your document. This is a shame, as there are many occasions (as we will see later) when including a standardized boilerplate file would be useful. However, there are three mechanisms that give us the ability to do something similar, and we will come to these in 'Bandwidth and graphics', p. 162.

Entering the WWW: references to remote systems

We have seen anchor tags that point to other anchors within local files and to other files on the same server. An extension of the same syntax is used to designate resources elsewhere on the Internet; the mechanism used is the **Universal Resource Locator** (**URL**), as defined in the RFC 1630 standards document. (RFC stands for 'Request For Comment' or 'Request For Compliance' – the two states in which a proposed or established Internet standard can exist.) A URL is actually a subset of a broader mechanism (the URI, or Universal Resource Indicator), which also encompasses URNs (Universal Resource Numbers, described in 'Flexible references', p. 182).

A URL identifies a protocol used to obtain the remote resource; the host from which the resource is available; and the location of the resource on the host. By using a URL, a web browser can retrieve a resource. For example:

```
http://www.yahoo.com/computers/world_wide_web/
```

means 'use the HTTP protocol to contact the host www.yahoo.com and retrieve the object */computers/world_wide_web'*.

A URN is a unique identification name for a resource. A central repository keeps track of the locations of a resource, for example, a file. When the file is moved to another host, its owner need notify only the central repository; thereafter, all requests for the URN are redirected to the new location. This is in contrast to a URL, which is 'hard wired' to look at a specific place on the Internet – if the file is moved, the web browser will be unable to locate it. For example:

```
http://www.tardis.ed.ac.uk/~charlie/whoami.html
```

refers to the entity *~charlie/whoami.html* on www.tardis.ed.ac.uk. (On UNIX systems, the notation *~username* refers to the home, or public, directory owned by the user *username*. In this case, the web server is configured so that each user on the system has their own home directory.)

However, if I rename the file *whoami.html* to *biography.html*, the above URL will no longer work.

Because of the plastic nature of the world wide web, everyone agrees that a URN mechanism is in principle superior to the URL – but it has not yet been formally proposed, and will probably not be phased in before 1998.

Understanding URLs

A URL (to a web page or file) consists of three parts:

1 the service protocol

2 the destination site

3 the path to the resource

The service protocol, followed by a colon:

HTTP:	HyperText Transport Protocol (used for HTML)
Gopher:	An alternative textual transport mechanism used for plain text
News:	Usenet news
Mailto:	Electronic mail
FTP:	File Transfer Protocol (used for bulk file transfers)
WAIS:	Wide Area Information Service (a subset of Z39.50, used for accessing large text databases)
Telnet/TN3270/rlogin:	Remote login access to other computer systems

The destination:

ftp, HTTP, WAIS, Gopher:	A hostname, preceded by two slashes, for example: //www.demon.co.uk. The hostname is the name by which the computer is known on the Internet; alternatively, the computer's IP address (a series of four decimal numbers separated by periods) can be used instead.

Most of the time, these protocols are handled by a server running on a 'well-known port' (a numbered TCP/IP port between 1 and 32 327). If the protocol is running on a different port, the port number is appended to the hostname, separated by a colon. For example:

http://www.demon.co.uk:8080

indicates an HTTP request directed to host www.demon.co.uk, on port 8080 (instead of port 80, the 'well-known port' for HTTP).

news: A usenet newsgroup name: for example,
                             `comp.infosystems.www.misc`.

mailto: This is a person's email address in the format
                             specified by RFC 822, for example: `charlie@`
                             `antipope.demon.co.uk`.

The path to the resource:

HTTP: The path to the resource is the pathname of the
                             HTML file to retrieve, from the web server's
                             document root directory. Slashes '/' are used to
                             separate directory and filename components. A
                             leading slash is always used to separate the
                             pathname from the name of the host that stores
                             the file. If the last component of the pathname is
                             a directory, the web server should return a list-
                             ing of the files in the directory; if it is a directory
                             name followed by a slash, the server should
                             return the default file for that directory.

FTP: Follows the same model as HTTP. It is a differ-
                             ent protocol, however, and does not retrieve a
                             default HTML file. (It also tends to be slower at
                             establishing a connection, but faster at retrieving
                             binary data.)

The other protocols all follow their own models, and have a rather different syntax for retrieving files. These will not be discussed in depth here, except
by example where necessary, and they are documented in full in the RFC.

For the time being, all we need to understand are HTTP URLs. Let's look
at one:

```
<A HREF="http://www.w3.org/index.html">
press here
</A>
```

Once you strip away the HTML anchor, you are left with:

```
http://www.w3.org/index.html
```

This means (reading from left to right): using the HTTP protocol, go to the
host `www.w3.org`, and retrieve the file */index.html*.

HTTP uses port 80 (under TCP/IP, all hosts can have 32 767 ports available for communication channels). We could equally well write:

```
http://www.w3.org:80/index.html
```

The file pathname bears some description. The file */index.html* does not
exist in the root directory of the computer hosting the web server. Rather, it

exists in a subdirectory, designated by the server as being the root of the visible filesystem. So in actual fact, its pathname on the server might very well be */usr/local/etc/httpd/docs/index.html* (if it is a standard NCSA httpd installation), but as far as other systems are concerned the root directory visible on the web server is */usr/local/etc/httpd/docs*.

Weird URLs – cgi-bin queries

Not all HTTP URLs are as easy to read as the ones above. Sometimes you will come across complex forms that contain buttons to send information back to an HTTP server. You send information to a server by submitting an unusual URL. One might look something like this:

```
http://odd.host.com/cgi-bin/search?arg1+arg2+arg3
```

What does this mean?

Firstly, note that the request is going to the *cgi-bin* directory. CGI is an acronym for **Common Gateway Interface.** CGI scripts are programs which are executed by the HTTP server, in accordance with a standard calling protocol. In this instance, the program is called **search**. The text following the question mark is passed to **search** as arguments; the arguments are separated by + symbols. (If you need to send a literal plus sign or question mark as an argument, it should be sent as an ISO 8859/1 entity – + or ? respectively. In fact, if you need to send any unusual characters, they need to be specially encoded; see 'CGI scripting in PERL', p. 127 for details.)

CGI scripts are explained in detail in subsequent chapters. Note that not all web servers use a *cgi-bin* directory to contain their scripts; some (notably the CERN/W3O server) keep scripts just about anywhere.

Tables

One last feature of standard HTML deserves a look: the table.

Tabular representation of data is pretty important in most forms of text. Tables logically group units of information in a way that is more easily understood than an outline or list structure.

Tables are relatively new. NCSA X Mosaic has supported them only since release 2.5 (late 1994), but Netscape 1.0 and 1.1 included full table support. Not all browsers can cope with them (notably the Microsoft web explorer 1.0 browser included with Windows 95).

Tables consist of cells of data, arranged in rows and columns. The cells are automatically resized and realigned to fit the data inserted into them. It is possible to specify that a cell spans two or more columns, or two or more rows; this allows us to create cells containing captions for a block of child cells.

A table is enclosed in the <TABLE> ... </TABLE> tag. Each row in a table is introduced with a <TR> (table row) tag; the </TR> (end of table row) tag is implied by the occurrence of either another table row, or the end of a table. Each cell within a row is introduced with a <TD> (table data) tag. (This is implicitly terminated by the next table data, table row, or end of table tag.)

Note that tables don't have any visible border unless you specify that they should have one, using the optional BORDER attribute. For example, <TABLE BORDER="4"> specifies that the table should have a visible four-pixel thick border.

Tables without a visible border are particularly useful if you need to lay out cellular, or columnar, text. For example:

```
<TABLE BORDER="1">
<TR><TD>Column 1<TD>Column 2<TD>Column 3
<TR><TD>Something here<TD>Something there<TD>Something
everywhere
</TABLE>
```

gives rise to:

Column 1	Column 2	Column 3
Something here	Something there	Something everywhere

The parameters ROWSPAN and COLSPAN make a cell expand to span the specified number of rows or columns. For example:

```
<TABLE BORDER="1">
<TR><TD><TD COLSPAN="2">Horizontal caption
<TR><TD ROWSPAN="2">Vertical caption<TD>A<TD>B
<TR><TD>C<TD>D
</TABLE>
```

this gives rise to:

	Horizontal caption	
Vertical caption	A	B
	C	D

(The first non-vacant cell spans two columns; the first cell of the second row spans two rows.)

Non-standard HTML

So far, this chapter has given a whistle-stop tour of the main elements of HTML 2.0. HTML 2 is the general standard for HTML, released in 1994; it draws together and formalizes the earlier HTML 1.0 and HTML+ standards, and does away with a number of obsolete or inconsistent tags. See RFC 1866 for further details of HTML 2.0.

At the time of writing few browsers support a full set of HTML 2.0 tags. The IETF specification lists three levels of conformance; level 0 (mandatory), and levels 1 and 2 (different discretionary levels). Most level 0 tags – the ones in this chapter – are supported universally. But the discretionary features are not universally available yet.

To make matters worse, some software companies have added their own non-standard HTML tags.

The most obvious culprit is Netscape, the browser produced by Netscape Communications Corporation. Netscape currently has 80% of the user base, and thus plays the tune the rest dance to. (Already TradeWave, inheritors of the EINet web browser, and NCSA, owners of Mosaic, have announced integration of some Netscape HTML features in their next-generation browsers.)

A second culprit is Microsoft, with Microsoft Internet Explorer for Windows 95. However, whereas Netscape have at least submitted their extensions to the World Wide Web Organization for input to the HTML 3 standards process, the additional tags in the Microsoft product are not part of any public standards process.

Netscape HTML extensions

Be warned that there is no guarantee that these tags are compatible with other web browsers! Although Netscape is popular and widely used, documents which use this dialect of HTML may cause unpredictable results when loaded into any other browser. (NCC say the tags are designed not to break other browsers; this is quite correct, as long as the browser in question handles HTML tags correctly, that is, by ignoring unknown ones. Unfortunately not all browsers work this way: some of them are alarmingly ad hoc in the way they parse input.)

The general intent of the Netscape extensions is to provide enhanced formatting control in documents. That is, rather than sticking to the abstract semantic markup model, they tend to roll their sleeves up and muck around with issues like font size and the position of items on the screen. This is really dubious in view of the distinction between information content and rendered document that is implicit in the whole HTML model, but it makes sense from a pragmatic viewpoint; documents are there to be read, not to conform to some theoretical ideal of well-formed documentdom.

As a rule of thumb, Netscape extensions should be used if you know that your web users will all be using Netscape. If not, you really should consider avoiding them entirely – or at least, providing an alternative web, stripped of tags that might confuse other browsers.

They fall into the following categories:

- graphics

- design elements

- document structure

- forms

- client-side imagemaps

Graphics

Firstly, Netscape supports inline JPEG images. JPEGs tend to be smaller than GIF format files, but as JPEG is a 'lossy' compression medium you probably shouldn't use it if exact graphical reproduction is essential. Furthermore, the lossy compression renders JPEG unsuitable for steganographic fingerprinting purposes, and to cap it all the DCT compression algorithm in JPEG tends to be more computationally expensive than the LZW compression used in GIF87a and GIF89a (meaning it takes longer to display).

Secondly, Netscape can handle interlaced GIF files. Rather than unpacking one bitmap line after another from the top down, as ordinary GIF files do, interlaced files unpack bitmap lines from alternating segments of the image, filling in the gaps. They take no less time to download, but a progressively unpacked interlaced image becomes recognizable long before a normal sequentially unpacked image. As Netscape can abort a connection and connect to a new URL while unloading proceeds, this means that users constrained by a modem's bandwidth can see what is happening much faster; it provides a significant illusion of speed. In fact, interlaced GIF files are usable with all Web browsers (although many make no special use of the format), and so can be unreservedly recommended.

Thirdly, the <IMG> tag has been hacked, almost out of recognition.

Under HTML 2.0, the IMG tag recognizes very few ALIGN options; just top, bottom and middle, where the positions apply to the subsequent line of HTML text.

Netscape retains the top, middle and bottom options. It adds new options: left, right, texttop, absmiddle, baseline and absbottom :

"left", "right"	Produce floating images. The images float to the corresponding side of the window, and text wraps around the side of the window (right or left, respectively).

"texttop", "absmiddle", "baseline"	Behave quite similarly to "top", "middle" and "bottom"; the main difference being that they are more precise.
texttop	Aligns the graphic with the top of the tallest text in the line (usually the same as that which top would align with).
absmiddle	Aligns the middle of the graphic with the middle of the current line (while middle aligns the middle of the graphic with the baseline of the text in the current line).
baseline	Aligns the bottom of the graphic with the baseline of the current line of text (as with bottom).
absbottom	Aligns the bottom of the graphic with the bottom of the current line of text (that is, with the descenders in the text that dip below the baseline).

An example of image alignment is shown in Figure 2.10.

Demo of image alignment

 Here is a paragraph with an inline image as the first item. The tag to produce it was <IMG SRG="file.gif" ALIGN="left">, and as you can see it is floating to the left of the paragraph.

This is the next paragraph. Because it extends below the image it has filled back to the left margin.

Figure 2.10

In addition to positioning commands, Netscape can speed up rendering of inline images. The normal process of displaying an image begins when the document is downloaded. The browser scans for included images, then opens sockets to the server and slurps them in. As it does so, it begins to render the page. It cannot make allowances for the size of the images until they are available; at that point, the browser can calculate how much display space to leave for the bitmap.

The WIDTH and HEIGHT options were added to IMG to short-circuit this problem. They take parameters measured in pixels, for example:

```
<IMG SRC="fred.gif" WIDTH="512" HEIGHT="384">
```

This specifies that *fred.gif* is 512 pixels wide and 384 pixels high. Netscape therefore knows how much space to leave for *fred.gif* before it begins to download the inline image – and can therefore format the surrounding text faster.

45

```
<IMG VSPACE=value HSPACE=value>
```

The VSPACE and HSPACE options control the vertical and horizontal space around the image, to prevent the image from pressing up against the surrounding text. For example,

```
<IMG SRC="fred.gif" WIDTH="512" HEIGHT="384" VSPACE="12">
```

indicates a gap of 12 pixels should be reserved above and below *fred.gif*.

Finally, images are usually surrounded by a border. The BORDER option permits the author to specify the thickness of the border around the image, in pixels. Note that images contained in cross-reference anchors are usually surrounded by a border, so setting BORDER="0" in such an image might confuse your users. For example:

```
<HREF="http://localhost/foo.html"><IMG SRC="foo.gif" BORDER=
"0"></A>
```

will display a graphic (*foo.gif*) without a border, so that it does not appear to be a clickable anchor.

Design elements

Netscape provides a number of extensions and modifications that affect the actual layout and design of a web page. These enhance the visual appearance of horizontal rules, add positioning control and add rudimentary font management commands to HTML. (The last is a particularly suspicious issue insofar as it breaks the ability of the user to determine how the web documents are displayed; designs based on extensive font changes are probably inappropriate for general use.) In addition to control over font size, Netscape permits font attributes to be applied cumulatively. For example, <I><B> italic bold</B>text</I> can be rendered properly. Arguably, this is a good idea. (The only problem is that it is non-standard, so text formatted for display with Netscape may appear different on other browsers.)

The <HR> tag specifies a horizontal rule across the page. Netscape adds four optional paramenters:

<HR SIZE="value"> Specifies how thick the horizontal rule should be. (value is an integer that indicates the rule thickness in pixels.)

<HR WIDTH="value"> Specifies how wide the rule should be. value can be a percentage (of the window width), or an absolute value in pixels. By default, rules are as wide as the window in which they are displayed.

<HR ALIGN="value"> Where value is one of *left, right,* or *centre,* specifies whether the rule should be centred, right aligned, or left aligned relative to the window.

`<HR NOSHADE>`   Specifies that the rule has no drop shadow beneath it: a solid line is displayed.

Note that rules that are of a given width (in pixels) may not be displayed properly on systems with a different display resolution – clipping is likely to occur. (For this reason, I would advise you to stick to specifying rule widths in percentage format.)

Normally, HTML text blocks are wrapped at the discretion of the browser. Netscape provides the following commands for controlling line breaks:

- `<NOBR>` . . . `</NOBR>` specifies NO BReak. This prevents the browser from breaking lines between the start and end tags. (Particularly useful in source code listings where the language is whitespace sensitive but a display format is inappropriate.)

- `<WBR>` specifies Word BReak. Permits the browser to insert an (optional) line break at this point in a `<NOBR>` . . . `</NOBR>` text block.

- `<BR>` accepts the following additional options to help handle floating images:

  `<BR CLEAR="left">`   breaks the line, moves down vertically until there is a clear left margin (with no floating images between the text and the margin)

  `<BR CLEAR="right">` breaks the line, and moves down vertically until there is a clear right margin (with no floating images between the text and the right margin)

  `<BR CLEAR="all">`   moves down until both margins are clear of images

- `<FONT SIZE="value">` permits rudimentary control over font size. value is an integer in the range 1–7; the default text size is 3. Font size directives can be absolute (for example, `<FONT SIZE="4">`) or relative to the base font size (for example, `<FONT SIZE="+1">` or `<FONT SIZE="-2">`).

- `<BASEFONT SIZE="value">` sets the base font size. All relative `<FONT>` size changes are tracked with reference to the base font size.

- `<BIG>` . . . `</BIG>` uses a font larger than the standard font size. `<SMALL>` . . . `</SMALL>` specifies a smaller than usual font. `<SUP>` . . . `</SUP>` and `<SUB>` . . . `</SUB>` respectively select superscript and subscript.

- `<centre>` . . . `</centre>` centres the text lines between the left and right margins.

Document structure

In HTML 2.0, list entities are tagged with a progression of different bullets, depending on their level of indentation.

Netscape permits you to specify the TYPE of element used as a bullet:

```
<UL TYPE="element">
```

legitimate values are "disc", "circle", or "square".

In HTML 2.0, ordered lists increment a count in arabic numerals (1, 2, 3, ...).

Netscape permits you to specify the TYPE of number system used for list items: "A" (capital letters), "a" (lowercase letters), "I" (capital roman numerals), "i" (lowercase roman numerals), and "1" (default, arabic numerals).

The START tag can be used to start a numbered list at a value other than 1. It accepts an integer parameter. For example:

```
<OL TYPE="I" START="3">
```

specifies that list items should be in uppercase roman, starting from 3 (III).

In addition to these changes, individual list items can have their TYPE reset. If you change the type of a list element, subsequent elements in the list change to match. Thus, you can create a bulleted list that switches to numbers halfway down, the VALUE option can be used to change the index count of numbered list items. For example:

```
<BL TYPE="disc">
<!-- bullet list, using discs as tags -->
<LI>first item
<LI>second item
<LI TYPE="I">Switch to ordered list, uppercase roman numerals
<LI VALUE="2">... and count backwards!
</BL>
```

(A note of caution: the ability to change the type of a list from inside a component element flies in the face of the tree-like inheritance of attributes that is characteristic of SGML-based applications. It might appear superficially useful once in a while, but it's a real can of worms.)

Netscape 2.0 adds support for the <DIV> text division, and adds the ALIGN attribute for both paragraphs and divisions. This permits left, right and centre alignment; for example <P ALIGN="right"> specifies that the next paragraph is to be aligned with the right margin of the window.

Other document structure changes include Framesets (in Netscape 2.0); these are described in 'Framesets', p. 202.

Forms

The ISINDEX tag has been augmented with a PROMPT option. ISINDEX indicates that a document is a searchable index. PROMPT specifies the message that is printed in front of the text input field. Its default value is:

```
<centre>This is a searchable index. Enter search
keywords:</centre>
```

Client-side imagemaps

See 'Imagemaps', p. 147.

Summary

So far we have focused on HTML at the file level. Although we have introduced the concept of URLs, we have not yet examined how to use them
effectively. Nor have we met some of the more exotic tags sometimes found in
the HEAD section of an HTML document (such as BASE, ISINDEX, LINK,
NEXTID and META), which are of some importance in defining the interrelation between HTML documents in a coherent web. We will see how these
work once we have examined the HTTP protocol in Chapter 3, p. 53. The information in this chapter is sufficient to write small to middling documents, but
stops short of being enough for a full-blown professional development effort.

In summary: this chapter introduced the structure of individual HTML
files, and the basic relationship between HTML files. Chapter 3 will explain the
structure of a web (that is, a tree of HTML files, access to which is provided by
an HTTP server), and some of the more subtle aspects of HTML and HTTP.

UNDERSTANDING THE HYPERTEXT TRANSPORT PROTOCOL

3

● ● ● ●

In Chapter 2, we saw that web documents are written in a fairly simple language (HTML) which is a functional subset of SGML. We examined the basics of URLs, and saw how documents can link to each other.

Nevertheless, most of the discussion so far has been based on the unwritten supposition that the files in the web are being browsed locally. There is a subtle difference between local file lookups and remote access. If you read a file locally, your web browser simply picks it up off your local filesystem. But remote file lookups are mediated via the HyperText Transport Protocol (HTTP).

An explanation of HTTP does not make sense without some basic knowledge of TCP/IP. Therefore this chapter starts with a very brief, non-technical look at TCP/IP. It then discusses HTTP in more detail, with reference to the MIME standard for transmission of multimedia information across the Internet. Having explained the symbiosis between HTTP and MIME, it is then possible to look at the additional tag types not described in Chapter 2 (including those that invoke server-side scripts and those that govern the relationship between web documents).

A potted anatomy of TCP/IP

TCP/IP (the IP is short for Internet Protocol) is a 'protocol stack;'; it services requests from software that understands the high-level interface it provides, passes the requests down through several levels to the underlying transport mechanism, exchanges data (at the lowest level) with other computers running TCP/IP, and passes incoming data back up to the software. TCP provides a high-level, reliable, interface to applications, and exchanges data via IP. It is packet-based, meaning that it splits messages into packages before transmission and reassembles them in the correct order at the other end, and reliable, in that it ensures that all the necessary packets in an exchange are received correctly and without errors. IP is the low-level protocol that mediates the connections; it is 'unreliable', leaving error correction to the higher levels. (Other high-level protocols also run over IP, notably UDP and ICMP; some of them, such as TCP, are reliable, while others, such as UDP, are not.)

TCP applications can rely on their data stream: they don't need any built-in error tests and don't have to worry about data being corrupted en route. If a packet arrives mangled, the receiving TCP stack simply doesn't tell the application it arrived – it sends off for a new copy.

Because TCP/IP sits between the user's applications and the actual physical network, it provides a standard model for all networking software. The physical connection beneath a TCP/IP stack can be Ethernet, a fibre-optic FDDI network, a modem running one of the SLIP or PPP driver protocols, or an aviary full of carrier pigeons. It doesn't matter: TCP/IP simply sends a stream of numbered and addressed packets down to the transport level 'listens' for incoming packets coming back from the transport level, and reassembles them into an image of the original data. This abstraction of the protocol from the hardware is important: it means that TCP/IP can provide a common interface for everything from an IBM PC or a Macintosh to a UNIX workstation, a VAX minicomputer, or an IBM mainframe.

TCP/IP relies on computer-to-computer connections (or carrier pigeons) to route packets to their destination; as with the telephone network, your computer doesn't need to be physically wired to another computer to send data to it, as long as both are connected to the network. Packets are tagged with a destination TCP/IP address, and intermediate machines route them towards whichever adjacent computer they believe to be nearest to the ultimate goal. All TCP/IP-running computers must have a unique address. This takes the form of a 32-bit integer, usually represented in numeric form as four 8-bit words separated by periods: for example: 158.152.11.49. You won't often see addresses like this; they are mapped to symbolic names by the client–server software, which invokes a subsystem called the Domain Name System for this purpose. (DNS is a distributed database of hostnames which – you guessed it – is maintained over TCP/IP connections; See Figure 3.1.)

TCP/IP addresses are not allocated at random. Virtually all of them are allocated within a network – a cluster of addresses, usually granted to an organization. For example, all the IP addresses that have a first number in the range 0–126 are allocated to separate Class A networks. A Class A network consists of systems with IP addresses beginning with the specified number;

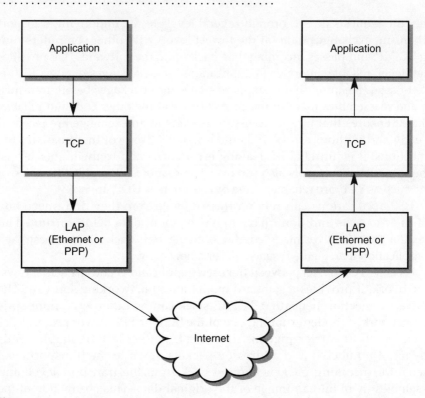

Figure 3.1

the administrator of the network is then free to allocate any permitted IP address starting with that number to a given machine.

Each of the mammoth Class A networks can have 16 million or so clients. Another cluster of IP addresses are allocated to the Class B networks, each node of which has the same first two IP numbers. (There also exist Class C networks; a Class C network can support a maximum of 254 hosts.)

Because TCP/IP is limited to an address space of 2^{32} hosts, various compromises have been made to prevent the address space from being overloaded as new systems come on-line. For example, local networks can be connected to the Internet via a gateway, and configured to use a subnet. (The computers on the subnet use a netmask to distinguish the host part of the IP address from the network component; this allows them to tell the difference between local and remote addresses.) An extended TCP/IP standard is under discussion; this standard will be upwardly compatible with the current one, but will provide an address space of 2^{64} hosts.

A computer running a TCP/IP stack needs to be able to allocate bandwidth to several programs executing in parallel. For this reason, two additional chunks of information are transmitted in any TCP/IP transaction; the port number and protocol number of the destination (and the port number of the originating host). TCP/IP can handle up to 2^{16} ports and 2^{16} protocols; as protocols can share ports, there is usually no trouble in allocating a communications socket the use of a unique port.

Well-known ports are port numbers that are usually used for a specific network protocol. If you have access to a system running UNIX, look in the file */etc/services*; this contains a list of recognized network services and the ports they run on. For example, almost all Internet news traffic is carried by connections on port 119 (which is reserved for NNTP, the net-news transport protocol). The world wide web is less standardized, but usually uses port 80; the URL specification makes allowances for a different port to be used. Thus, a web server listening for connections to port 80 of a host will grab any incoming packets and interpret them as HTTP commands.

A protocol in this context is simply a set format used for carrying out transactions between a client and a server. The client issues commands and the server carries them out and sends back some response to which the client may in turn respond, maintaining a dialogue. In many respects, a protocol can be viewed as a simple programming language. For example, NNTP or SMTP have an accepted repertoire of commands with various parameters, and return error values if an incorrect command is received.

The HTTP protocol

HTTP 1.0 is a fast, stateless protocol for the exchange of textual information. 'Stateless', in this context, means that the server doesn't remember any information about a query after it has been responded to. In NNTP, for example, a state-bound protocol, the client usually issues a GROUP command to specify a newsgroup to read. The server switches to that group, and applies the next command the client issues in the context of the current group. HTTP, however, is amnesiac; if you send two commands to an HTTP server, the result of the first command should not in any way affect the second command (except in some limited, unusual, circumstances: for example, when a CGI script is tracking state information associated with a browser's interaction with the server).

An HTTP exchange takes place over a TCP/IP socket. The client opens a socket, connects to the HTTP server via the port the server is listening to, and issues a command. The command is routed to the server via the Internet. The server receives the command and does something, typically involving a file lookup (Figure 3.2).

The second part of the transaction occurs when the server encodes the results of the request as a MIME-encapsulated document, pumps it back down the socket, then closes the connection. What happens after that is typically up to the client: normally it parses the response and either issues another query or renders the response and displays it (Figure 3.3).

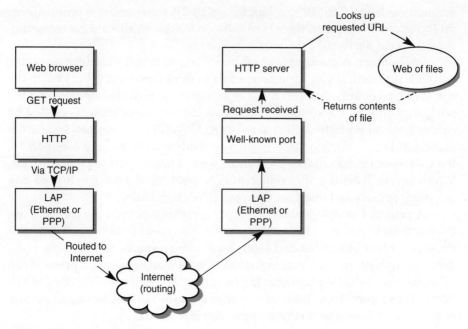

Figure 3.2 Stage one: the client makes a request.

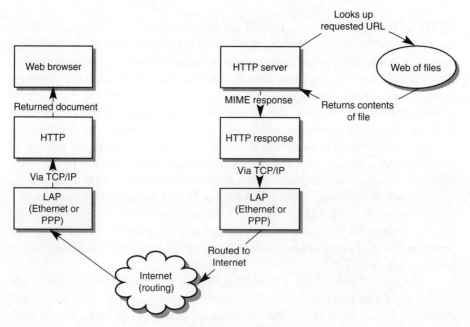

Figure 3.3 Stage two: the server returns a file.

Types of HTTP request

There are two types of HTTP request: simple requests and full requests.

A simple request is a command to get a URI. For example:

```
GET http://info.cern.ch/<CR><LF>
```

<CR> is a carriage return character; <LF> is a line feed character.

The server's response is to send the object specified by the GET request back to the client via the socket. In the case of a simple request, the object is simply sent back to the browser. In the event of a full request, the object is encapsulated using the MIME protocol, and a descriptive header precedes it on its way to the client.

MIME is the Internet standard for multimedia email, and it is described in the Internet standards documents RFC 1521 and RFC 1522 (formerly RFCs 1341 and 1342). Because a lot of mail gateways and network connections cannot handle full 8-bit binary data, or even 8-bit text, or long lines of text, MIME 'encapsulates' files for transport; a MIME message consists of a header (specifying the encoding method used) and an encoded form of the file, that is intended to pass through any mail gateway, however primitive. For example, a valid MIME content-type might be:

```
Application/postscript
```

indicating that the file in question contains application-specific information, of type postscript.

Use of the MIME protocol gives HTTP two advantages. Firstly, it can send ASCII-only connections and handle data passed through email gateways. Secondly, it serves to identify the type of data in the transmission. HTTP is not restricted to sending HTML; the MIME header identifies the method that must be used to unpack the document, and the format of the document. (We will examine the implications of MIME encoding in more detail later in this chapter. See 'Content-types', p. 59.)

A full request is somewhat more complex. It is a text message from the client, encoded in accordance with RFC 822 (originally used to define the header of email messages). It has this form:

```
Method URI ProtocolVersion <CR><LF>
[*<HTRQ Header>]
[<CR><LF> <data>]
```

- Method is actually a command to the server. GET is a method; there are others, and we'll see them shortly.

- URI is short for Universal Resource *Indicator*. At present, this is just a URL; however, the URI specification subsumes URLs and other, as yet unused, types of resource. (We'll see more about URIs in Chapters 4 and 6.)

- ProtocolVersion is usually a fixed piece of text that indicates the version of the protocol in use. At present it is HTTP/1.0, but this allows for change when HTTP 1.1 and HTTP-NG become available. (These future protocols are described in Chapter 10 'What they imply about the web'.)

Here is an example full request:

```
METHOD GET http://info.cern.ch/ HTTP/1.0<CR><LF>
```

The METHOD GET part of the request indicates that it is a GET request, as opposed to a POST or PUT or some other type. The HTTP/1.0 following the URI indicates that the request uses the HTTP 1.0 protocol.

- The HTRQ Header is an optional element or elements, separated by <CR><LF> pairs. They are encoded in RFC 822 format, so that each line consists of a keyword, followed by a colon, then a value or values. They are used to transmit control information about the transaction (such as who it originates from, what types of MIME-encoded data the client can accept, how they should be encoded, and what language version to send if the document specified by the GET command is available in multiple versions in different languages.)

- The Data portion is optional. Again, it consists of a MIME-encoded message. It is determined by the earlier information in the request; for example, a PUT command (which uploads a URL to a server) supplies the file to upload in the data portion of the request.

Methods

The method determines what the server is to do with the URL supplied in the query. Many methods are possible; you can extend the list and add new methods by registering them with the central registration authority. Here are the commonest: note that they are case-sensitive (unlike URIs).

GET   Retrieve whatever is indicated by the URI. If the URI points to a file, the server should return the file. If it points to a CGI script, the server should execute the script (with the remainder of the URI passed as parameters) and return the scripts output.

HEAD   Retrieve the HEAD portion of the specified URI. The HEAD portion of an HTML file stores various information, including some tags not discussed in the preceding chapter; notably, you can use it to store an indication of the last modification date. HTML HEAD elements are typically much smaller than the BODY elements. This command is really useful for caching web clients that store HTML files after each lookup, such as Netscape. When visiting a file that is stashed in the local cache, the web client grabs the HEAD of the file and checks the modification date. If it has been modified since it was last loaded (and stored in the cache), the browser issues a GET command to retrieve the body; otherwise, it displays the locally stored copy (which saves net bandwidth and time).

POST   Used to send a file, or data, to the server. The data is MIME encapsulated, and may be stored on the server as a file (if the server is so configured). Used by fill-out forms to send large amounts of data to a server. If the POST data is used to create a file, a URL corresponding to the new document is created and returned to the client.

PUT   Stores the information in the body portion of the request under the specified URL (which must already exist – typically created by a POST command). (Not commonly implemented.)

DELETE   Causes the server to delete the information stored under the specified URL. (This causes the URL to become invalid for future requests.) (Virtually never implemented, for security reasons.)

TEXTSEARCH   The specified URL is to be searched, using the query part of the URL (that is, the chunk following a question mark in the URL). (Searching will be covered in detail in Chapter 5, see 'A simple search script', p. 137. This method is virtually never implemented as such.)

Several other methods are available. Notably, LINK and UNLINK are used to connect or disconnect objects from each other. SPACEJUMP is used to indicate that the target of a GET method accepts a query consisting of the coordinates of a point within the object; this is used in implementing imagemaps. CHECKIN and CHECKOUT are similar to PUT and GET, but lock the object being checked in or out against changes by other users; they are deprecated, but were originally intended to facilitate common document source code management (such as a distributed version control engine). These methods are not actually used by most servers, because they imply a degree of interactivity that is inappropriate to the web's current usage model as a publishing medium. They are an historic legacy of the early web, which was implemented at CERN as a platform for collaborative working – the idea being that the web server would not be merely a publishing mechanism, but a project tracking and version control system with built-in text searching.

HTTP request fields

These fields are included in the query in a form similar to headers in an RFC 822 specification email message. Their function is to modify (or clarify) a method. Standard request fields are:

From: Identifies the username of the originator of the query. (Note that this is not trusted for secure communications.)

Accept: Contains a semi-colon separated list of content-types that the browser can accept and format. (Content-types are defined within MIME; see the next section for more information.) To save time it is possible to use wildcards in the Accept: field, for example, Accept: text.*

Accept-Encoding: Contains a semi-colon separated list of content-types that the browser can handle in the response. (For example, files that can be received and saved locally.) The Accept-Encoding field does not necessarily imply the ability to parse or display that content-type.

User-Agent: Contains the name of the browser or spider (web-probing robot) that originated the query. (This doesn't influence the returned response, but is used to provide the server with statistical information.)

Referrer: If present, contains the URL of the document from which the current query is derived. For example, if you are browsing a document (X) and select a URL (Y), the Referrer: field in your browser's HTTP request should be set to the URL of (X).

Authorization: Used for password/username/encryption information.

Charge-To: Used for account information; tells the server who to bill the request to. (The definition of this field is still being refined.)

If-Modified-Since: This field can be used to make a GET command conditional. If you are using a caching browser which saves visited files locally, it may use this field to ensure that the file is present only if it has been modified since the last time a local copy was stored. (It obtains the date at which the copy in its cache was written; puts that date in the If-Modified-Since: field; and if nothing is returned, knows that it is safe to display the version in the cache because it is still current.) Note that the format for dates is specified in the HTTP protocol. Dates are presented in a regular format, like: Tue, 15 Nov 1994 08:12:31 GMT.

MIME

MIME has been mentioned too many times to ignore in the past few pages. Originally, Internet email was transmitted in 7-bit ASCII code; this was an historical accident, dating to the early 1960s, when minimizing the amount of data exchanged was a priority, and the need to transmit 8-bit data had not yet been recognized. (Some systems today still have difficulty handling 8-bit information streams.) However, this was not exactly a satisfactory solution. It rendered the transport of complex binary data, or even ordinary text containing accented characters, impossible. MIME is a standard for Internet multimedia mail transport, specified in RFC 1521 (for details of specifying the format of Internet message bodies) and RFC 1522 (for details of a standard for transmitting non-ASCII text within MIME).

MIME messages look structurally similar to normal RFC 822 email messages, except for some additional header lines. Mime messages require the following additional header lines:

`MIME-Version:` The version of the MIME standard to which the message conforms (so that mail agents or web browsers know how to decode the message).

`Content-Type:` The type and subtype of data in the body of the message; specifies how the data is encoded. This usually consists of two values separated by a slash '/'.

`Content-Transfer-Encoding:` How the data is encoded to allow it to pass through mail gateways. (MIME usually uses a radix-64 encoding protocol to send binary files, but other encoding mechanisms are available.)

In addition, two other header fields may be used: `Content-ID:` and `Content-Description:`.

The point of MIME is simple; it provides a framework for sending canned multimedia information over the net. It describes the encoding and transmission of the body of a message, in a manner that is extensible. New content-types can be registered centrally with the Internet Assigned Numbers Authority (`IANA@isi.edu`). Thus, MIME was a natural choice for the world wide web.

Content-types

Common content-types include 'text' (contains textual information in a variety of character sets), 'multipart' (indicating that several different types of data are combined in one message), 'application' (indicating that the message contains binary data specific to some application), 'message' (for encapsulating other mail messages), 'image' (for transmitting graphics files), 'audio' (for transmitting audio or voice data) and 'video' (for transmitting video or moving image data).

Such formats are usually specified as type/subtype; for example text/ascii or image/gif, or text/richtext. (Richtext, defined in RFC 1341, looks suspiciously like HTML ...)

The purpose of the Content-Type field is to distinguish between different types of information. Web browsers can generally accept only certain types of file (notably HTML, text and some image formats). However, if they are informed what the content-type of a file is before it comes in, they can take appropriate action. This usually consists of checking a configuration mechanism that maps content-types to external programs that can deal with that kind of content; the browser then sends the incoming undigestible data to an application that can do something with it.

For example, a Microsoft Rich Text Format (RTF) file is probably meaningless to a web server and to a browser. However, if the web server is configured to signal that files ending in '.rtf' are of content-type `application/rtf`, and the web browser is configured to associate `application/rtf` with Microsoft Word, the file can be handed over to Microsoft Word for display.

Note that it is possible to specify a content-type as being 'multipart'. This means that several distinct objects are enclosed in the MIME-encapsulated data. (This is important for server-push documents, see 'Server push' p. 78.)

Putting it together

Now we've examined the standards, it's possible to explain what happens when you click on a hotlink in a document and your browser says, 'host contacted: waiting for reply'.

Firstly, your browser works out which URL you clicked on. It expands the URL, working out which web server the object referred to is stored on (assuming that it is not a local file). It then assembles an HTTP request.

If your browser supports a local cache (like Netscape), it checks the cache to see if a document matching the URL is present. If the document exists, it checks to see the last modification date on it. It then sends an HTTP HEAD request to the server. If the last modification date on the returned web document header is the same as the copy in the cache, it doesn't bother grabbing the document body – it displays the local copy, saving bandwidth and time. If the document on the server has been modified since the last request, it pulls in the new one with a GET request (and saves a copy in the cache behind the scenes while it displays it for you).

If your browser doesn't know about local caching, it just sends a GET request for the remote document. If nothing comes back, or an error message is returned (as defined in the IETF draft protocol for HTTP 1.0), then it tells you in no uncertain terms that it didn't find anything.

The process is more complex if you are using a proxy server. A proxy server is a local web server that acts as an external cache for web documents. You configure your web browser to send all its requests to the proxy server. The proxy then mediates your requests.

When you click on a hotlink in your proxy-aware client, it sends a GET request to the proxy server. The proxy server consults its cache, and basically does what the caching browser would do – it sends a HEAD, compares modification dates, and either passes the cached copy back to you or does a GET according to whatever it finds. Of course, your caching client might be set up to use a proxy server (effectively making a two-level cache). In this case, describing the transaction is a matter best accomplished with diagrams covered in sphagetti-like arrows.

As an aside: proxy servers perform the vital task of reducing long-distance traffic on the net. Because many local browsers can use a single proxy service, it reduces the number of GET requests considerably and replaces them with HEAD requests. Most documents have body parts that are much larger than their headers, so this reduces traffic to remote servers. (Local bandwidth is significantly cheaper than long-distance bandwidth.)

Of course, there are some points that need to be made about HTTP servers.

Firstly, although they listen to requests and reply by sending or receiving messages that look suspiciously similar to MIME email, they are *not* mail servers. An SMTP mail server does not store documents locally (except in a temporary queue); it tries to forward them as fast as possible to its peers. An HTTP server, on the other hand, doesn't know how to talk to other HTTP servers (unless it is a proxy server). It does, however, know how to find files that are stored locally.

Secondly, you can do lots of things with a private HTTP server that are not immediately obvious. The CHECKIN and CHECKOUT methods, although obsolescent, point the way: PUT and GET are more explicit. The Web was designed at CERN to facilitate collaborative authoring – not simply browsing, but group work to prepare documents. These features are not currently used to any great extent by web browsers; in fact, most current browsers are pretty much read-only, to the point where separate HTML text editors are being sold on the basis that people need an additional piece of software to help write web documents. This situation is not going to last for ever. Software like Microsoft HTML Assistant for Word shows the way towards combined browser/editors that use the web as a data repository, rather than as a passive publication medium. The ability to share documents (and lock them against third-party changes while editing them, and to store multiple versions) turns a Web server into an extremely powerful groupware environment.

Thirdly, a caveat: the version of HTTP described above is HTTP 1.0. This is a preliminary standard. An improved version, HTTP 1.1, is in the works; behind it, early studies are being conducted into the feasibility of HTTP-NG, a next-generation non-text-oriented protocol for high-speed data transfer that will nevertheless be a backwardly compatible superset of the earlier standards. HTTP 1.0 will probably remain standard for quite a while (as the installed base of web browsers and servers adds a certain inertia to it), but new features will appear – and the web is developing so fast that it is not possible to predict where they will spring up.

> There are more HTTP request header fields than those described above. We'll see some of them in action later in this book (notably the fields used by HTACCESS authentication). For the time being, if you need an exhaustive list of HTTP request headers, you need to find a copy of the relevent RFC standard for HTTP 1.0; this can be found on `www.w3.org`, among other places.

Response status messages

From time to time, you will click a link and see, not a pretty document or image, but a bald, bare, error message, usually with a number attached. In fact, every time you send an HTTP request, the web server returns a MIME header. The first line of the response consists of:

```
HTTP-Version<SP>Status-Code<SP>Reason-Phrase<CR><LF>
```

for example:

```
HTTP/1.0 200 OK
```

This is the standard response to a successful GET request for an HTML document. It would normally be followed by more header information, such as the Content-Type, the Content-Length and then the MIME-encapsulated document.
However, there are some other possible responses:

`Created 201`	Following a `POST` command, this indicates that a document was successfully created. The textual part of the response line indicates the URI by which the newly created document is known.
`Accepted 202`	The request has been accepted for processing, but processing has not been completed. (In other words, the request is being executed asynchronously.) The request may or may not eventually be acted upon; there is no facility for status reports on asynchronous operations.
`No Response 204`	The server has received the request but there is no information to send back, and the browser should stay in the same document view. This is mainly to allow

input for scripts to be received without the browser changing the document at the same time.

`Redirection: 300`   The target URI has moved (see below).

`Error 4xx, 5xx`   The 4xx codes indicate that the browser seems to have made a mistake, and the 5xx codes indicate that the server is aware that it has encountered an internal error. It is often impossible to distinguish these cases. The body section may contain a document describing the error in human readable form.

The commonest error messages are:

`Bad request 400`   The request was badly formed or impossible to satisfy.

`Unauthorized 401`   Returned by a server where access control (typically through HTACCESS) is in force. The parameter to this message specifies a set of authorization schemes which are acceptable. The browser should retry the request with a suitable `Authorization:` header.

`Payment required 402`   The parameter to this message specifies acceptable charging schemes. The client may retry the request with a suitable `ChargeTo:` header. (This is not in general use yet.)

`Forbidden 403`   The request is forbidden. Authorization will not help.

`Not found 404`   The server has not found anything matching the URI given.

`Internal error 500`   The server encountered an unexpected condition which prevented it from fulfilling the request. Typical causes of this message include a CGI script failure, or corrupt output from a script.

`Not implemented 501`   The server does not support the facility required.

`Service temporarily overloaded 502`   The server cannot process the request owing to a high load (whether servicing HTTP or other requests). The implication is that this is a temporary condition.

`Gateway timeout 503`   This is equivalent to `Internal error 500`, but indicates that rather than the server being at fault, the fault lies in some other service that the server was invoking to fulfil the request; the response from the other service did not arrive within the time that the gateway was prepared to wait. As from the point of view of the client the HTTP transaction to the other service is hidden within the server, this may be treated identically to `Internal error 500`, but has more diagnostic value.

Redirection codes (3xx) indicate that the request can't be handled by the server, but is not necessarily invalid; some action can be taken by the browser to fulfil the request. These codes are:

Moved 301   The data requested has been assigned a new URI. The change is permanent. (Browsers with link-editing capability should automatically relink to the new reference.) The response contains one or more header lines which specify alternative addresses for the object in question.

Found 302   The data requested actually resides under a different URL, however the redirection may be altered on occasion.

In general, HTTP return codes are not displayed by a browser unless something has gone wrong. They can be invaluable in debugging a web, though. For example, the commonest error returned by a malfunctioning CGI script is 500: malformed header from script. This means that the CGI script either failed to run, or returned something that wasn't a valid MIME-encapsulated response to the server, and is the cue to the programmer to check the server *error_log* file (for whatever error output the script produced).

Forms, ISINDEX and tags that go bump on the server

As we've seen, the HTTP protocol supports much more than just hypertext browsing. Its facilities for accepting data permit it to interact with client software in a variety of ways. We are now in a position to look at some of the more complex issues surrounding the web: namely, forms and scripts that run on the server, searchable document sets, tags that refer to document meta-information and server-push/client-pull.

These aspects of the web are the most difficult to deal with, but among the most rewarding; if you can give your users access to forms you can provide central access to some useful facilities – you can sell things to them, for example, or let them use a centrally maintained software tool, or make them tell you their name before you give them access to information. If you can make your web searchable, you can multiply its usefulness massively; navigating through hyperlinks forces your users to follow the railroad tracks of someone else's thoughts, but if they can search for document contents they can drive wherever they want to go. And document meta-information – information about the structure of documents – can be used to do some really nifty things (as described in Chapters 4–6).

Web servers can do more than serve documents; they can execute other programs and return the results to a browser. These programs are frequently called CGI scripts (after the Common Gateway Interface, which they use to communicate with the web server). For purposes of this discussion, programs executed via the CGI interface may be referred to as scripts, because many such programs are written in interpreted languages such as Perl. (Programs written in interpreted languages are frequently called scripts, to distinguish them from compiled binary programs.)

Note: Two other types of programmatic facility exist on web servers. These are: server-side includes and client-side applets. For the sake of simplicity, we're going to ignore these until we have examined the CGI interface in some detail.

When an HTTP server receives a request that invokes a program, as opposed to a file, it runs the appropriate program and sends its output back to the requester.

To allow useful interaction between a user and a script on a server, some sort of mechanism is needed to allow users to enter information that can then be transmitted to the server. HTML is fixed text; a dynamic, changeable medium is needed. In the HTML 2.0 standard, this is provided by forms.

Using HTML forms and CGI scripts, it is possible to interface an HTTP server to a big database so that it acts as a front-end, giving users many of the benefits of a distributed database without the corresponding disadvantages (Figure 3.4).

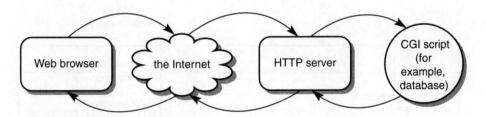

Figure 3.4 Web browsers and CGI scripts.

The relationship between a form and a CGI script is mediated through HTTP, using the web server as matchmaker. A form is an HTML document; it contains a URL that points to a CGI script (rather than to another HTML page). When you click this link (using a button on the form), your browser sends a complex request to the server, enclosing a package of data from the form. The server in turn runs the CGI script and feeds the data to it. The CGI script does something with the data, and prints some HTML (or another MIME content-type) to the standard output device; the web server reads this, and returns it to your browser (Figure 3.5).

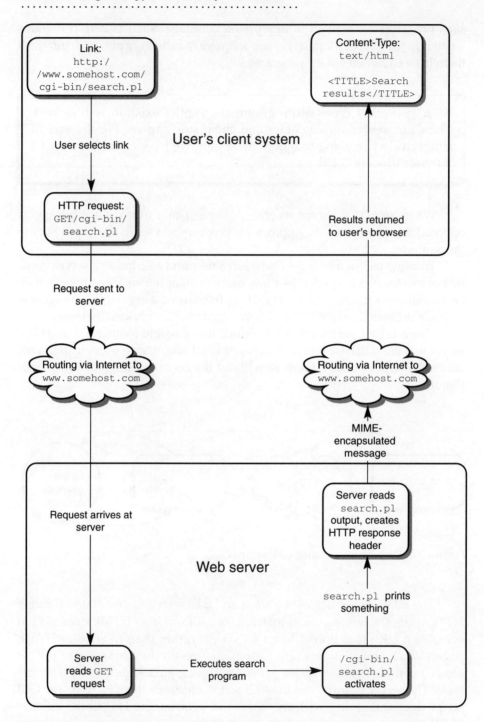

Figure 3.5 Flow of data in an HTTP request.

Forms

In general, a form consists of a section of an HTML document enclosed in the tags:

```
<FORM ACTION="url"> ... </FORM>
```

All the text between the tags consists of the body of the form; the URL specified in the ACTION parameter is the address of the program that handles the form back on the server. (We'll look at an example server-side script in some detail later on. For now, we're concentrating on the HTML interface to forms.)

You can specify the HTTP method used to send the form feedback to the server. In general, you can use the GET or POST methods; GET (the default) causes the fill-out form contents to be appended to the URL (like a query), while POST causes the fill-out form contents to be sent to the server in a data body attached to the HTTP request.

For example, to set up a form which will be processed by a server CGI program called *cgi-bin/server.pl* on myhost.com, using the POST method, you would do something like this:

```
<FORM ACTION="http://myhost.com/cgi-bin/server.pl"
METHOD=POST>
<!-- form contents go here -->
</FORM>
```

Within a form, you can use some new types of tag: INPUT, SELECT and TEXTAREA. An INPUT tag is used to display a simple element like a pushbutton or a text entry box on the form. A SELECT tag selects one of a number of options – in effect, you can use it to display menus. And a TEXTAREA is used to create a field you type text into.

INPUT

You use the INPUT tag rather like IMG (see, 'Pictures', p. 32); it requires no corresponding </INPUT> tag, but takes a number of parameters that define what it is. For example, <INPUT TYPE="checkbox"> displays a single checkbox (a box which can have a tick in it, indicating whether it is 'on' or 'off'), while <INPUT TYPE="reset"> displays a button which, when pressed, resets all the other fields in the current form. <INPUT TYPE="submit"> displays a 'submit' button; pressing this button causes the contents of the form to be sent to the named server URL via the method you (the author of the form) choose.

In addition to taking a type parameter, all INPUT tags require a symbolic name which identifies them. For example, in the following (bad) form:

```
<FORM ACTION="http://myhost.com/cgi-bin/server.pl"
METHOD="GET">
<INPUT TYPE="checkbox">foo
<INPUT TYPE="checkbox">bar
<INPUT TYPE="submit">
</FORM>
```

the browser can check the state of the two checkboxes – but as they are not named, it has no way of letting the server program know which of them is in a given state.

The correct version of the form gives each of the checkboxes a name:

```
<FORM ACTION="http://myhost.com/cgi-bin/server.pl"
METHOD="GET">
<HR>
This is an example form with two checkboxes
<P>
<INPUT TYPE="checkbox" NAME="foo">foo
<INPUT TYPE="checkbox" NAME="bar">bar
<INPUT TYPE="submit">
</FORM>
```

and it looks like Figure 3.6.

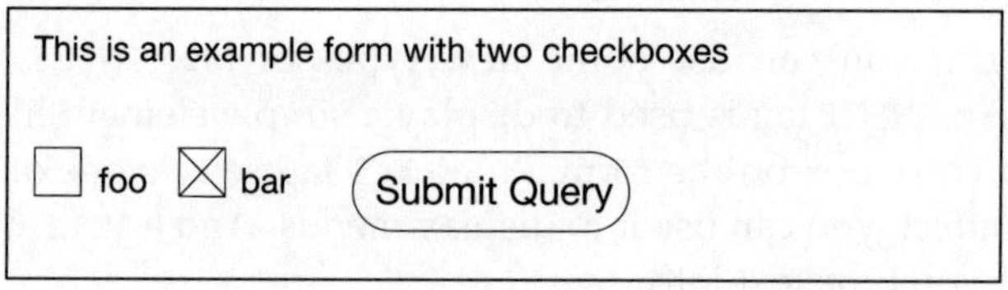

This is an example form with two checkboxes

☐ foo ☒ bar (Submit Query)

Figure 3.6

The two INPUT tags are both of type checkbox, but now they have different names.When you press the 'submit' button (which needs no name, because its value is not returned to the server), the browser can figure out the state each checkbox is in and send back to the server (http://myhost.com/) a request like this:

```
http://myhost.com/cgi-bin/server.pl?bar=on
```

When the server gets this URL, it will run /cgi-bin/server.pl, passing it (via the environment, if it is a UNIX server, or through some other means if it is not) the parameter:

```
bar=on
```

Note that checkboxes which are off are not passed back to the server (by default).

If we had specified METHOD=POST, then instead of tagging the returned values onto the end of the HTTP GET request, the client would submit an HTTP POST command to the server http://myhost.com/cgi-bin/server.pl, the body of which would contain those two parameters.

The main reasons for using the POST method rather than GET in scripts are:

- GET requests are passed to CGI scripts via the 'environment', an area of shared memory. Some systems place a limit (usually small) on the size of the environment, so a large form may not fit into it. In contrast, POST arguments are passed to CGI scripts via their 'standard input'. (UNIX views all programs as having a 'standard input' and a 'standard output', which are streams of bytes going into and out of the program). The standard input is unlimited in size – it is a stream of input data, not a preallocated block of memory.

- GET requests are sent to the server as arguments following the name of the CGI script to execute. They may therefore be 'captured' at the client side, for example by adding a GET request to a hotlist of frequently used URLs. POST requests, however, are sent as separate MIME-encapsulated messages, and cannot be captured on a hotlist. Thus, if you are writing a form-based login handler for your site, which forces users to enter their names and passwords every time they try to access it, you will probably want to use the POST method so that the name/password information can't be captured in a hotlist and passed on to persons unknown.

Here are the various attributes you can use with an INPUT tag:

TYPE   Specifies the type of input tag to display. It can be:

checkbox   A toggle button that can exist in two states (on or off).

hidden   A field that is present, and sent to the server, but that is not visible to the user. (A use for this option is discussed in Chapter 8, p. 192.)

image   Rather than displaying a button or field, this displays an image (specified using an additional SRC="url" tag). If the user clicks inside the image, the form immediately submits the mouse coordinates to the server. The coordinates are measured from the top left corner of the image in pixels; if the image field is named field then the X-coordinate is returned with name field.x, and the Y-coordinate is returned with name field.y.

password   A text entry field that conceals typed input with asterisks.

radio   A toggle button that can exist in two states (on or off). It may share a name with other buttons, in which case only one of them can be on at a time. (Think about an old-fashioned car radio with its preset tuning buttons.)

reset   A pushbutton that clears all the other input elements in the current form (it resets them to their default values).

submit	A pushbutton that causes the current form to be submitted to the server on the designated URL.
text	A text entry field you can type into (default).
NAME	Specifies the symbolic name of the input tag. This is required For all types except 'submit' and 'reset' (which are not passed back to the server). It permits the client to assemble a query string that distinguishes between different input tags. (The best way to think of this parameter is as a variable declaration in a programming language – you declare the name of a variable of a given type, and thereafter you can use it to store that type of data and can refer to the data it contains by name.) Note that the NAME attribute is not displayed in the form; it is defined purely to assist in communication with the server script.
VALUE	Used to specify the default contents of a text entry field or the state of a checkbox or radio button when it is checked. Normally buttons are 'on' when checked, otherwise they are 'off'; using VALUE you can set a checkbox to return some other value when it is checked. If you apply a VALUE parameter to a submit or reset button it changes the label on the button.
CHECKED	Specifies that the current checkbox or radio button is checked by default.
SIZE	The physical size of the input field in characters; it applies only to text and password fields. If no SIZE parameter is specified, these fields default to 20 characters.
MAXLENGTH	can be used to set an upper limit on the number of characters accepted in a text or password field. If it is not set, the text field scrolls to accommodate additional text, up to an unlimited capacity.

In addition to the INPUT tag types, there are other ways of getting information to a script, notably SELECT and TEXTAREA:

SELECT	The <SELECT> ... </SELECT> tag is used to present a menu-like mechanism for choosing between options. Within a SELECT tag, only OPTION tags are allowed. For example:

```
<SELECT NAME="image configuration">
<OPTION> Black and White
<OPTION> 4-bit Colour
<OPTION> 8-bit Colour
</SELECT>
```

This is displayed as a pop-up menu with three items (Figure 3.7). SELECT accepts the following parameters:

NAME	The symbolic name for this SELECT element. This must be present, as it is used when putting together the query

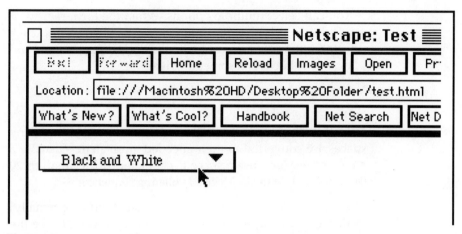

Figure 3.7

string for the submitted form. SIZE: if SIZE is 1 or unde-
fined, the SELECT is represented as a pop up menu. If SIZE
is 2 or more, the SELECT is a scrolled list; the value of SIZE
determines how many items in the list are displayed.

MULTIPLE   If present, specifies that the SELECT should allow multiple
options to be selected. The presence of MULTIPLE forces the
SELECT to be represented as a scrolled list rather than as a
menu.

OPTION   Can also accept the SELECTed parameter; this specifies that
the option is selected by default.

So we can now display a scrolling list of options like this:

```
<SELECT NAME="my-country" SIZE=4 MULTIPLE>
<OPTION>Greece
<OPTION>France
<OPTION>Belgium
<OPTION>Norway
<OPTION>Nepal
</SELECT>
```

This is displayed as shown in Figure 3.8.

Figure 3.8

You can select multiple options. When the form returns, it sends back a URL containing `mylist=` strings for each selected option. For example, if you tagged `One`, `Three`, and `Five`, it would contain something like.

```
...?my-list=One&my-list=Three&my-list=five
```

in the GET request.

Note: It is illegal to include space characters in a URL, so any spaces are converted to their encoded equivalent – usually a "`%20`" string (because a space is character 32 (decimal) or 20 (hexadecimal) in the ISO 8859/1 collating sequence).

TEXTAREA

The TEXTAREA tag creates a text entry field with (optionally) multiple lines and default contents in the form. Unlike the text entry version of INPUT, it takes separate options for ROWS and COLS (to indicate the size of the field); by default it creates a 4 row by 40 column area. A closing tag is required.

For example, a text area with some default text might look like this:

```
<TEXTAREA NAME="address" ROWS="5" COLS="60">
Please enter your residential address here
</TEXTAREA>
```

This is displayed as shown in Figure 3.9.

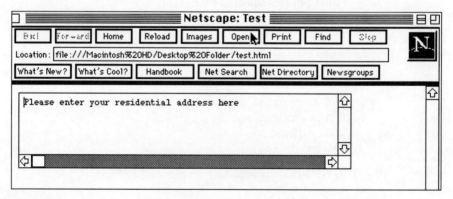

Figure 3.9

Obsolete forms

To all intents and purposes, a searchable server index is just another kind of form. The difference is that while the forms we've just seen bundle up a bunch of data to send to a script on the server, the index specifically looks for a keyword on the server and returns a document containing it. Thus, it's a special – somewhat simple – example of a form.

The ISINDEX tag designates a document as being a searchable index. It is not enclosed in a <FORM> ... </FORM> tag; rather it appears in the <HEAD> of the document. ISINDEX documents automatically include a search field; if you type some text into it and press return, the text (with words separated by + symbols) is returned to the URL of the ISINDEX form.

ISINDEX is effectively obsolete; it predates the existing form standard. These days, it is more appropriate to write a form that queries a server script than to use an ISINDEX document. When they are used, ISINDEX documents are generated automatically by a search script; this is discussed below. However, it is common practice to see ISINDEX tags embedded in the body of an HTML document where a single text entry field is desired.

ISMAP is a similarly obsolescent attempt at defining a protocol for handling clickable images. It is being replaced by the <SUBMIT TYPE="image" SRC="url"> tag, which is cleaner and more consistent with the general form handling mechanism. However, with the exception of HTML 3.0 compatible browsers (such as Netscape 2.0), which support client-side imagemaps, ISMAP is in general use. We will examine its use in Chapter 6.

CGI scripts

CGI scripts are programs executed by the HTTP server software that accept certain information (passed in accordance with the specifications of the CGI), do something with the information, and (usually) print out an HTML document to return to the client. This, of course, begs the question: what does it do? The answer can only be embarrassingly vague ... anything you can think of programming can be done using CGI scripts. The following example carries out a text search on a directory of files. More sophisticated CGI scripts can handle bulletin boards (HyperNews), mediate complex symbolic naming schemas and access control protocols, or even serve as the front-end to a complex graphical user interface (as with W3Kit, http://www.geom.umn.edu/ docs/W3Kit/W3Kit.html, a system for controlling 3D rendering systems remotely). CGI scripts can also be used to constantly update a flow of data to a browser, using two methods, server push and client pull. These are used by coffee percolator and fishtank-observing web sites and other novelties, not to mention pieces of complex software like SATAN, the network security analyser (which uses the web as a control interface).

The CGI interface works fairly simply. A directory or set of directories on the web server are given over to scripts; these are user or webmaster-written programs that are 'trusted' to run on the server. The directory containing scripts is usually called *cgi-bin* (at least, on the NCSA and Apache servers), after the standard introduced in the NCSA web server in 1992, and it is located in the web server's root directory. Some servers, such as NCSA HTTPD, Apache and Netsite Commerce Server, can handle CGI scripts in subdirectories of */cgi-bin*. Other servers, notably CERN HTTPD 3.0, can handle only a single */cgi-bin* directory, but permit individual users to have their own script directories. And some servers recognize scripts located anywhere, by virtue of their filename extensions.

When an HTTP GET or POST request is received by the server, with a URL pointing to a file in a directory designated as containing scripts, the server attempts to execute the script and pass it the query information for processing. The query takes the form of parameters following a question mark in the case of a GET request, or the MIME-encapsulated message in a POST request. The server then takes the output from the script and returns it to the client in the body of the HTTP server's response.

If the script is invoked via GET, it finds the submitted information in the environment variable QUERY_STRING. If it is invoked via POST, the submitted information can be read from the standard input. The server tells the script where to read its input information from, by setting the environment variable REQUEST_METHOD to either "GET" or "POST" depending on the nature of the query.

Of course, this is a fairly UNIX-specific protocol. HTTP servers run on just about everything. There are several flavours of server for UNIX; there are also servers for the Macintosh, for Windows, and for big metal systems like VAX/VMS and even IBM's MVS. Unfortunately, these systems don't all support the same scripting languages. They don't have common filename semantics, or a universal standard for passing variable information between programs: they don't even all use the same native character set. So it is not possible to expect a CGI script from one server to run on another without modification. At the point of pressing 'submit', what happens in the world of HTML stops being standardized and descends into a hodgepodge of machine-dependent conditions and outright eccentricity.

To keep things simple, I'm going to show a short example that works only on a UNIX system. UNIX is a convenient platform for web server development; its filename conventions are the same as those used for URLs, and it provides a handy mechanism for passing parameters to a program.

When a CGI script runs in response to a GET request, the server passes all the form options to it on the command line. The options are passed in the form of variable=value pairs. For example, the request:

```
http://myhost.somewhere.com/cgi-bin/myscript.pl?
box1=on&box2=on&password=xyzzy
```

will be passed to the script *cgi-bin/myscript.pl*, with the parameters:

```
box1=on box2=on password=xyzzy
```

present in an environment variable (QUERY_STRING).

The script then needs to:

- split the variable up into separate arguments

- decode any encoded escape characters

- set internal flags accordingly

- do something (!)

- print an HTTP header that can be sent back to the client application

- optionally, print some data that can be sent back to the client in the body of the HTTP transaction

A simple query

Suppose we want to allow users to search all the documents in a directory on our web server (which just happens to be running UNIX). The searchable files are held in a directory at the same level as *cgi-bin*. A map of the system looks like Figure 3.10 (if you oversimplify grossly and ignore the other 18 000 files on the UNIX system).

The file *documents/index.html* contains a form that permits you to search the files in */usr/local/http/documents*. It looks like this:

```
<HTML>
<HEAD>
<TITLE>Index to "documents"</TITLE>
</HEAD>
<BODY>
<H1>Search form</H1>
Welcome to myhost.com. A number of documents are available
on this server. You can browse the documents by name (from
the list below) or you can search the documents using the
search form:
<P>
<HR>
<FORM ACTION="http://myhost.com/cgi-bin/search.pl"
METHOD="GET">
<INPUT TYPE="text" NAME="srch">Text to search for
<INPUT TYPE="submit" VALUE="Begin search">
<INPUT TYPE="reset" VALUE="Reset form">
</FORM>
<HR>
<H2>List of files</H2>
<A HREF="document1.html">document1.html</A>
<A HREF="document2.html">document2.html</A>
<A HREF="document3.html">document3.html</A>
</BODY>
</HTML>
```

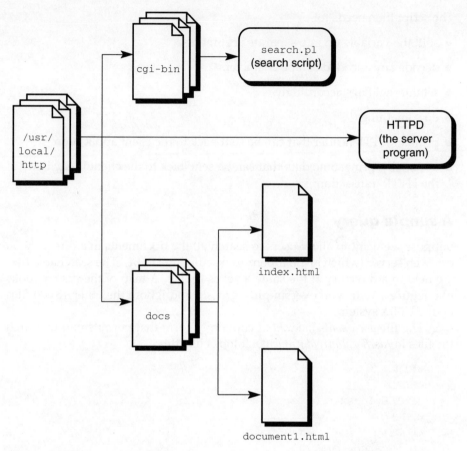

Figure 3.10 Map of the filesystem

This looks (to Netscape, running on a Macintosh) like Figure 3.11.

When you enter some text (for example, the word 'value') in the search field and press the 'Begin search' button, it sends a GET request to myhost.com:

```
GET http://myhost.com/cgi-bin/search.pl?srch=value
```

When this arrives at the *myhost.com*, the HTTP server looks in */cgi-bin* and executes the program *search.pl*, passing it the single option: srch=value (meaning the field srch had the contents value typed into it). The script is described in detail in Chapter 5; see 'A simple search script' p. 137. It embeds its output in a stream of HTML, then exits. What comes back to the client from the script might look like this:

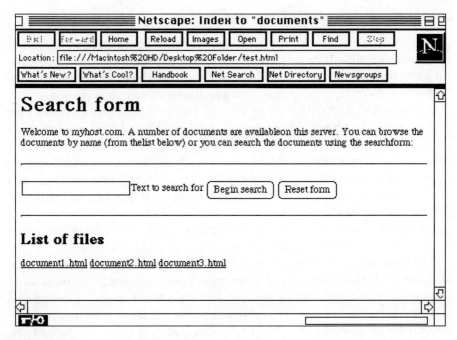

Figure 3.11

```
<BODY>
Results of server search on <B>myhost.com</B>:
<P>
document1.html
document4.html
<P>
<A HREF="index.html">Back to index page</A>
</BODY>
```

Note that this is a fairly crude CGI script. It doesn't attempt to:

- check that it is being invoked by an authorized user or source

- check its arguments for correctness

- invoke any external programs

- print an alternative output if nothing was found

Every one of these omissions serves to render it less than pleasing. Nevertheless, it should be clear what's going on.

Dynamically updated documents

Up until now, we've looked at HTML documents as being essentially passive, like paper. Admittedly, paper does not support pop-up menus and hypertext links, but the web documents we've seen are essentially static between downloads. They do not spontaneously change without human intervention.

Also noted in passing are those web pages that are connected to the external world by some kind of interface, be they a digital camera pointed at a lizard in a terrarium (`http://iguana.images.com/dupecam.html`), or a controller and a robot arm with attached camera. These operate via a CGI script; a request to the script causes the camera to package its most recent image as a GIF file and return it via HTTP. Such pages are interesting, but serve little purpose unless they can be updated automatically and regularly.

There are two ways to drive the regular update of a document; either from the client end (client pull), or from the server end (server push).

In a client-pull system, the web browser receives a document that contains special HTML meta-information tags. These tags cause the browser to take some action automatically at a specified time, for example, by reloading a page every few seconds, with a new image each time. (Currently, the only browser that supports this is Netscape, although it is likely to spread.) The client 'pulls' in data repeatedly. The repetitive GET requests may also include some control information to tell the server to modify the file being delivered to the client, for example by changing the time interval at which pages are pulled in. There is no need for the server to understand 'client pull' in any way; all it does is respond to client requests.

In a server-push system, rather than the client pulling pages regularly, the server sends a document then holds the HTTP connection open and sends successive MIME-encapsulated objects through it. This system is mediated by HTTP rather than by HTML; both client and server need to know about 'multipart/mixed' MIME documents, but there is no requirement for the client to understand the special HTML tags used in client-pull systems.

Server push

MIME permits multiple objects to be included in a message by specifying that the content-type is 'multipart/mixed', and by adding a boundary that can be used to delimit the objects. HTTP uses the content-type 'x-mixed-replace' to indicate that the second and subsequent objects should replace their predecessors. For example:

```
Content-type: multipart/x-mixed-replace;boundary=---=====--
```

This is then followed by a series of MIME-encapsulated objects, separated by lines containing only the boundary string, `--=====--`. For example:

```
Content-type: multipart/x-mixed-replace;boundary=--=====--
--======--
Content-type: text/html
[[ an object goes here, containing text ]]
--======--
Content-type: text/html
[[ the second and final object goes here ]]
--======--
```

The first object is received by the browser and displayed, but the connection stays open until the second object has been received. This blocks up a socket from the server to the client until the last in the series of files has been transferred (although a user can end the session at any time by telling the browser to 'stop' the connection).

One use of this is to send a sequence of images that change over time. Because the subsequent objects replace their predecessors, you can use server push to update an inlined image in a web page regularly. Thus, you can effectively use the web as a delivery mechanism for (very) slow-scan video.

Note that when sending objects down a connection using server push, it is a good idea to ensure first that the CGI script driving the connection terminates as soon as the connection disappears. Otherwise, every time somebody connects to your server, a new process will be spawned that will continue running after the user moves on elsewhere.

Client pull

Client pull relies on a special HTML tag in the HEAD section of a document:

```
<META HTTP-EQUIV="Refresh" CONTENT="1;URL">
```

The META tag indicates that this is meta-information describing the document. It sets the variable in HTTP-EQUIV named "Refresh" to whatever is described in CONTENT. (HTTP-EQUIV allows an HTML document to specify information equivalent to the HTTP response header from the server).

If CONTENT contains just a number, Netscape responds by reloading the document that many seconds later. If CONTENT is something like: "1;URL=http://www.w3.org/index.html", Netscape waits for one second, then loads the designated URL.

Note that if the newly loaded document does not also contain a refresh directive, it will not be reloaded again; the new document replaces the original, and the meta-information associated with the original is lost.

If you create a file with a refresh directive in its header, then load it, your browser will automatically reload it from here to eternity, unless you explicitly go to a different URL or close the window you are viewing it in.

Client pull is probably more useful with a CGI script. For example, the HTTP response:

```
Location: URL
```

is used to redirect browsers to another location; it causes a web browser to load the specified URL. The HTTP response:

```
Refresh: n
```

(recognized by Netscape – it's the server version of the `HTTP-EQUIV` meta-tag described above) makes the browser reload the current URL. You can combine the two:

```
Location: somewhere.html
Refresh: 10
```

thus giving yourself 10 seconds to look at *somewhere.html* before your browser reloads the current URL.

We will see how to emit custom HTTP headers from inside CGI scripts in Chapter 5.

One point to note is that each refresh operation constitutes a new HTTP request. There are some overheads for setting up a connection from a browser to a web server; thus, client pull is less efficient at loading long sequences of files than server push.

THE BABEL OF THE WEB

• • • •

Formatting languages, style sheets, PDLs and scripting systems

The world wide web is a veritable Tower of Babel; a vast, seething mass of information represented (and transported) using a myriad of languages. In the preceding chapters I've discussed parts of the HTML 2.0 language (including the table extensions), and the HTTP 1.0 protocol, and have confined my excursions into other languages as much as possible. Unfortunately there comes a point when it's necessary to start exploring other dialects.

In the beginning, the lingua franca of the Internet was the US ASCII character set. Email between some networks could be exchanged only in this format; adding formatting or markup information to documents was simply not possible (at least, not without complex work-arounds). This made sense back in the pioneering days when networking was something of a feat in its own right and the emphasis was on just getting your system hooked up to one of the early Internet IMPs or a UUCP feed. However, it was a lowest common denominator approach: if you couldn't send a complex document over your network protocol, you had to send a simple one instead. This approach worked, but it left a legacy of problems that are only now being addressed (by the new open document exchange protocols that are described in this chapter).

Why ASCII is a problem

The US ASCII character set is a simple 7-bit representation of the English alphabet, plus some spare control characters, numbers and symbols. As a standard for information exchange it gained ground from the late 1950s, becoming ubiquitous in the 1970s. A variety of 8-bit derivatives were designed, which used the extra 126 characters for various purposes; the most important of these (for our purposes) is ISO 8859/1, the Latin-1 codeset (which can represent most Western European languages and is used by HTML 2.0).

There's nothing inherently wrong with ASCII; you can read it on nearly anything, and what it loses in monotonous appearance it makes up for in portability. However, ASCII is inadequate for publishing complex information. It contains no formatting codes to select typeface, weight, point size or emphasis. Nor does it contain semantic tags to indicate the nature of tagged information. For example, it is possible in principle to publish a book as raw ASCII text, but it is not possible to apply italics or large print within it: nor is it convenient to use the text as a reference, by tagging the elements within it.

Most text searches simply attempt to match a target string within a file. A semantically tagged file is more useful; it becomes possible to match target information types within a file. For example, if the file is a manufacturer's price list, it might be possible to search for all widgets matching a specific price – because the price of each item would be semantically tagged and therefore identifiable within the document. For example, consider an HTML file with the following head:

```
<HEAD>
<TITLE>Inventory description: Widget 43</TITLE>
<META NAME="Widget" VALUE="43">
<META NAME="Colour" VALUE="Blue">
<META NAME="Price" VALUE="3.00">
</HEAD>
```

The <META> tag lets us embed information about the content of a document within it. Each of these tags declares that a named attribute (such as "Widget") has a given value (such as "43"). The <META> tags are not rendered with the document, but nonetheless they associate certain information with it. By searching through the <HEAD> sections of a collection of documents that contain these tags, we can use the tags as if they are key fields in a database (within which each HTML file is a single record).

Gopher, an early (late 1980s) distributed information system and forerunner to the world wide web, uses ASCII files. Its shortcomings are most evident after you have tried the world wide web. Notably, although Gopher is an efficient mechanism for providing access to files, it doesn't support any kind of formatting or semantic markup: the files on a Gopher archive appear in whatever default typeface your browser displays, and you can't search then on the basis of their meaning – only on their literal textual contents (Figure 4.1).

WAIS, an early (late 1980s) implementation of the Z39.50 standard for searchable text databases, also suffers from the lack of semantic markup. A WAIS server maintains an index of every word in all the files on the server; complex boolean searches and word frequency searches can be specified. However, WAIS engines don't handle the semantics of a document – they

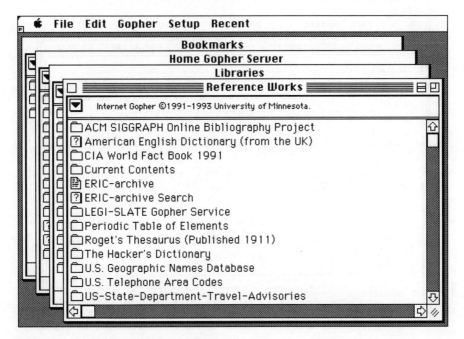

Figure 4.1 TurboGopher (Macintosh).

treat each file as a raw stream of text. So you can't tell a server to search the title and abstract of every file stored on it for some target text; it searches the whole text, or none (Figures 4.2 and 4.3).

Email was also handicapped by ASCII. In fact, sending anything except straight ASCII through an email system was an angst-inducing experience until quite recently. (For real fun and joy, try sending some email containing lines beginning with a period followed by some random letters through a UNIX MMDF or sendmail system. You might find the result enlightening: just don't do this with any file you consider valuable!)

The MIME standard, proposed in 1991, was intended to get around this problem by allowing complex documents to be exchanged. It permits embedded objects – such as word processor files – to be transmitted; they are encoded in a 7-bit format that any MIME-compliant mail agent can unpack at the receiving end. However, most text processing file formats are proprietary; you need a (commercial) program to read them. The MIME standard therefore included a simple Richtext format in order to provide an alternative to using raw ASCII. Richtext (not to be confused with Microsoft's Rich Text File format) was based on the idea of 'tagged' ASCII, with markup to indicate italicized or emphasized text. In fact, if you look at the specification (in RFC 1521) it looks like HTML.

There's a reason for this. Richtext and HTML are cousins; they are both applications of SGML. But what is SGML, and why does it keep sneaking into

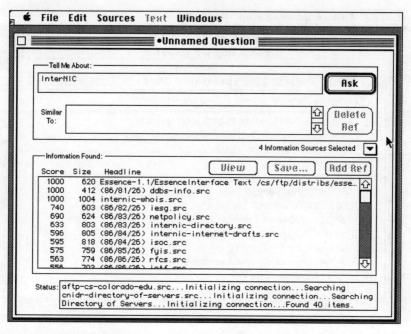

Figure 4.2 MacWAIS Query.

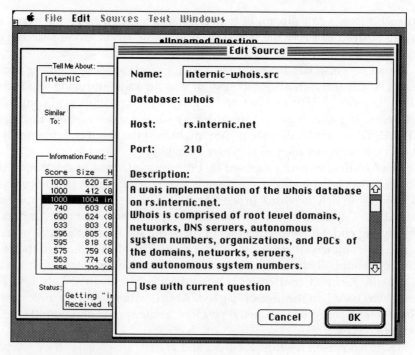

Figure 4.3 MacWAIS Query result.

the world wide web business? To answer this question, I'm going to have to make a short detour ...

Text processing and markup languages

Let's backtrack a bit and look at a completely different field – one which has little obvious connection with the Internet, but everything to do with the ancestry of the languages used on it.

Computers were in use for text processing and typesetting well before the first microcomputer word processing packages were developed in the late 1970s. UNIX, for example, was developed as a text processing platform within AT&T between 1972 and 1976. Using the troff typesetting languages, it was possible to use a PDP-11 minicomputer running UNIX and an appropriate typesetting machine to produce publication-quality books and articles. Like any large business, AT&T generated huge amounts of paperwork and procedures that needed documenting: in fact, UNIX was first deployed and supported as a typesetting support system within the phone company.

Computerized typesetting had two advantages:

1 The documents were reusable: they could be edited and retypeset much more easily than was possible using the old hot lead process.

2 They could be searched easily while stored on a computer, making the computer a feasible alternative to bulky microfilm and card archives.

Computer typesetting also brought with it two disadvantages.

1 When a source document – one that can be fed to a typesetting program, such as troff or T_EX – is stored on magnetic media, it is only usable as long as you can lay your hands on a computer and suitable software to read it with.

2 Most computer typesetting systems concentrated on adding control codes that determined the visual representation of the document, embedded within a stream of ASCII text. The semantics of the data had no direct bearing on their printed appearance, or on their online searchable form.

It was recognized quite early that the ideal document text retrieval system would scan documents on the basis of the meaning of their contents or structure, not their raw text content or visual appearance; as more information was stored online, it became clear that online searching would be a major growth area.

During the 1970s and 1980s, document management turned into a big business. User manuals come in all shapes and sizes, from the pocketbook to the shipping pallet. When the Royal Navy placed the engineering manuals for their Type 23 destroyers on CD-ROM, they saved 2.1 tons of dead weight on each ship. Meanwhile, the Pentagon attributes 30% of peacetime fatalities in the US Army indirectly to 'documentation errors'. Finding the important information in a large document is a real problem, especially when it is time-critical or when failure can lead to loss of life.

To make matters worse, a lot of early computer typeset documents are no longer available. The tapes they were recorded on have oxidized, or the programs they were typeset by have been lost. It became apparent that not only was it useful to be able to make typeset documents available in a search-able form, but that it was also essential to record them in a manner that was maintainable and usable.

Enter IBM. As the world's largest computer company (until the early 1990s) IBM also had a serious interest in preserving information and provid-ing access to legacy systems; machines and software installed during the 1950s, and used far beyond the expectations of the managers who commis-sioned them. As the world's largest computer corporation, IBM spent more money on research and development than many countries, and their Thomas J. Watson research lab was famous for its steady acquisition of Nobel prizes. (For example, it was at IBM that Codd developed the relational algebra and the theory of relational databases, which has more or less rendered the old COBOL-based information systems obsolete.) And it was at IBM that GML, the Generalized Markup Language, was created by Charles Goldfarb, Edward Mosher and Raymond Lorie (G, M and L, respectively) in 1969. GML was adopted by IBM as its main internal publishing system during the 1970s; meanwhile, various additional features were added by the development team, and the extended superset of GML evolved into the ratified ISO SGML stan-dard during the 1980s.

SGML is a markup language for documents. Unlike troff or T_EX, rather than tagging text with typesetting directives, it tags text entities with generic identifiers. The relationship of the identifiers to one another is defined in a separate file (the Document Type Definition, DTD). By referring to the DTD, you can analyse the SGML document, and by using a different DTD you can in principle impose a different structure on an existing file. For example, the HTML DTD describes the relationship between the tags in an HTML docu-ment. Indeed, the DTD is basically a description of the structure of the information that says nothing about its printed appearance but everything about its semantics. Another way of looking at SGML is that it is a meta-language for describing document typesetting systems; each DTD effectively defines a different document structure and set of typesetting rules.

Documents coded in SGML are searchable in ways that documents coded in typesetting macros are not. For a trivial example, by defining entities in a DTD to represent keywords or article headers, you can establish a reposi-tory of papers that can be searched on the basis of keywords or headers. By using a DTD to describe the relationship between entities in a document, you acquire the ability to conduct complex searches that take into account the structure of the document rather than simply its constituent words.

A number of parser programs exist for SGML. Such programs read in a DTD and analyse it, then read in a document written to be used with that DTD. If the elements in the document are badly formed, the parser flags them; effectively it does the same job for a document that a compiler does for a programming language, validating the SGML file and translating it into some output format. SGML documents must be structurally correct, unlike documents written in, say, T$_E$X, which can be printed despite some errors, but which might not be very readable.

SGML does not, however, say anything about the appearance of a document. When you take an SGML document and attempt to typeset it, a fairly complex chain of events takes place. Firstly, you need a formatter that can assign styles – visible typographical formats – to different document elements. The formatter must read the DTD and a style sheet, work out the correspondence between styles and SGML entities, and then slurp in the source file. Secondly, the formatter must spit out a file in some format that can be printed on an output device.

The commonest way of driving a printer today is Postscript. Postscript should require no introduction; most laser printers use it. It is a simple programming language that can be used to inscribe patterns on a large bitmap: this is rendered by dumping it to a printer. For this reason, Postscript is known as a 'Page Description' Language (PDL); a Postscript program is a description of the appearance of a printed page. Fonts are effectively subroutines. The program calls the subroutine for a character in a given font, passing it the appropriate weight or point size, and Postscript interprets the font description and places it at the desired location on the page.

In principle, any Postscript printer, given the same Postscript input file, should produce a page that looks the same – only the physical resolution should differ. In practice this is not always the case, as there are different levels of Postscript language compatibility and not all printers have the same sets of fonts or use the same default page size, but to all intents and purposes Postscript is a device-independent way of describing the appearance of a page. Only one point should be noted. Postscript is concerned entirely with the visual appearance of the page. Consequently, it may be totally impossible to read a Postscript file and extract the original information from it; the semantic content is so obscured as to be irretrievable.

SGML is all semantics and no appearance. Postscript is all appearance and no semantics; it lies too close to the underlying hardware, to the extent that a Postscript document designed for a given page size will not print effectively on a different size of paper. The formatter that turns SGML into Postscript itself needs a way of mapping semantic content to appearance. A new (draft) standard, DSSSL, the Document Style Specification and Semantics Language, is in the making.

DSSSL is a declarative language, based on Scheme (a descendent of LISP). It has two purposes:

1 to permit SGML documents constructed in accordance with one DTD to be transformed into compliance with a different DTD,

2 to permit SGML to be transformed in accordance with a DSSSL program into some other output format (such as a Postscript program).

Both tasks are achieved by reading in the DTD and SGML document to construct a tree structure representing the document. The tree is then transformed by means of a process referred to as the SGML Tree Transformation Process (STTP) built into the DSSSL interpreter. The STTP requires an output definition; this is a DSSSL program specifying that the tree should be transformed into one that matches a different DTD, or that nodes in the tree should be fed into the Standard Tree Formatting Process (STFP), which is used to produce output in accordance with a DSSSL style sheet.

Note that from the point of view of HTML, DSSSL prescribes exactly how the areas that are simply declared by HTML will be handled. A DSSSL style sheet describes how to format and print (usually to Postscript or some other PDL) a document composed in accordance with a corresponding DTD. DSSSL thus fits in the gap between SGML and the PDL. (According to the ISO DSSSL standard, the proposed output format for DSSSL is an as-yet unspecified Standard Page Description Language – likely to be Postscript by any other name.)

Semantic markup languages, PDLs and style sheet languages all have different characteristics. Of the three, the style sheet language is of relatively minor significance to the end user; an end user is mainly going to be bothered with reading documents (formatted into the PDL), or searching the source data structure (in the markup language). Ideally, the process of turning a source file into something readable should be invisible to the end user (Figure 4.4).

The world wide web is about more than making pretty pages in HTML accessible over the Internet. It was designed as an experiment in collaborative authoring and publication of documents. The goal of the web was to produce a system that was ubiquitous, not tied to any one hardware or software

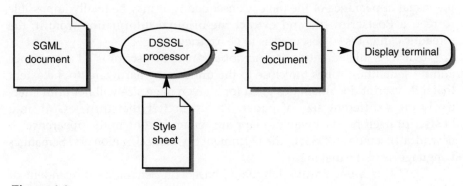

Figure 4.4

platform. Web documents are intended to be searchable – their structure and contents are public. They are also intended to be readable on any display device that comes to hand.

The HTML formatting language was developed to meet the requirements of the web. It was designed as a markup style that could be specified by a simple DTD in SGML. (Along the way, it spawned the MIME Richtext, content-type, a simple markup standard for email). But it rapidly became apparent that HTML was not suitable for all possible publication requirements. A lot of high-quality documents are today published on the web in Postscript. This is undesirable. Although such documents can contain formatting or visual information that can't be encoded in HTML, they cannot be searched, they cannot be edited, and they tend to be big. (Postscript page images produced by a poor-quality formatter can run to over 100 kb per page, compared to roughly 5 kb per page in HTML.) But, prior to the HTML+/ HTML 3.0 standard, HTML had no provision for handling chemical or mathematical formulae or tables. Such elements had to be included as inline images or as crude ASCII line-drawings. (This meant that they weren't searchable, weren't editable, and tended to be big.)

Richtext, augmented with URLs, became HTML 1.0. It was deliberately oversimplified in the first instance, to encourage early adoption. A later standard, HTML 2.0, formalized the extensions found in NCSA Mosaic and other browsers to add form support and some revised tags.

Going beyond HTML 2.0, the World Wide Web Organization began laying the groundwork for a next-generation system (HTML+) in 1993. HTML+ was to address all the shortcomings of HTML 2.0, adding functionality which would take HTML on a gently converging course with full SGML. HTML+ evolved over time, and with the sudden explosion of interest in the Web during 1994 it became the nucleus for the emergent HTML 3.0 standard.

HTML 2.0 was due to be superseded during 1995, by HTML 3.0 (formerly HTML+), a language containing additional tags for tables, chemical and mathematical formatting, enhanced formatting directives, a degree of extensibility and a full SGML DTD. Netscape Communications Corporation's Netscape 1.1 browser already supports some HTML 3.0 entities, such as tables; the Arena browser is already compliant with the HTML 3.0 specification, and can be used as a reference model for exploring HTML 3.0 compatability issues.

Unfortunately, HTML 3.0 fell victim to the very explosion of interest which made it seem so attractive. The web grew amazingly fast during 1993–95, averaging 100% compound growth every 60 days. This growth brought with it a tremendous degree of inertia. There are tens of thousands of public servers now operating that adhere to current standards; all would need to be updated to conform to any new standard in the HTTP. The situation is even worse for HTML authors. Literally hundreds of thousands of people have each written between one and one thousand documents in HTML. Updating the published information content of the web to take account of a new standard would be a staggering task. Finally, and most importantly, for new standards to be adopted, new software would need to be made available to web publishers and readers. In the early days at CERN the web consisted of a single piece of server software (the CERN httpd), a library of common code, and two or three web browsers based on the library. Today, however, there are dozens of commercial web browsers and web servers, and to change the standards you need to be able to convince both a multitude of users that they need to adopt your new ideas, and a large group of developers to update their software to support the required features.

The issue of updating HTML was hijacked during the course of 1995 by corporate interests. There are two (or three, depending on your point of view) contenders: Microsoft and Netscape Communications Corporation (in alliance with, or competition with, Sun Microsystems).

Netscape Communications Corporation, as of late 1995, had the lion's share of the web browser market to themselves. The company was formed in late 1994 by programmers from the National Center for Supercomputing Applications (NCSA), who had previously written Mosaic – the groundbreaking web browser that demonstrated the visual potential of the web. The initial goal of Netscape corporation was to become the main player in the visibly developing web software market. Their chosen technique was to market a web server suitable for commercial applications, and to ensure that people used it (and the security features it offered) by making a secure web browser freely available (or, more accurately, available as try-before-you-pay shareware).

Netscape, the web browser, caused a stir when it came out, for two reasons: firstly, it was a far more professional and polished piece of software than NCSA Mosaic; and secondly, it added 'extensions' to HTML that fitted no formal standard. For an example of the first category, Netscape was optimized for modem communications (then the fastest growing segment of users); by using multiple simultaneous connections, it downloaded inlined GIF images far faster than Mosaic or any other first-generation browser. In the second category, Netscape extended HTML. For example, the <BLINK> tag is meaningless to a standard HTML 2.0 browser (or an HTML 3.0 one, for that matter), but in Netscape text tagged as <BLINK> blinks – unpleasantly.

Netscape is (as of late 1995) the most commonly used web browser; versions run on Windows, MacOS and most common flavours of UNIX, and an estimated 70% of web users use it (an estimate based on logged counts of which browsers users pointed at a popular site).

Some parties ascribed uncharitable motives to Netscape Corporation in providing these extensions. In general, judicious use of Netscape-enhanced HTML can make pages more visually attractive. So a lot of HTML authors immediately began preparing pages for Netscape users only – with the effect that people were forced to use Netscape. This led to accusations that Netscape Corporation was going to hijack the standards process, by bringing out more and more non-standard extensions and forcing other users and software producers to follow suit in order to retain compatibility.

Netscape 2.0 will be discussed at greater length later; in addition to yet more HTML enhancements, Netscape 2.0 supports Java (described later in this chapter). However, the extensions to HTML introduced in Netscape 2.0 appear to conform fairly closely to HTML 3.0, and the earlier non-standard Netscape extensions have been submitted to the standards body for consideration. It therefore looks as if Netscape Corporation is converging on HTML 3.0 (probably achieving full compliance, if current rates of progress are maintained, some time in 1996–97).

Meanwhile, in mid-1995, Microsoft Corporation finally noticed the world wide web (or admitted it in public). With the release of Windows 95, Microsoft – the 'King Kong' of the software business – also announced their public Value-Added Network (VAN) business, Microsoft Network. MSNet is compatible with the Internet from the outset to a greater degree than was possible for earlier VANs such as CompuServe or Delphi. In addition, the Microsoft Network software includes a web browser, with numerous Microsoft-designed extensions: behind it lies a barely visible strategy for networked information browsers.

Arguably, both Netscape and Microsoft are used to shaping public standards in their own interests. Only a company with a huge user base can today hope to change the structure of the web radically. However, this may change in the near future (1996–97), if the third player (Sun Microsystems) gets its way.

Sun's offering in the web standards camp is a language called Java. Java is not strictly anything to do with HTML; it's a programming language, similar to a cleaned-up version of C++, and it is designed to run safely over networks of embedded processors. We'll see how Java could upset the balance of the web standards later in this chapter. (See Figure 4.5).

Today there are three visions of where the web will go:

The academic vision

The eventual destiny of the web (as it is conceived of by the academic community) is to converge on SGML as a document delivery medium. Ninety-five per cent of the web will still consist of HTML, but browsers will be able to parse and display true SGML documents with a variety of DTDs, and their on-screen appearance will be managed by DSSSL-Lite – a derivative of DSSSL designed specifically for formatting HTML 3.0. This will ensure that the web remains searchable and editable, while permitting an almost endless variety of document types to be produced and ensuring that they are all displayed correctly by the browser. (Richer solutions are also being discussed, but no final solution has yet emerged as the clear winner.)

The underlying purpose of the web (according to this vision) is to permit academic collaboration and sharing of information. Thus, a heavy emphasis on conferencing systems, annotation mechanisms and searchability is mandated. The primary user base is therefore academic researchers, staff, students and scientific information providers.

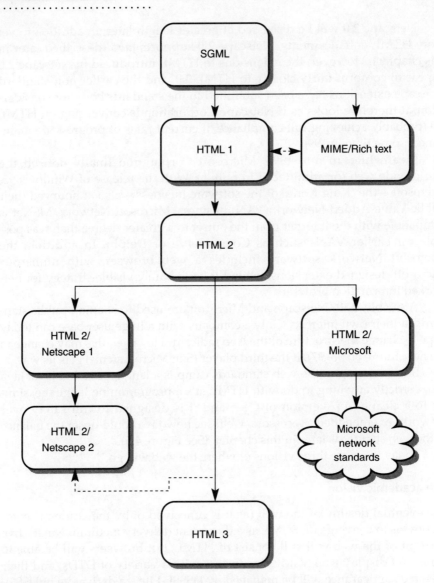

Figure 4.5

The commercial vision

The main commercial users who have leapt on the web so far (early 1996) appear to be advertising and marketing corporations, and those retail sectors which provide lots of information and consultancy about their product prior to the actual purchase (for example, estate agents and software companies). A secondary market for actual information services is appearing (direct banking, financial services, newspapers and so on), with retailers waiting in the wings (bookshops, computer shops and retailers of high-value goods). These commercial users have the money to pay for site design and development, and they place a premium on visual impact – a lesson they learned from experiences of marketing in other media.

Thus, their main representatives in the field are designers and advertising specialists, some of whom have difficulty coming to terms with the limitations of the web as a presentation medium. For example, some graphic designers use one-pixel GIF files, masked into transparency, to adjust interword or intercharacter spacing on the screen of Netscape users. This renders their documents valueless for searching and editing purposes, although their visual appeal cannot be denied.

The other vision

There are far more uses for the web than the two earlier groups can envisage. For example, the world wide web provides a beautiful opportunity for far-flung companies to consolidate their information processing requirements. Already, some larger companies are beginning to re-engineer their business processes around the world wide web, using it for information sharing (initially) and then as a backbone computing resource. In this vision the web server takes the place of the old backroom mainframe and the web browser (be it on a laptop in another country or on a workstation on the programmer's desk) stands in for the terminal. By providing cheap, easy communications and a uniform interface, the web is letting these companies re-invent their internal information systems. It also provides them with an easy-to-program way of interfacing their internal systems to a customer or contractor company's systems – a task which was virtually impossible (or at least very, very expensive) before the web.

Although much of this activity is invisible to the public, I believe that it will inevitably far outstrip the other two sectors in its long-term impact. Companies are prepared to pay far more than consumers or academics if it is necessary to do so to ensure their long-term survival, and investment in internal IT functions has been a mission-critical necessity for decades. And their requirements include: secure, reliable communications, graphical user interface elements (like forms, but richer), the ability to send files to a central repository, get them from the repository, and edit them in the browser, and the ability to interface easily to back-office applications such as large database servers.

Other approaches: HDL, setext and Acrobat

For the time being, we are going to concentrate on document and information management rather than on graphical interfaces and presentation. The academic vision of the web is not incompatible with the internal corporate re-engineering vision, and between them they are likely to exert more pressure on the long-term development of the web than the requirements of graphic designers. Information management is the key to both these visions, and it depends heavily on the type of documents being managed.

SGML is a heavy-duty tool for document management. DSSSL is a pretty mind-numbing mechanism for general purpose document formatting. And Postscript is total overkill for many display devices. The pyramid of three disjoint document definition, format definition and page definition languages appears to totter when exposed to the fairly slapdash manner in which most electronic documents are composed. Short of enforcing the use of language-sensitive editors on pain of death, it's going to be hard to expect a rigorous standard to be used by all writers. This problem becomes especially difficult when we consider that there is no central control of the Internet or the world wide web. Many people contribute valuable information to the web, yet are ignorant of or unconcerned with the issues of document management that should concern a webmaster. Is it anyone's job to tell them how to write their files? HTML is sufficiently simple that, with the aid of some basic tools for checking consistency, it results in usable text; this is its main strength.

Rather than insisting that full SGML should immediately be implemented as the delivery vehicle for web documents, a proposal surfaced in 1994 in the IETF HTML Working Group for a new language – HDL (Hypertext Delivery Language). HDL is seen as a descendant of HP's Semantic Delivery Language (SDL), which was developed as an SGML application language to permit rapid delivery of online help information to UNIX workstations. SDL had numerous design 'wins' in terms of hypertext: notably, it was intended to parse and display rapidly, support infinite structural depth, support advanced document retrieval functions and run on systems with relatively limited memory and CPU resources. It also permitted direct control over the typographical rendering of documents, within the limitations imposed by the display device, by delivering style information along with the document's semantic content. And, unlike HTML, SDL was optimized for information content rather than for readability. (Note that one 'loss' for SDL is the relative complexity of its markup language. This adds size to SDL documents, relative to their simpler HTML equivalents, so that a system based on SDL would consume more bandwidth.)

The proposal was based on the idea that it is relatively easy to write a program that transforms HTML 3.0 into SDL (or rather, into HDL – the version of SDL proposed for the web). Therefore, authors could transport existing HTML documents into the new system automatically, and could still write in HTML – the documents would simply be translated into HDL before delivery. SDL lacked some of the features needed for a web language (notably forms, horizontal lines, embedded widgets and platform-independent font handling), but all these features are addressed in the draft HDL documents that are circulating.

The focal point of HDL is pragmatism. Most users cannot easily learn a markup language more complex than HTML without the aid of a sophisticated language-sensitive editor that can insert tags automatically and attempt to display them in an eyeball-friendly manner. Furthermore, many users have already learned HTML, and it's notoriously difficult to get someone to adopt a new form of behaviour just so that they can conform to a seemingly arbitrary standard laid down by The Powers That Be. Finally, the web is still evolving rapidly. While a full SGML/DSSSL/SPDL system can handle the simpler HTML/HDL system, it is difficult for a small company or programmer to assemble such a complex piece of software single-handed; insisting on a complex standard effectively raises a barrier to active participation by those people who don't have the resources to compete. So a proposal that lets the technical managers at large sites adopt ISO standard document processing methods, while permitting freelance programmers to churn out useful web tools and HTML pages on primitive equipment is more likely to receive global approval than a proposal which alienates one or more sectors of the user base.

There are a couple of additional contenders for the web, although as of early 1996 they appear unlikely to move out of a niche role into centre stage.

Firstly, there is a rather informal standard called setext. Setext arose out of the habit of some email users, accustomed to the vagaries of raw ASCII mail, to add emphasis to their ASCII documents. For example, a word might be indicated as underlined _thus_ (by surrounding it with underline characters), or italicized like *this*. The setext method works fairly well in ASCII text which is not fed through a formatter of any kind (insofar as readers can distinguish emphasis in documents without the aid of such relatively crude tools as emoticons :-). Setext was a formalization of this approach; that ASCII documents could be marked up in such a way that a user could read the emphasis in it with minimal effort. However, setext is likely to be superseded in the near future by machine-readable markup standards like Richtext (in email) or HTML (on the web) for most purposes; the ubiquity of HTML is now a barrier to the use of other standards.

Secondly, there is Adobe Acrobat 2, or HyperPostscript. Acrobat was developed by Adobe in an attempt to counter some of the perceived defects of the Postscript page description language. Postscript was designed initially to drive printers: machines for making marks on paper. Implicit in this was the idea that the page on which the marks would be made were of a constant size. Whoever heard of a piece of paper that you could stretch or shrink? Just such a problem applies when you try to display ordinary Postscript on a monitor, using a Postscript interpreter. The electronic document does not scale effectively, nor is it possible to embed links to other files in it.

Acrobat was developed as a way of producing portable, scalable Postscript files that could be displayed on any output device. The initial idea was to facilitate exchange of Postscript documents between sites which had different display or printing systems (for example, different font sets or resolutions). However, with the addition of support for hyperlinks, Acrobat turns into a potential world wide web delivery mechanism. Acrobat files are typically smaller than normal program-generated Postscript, can contain hotlinks to other files, and can contain semantic information – notably, they may be indexed for free-text searches.

Acrobat is fundamentally a publishing mechanism; you cannot take the information in an Acrobat file and load it into a text editor (although systems capable of importing and editing Acrobat files do exist). While it might be useful for the dissemination of copyrighted text, it is less useful for the collaborative authoring envisaged for the web. However, for commercial web applications such as advertising and marketing, where collaboration and interoperability are less relevant than eye-catching design and typographic sophistication, Acrobat may be considered superior to HTML.

Thirdly, there are the general-purpose multimedia tools that have been developed for giving presentations on ordinary workstations and standalone personal computers. In May 1995, Netscape Communications Corporation announced that they had licensed the runtime package for Macromedia Director, one of the commonest multimedia scripting systems. A future Netscape product, it was indicated, would have the ability to play Macromedia documents, which can combine animation, video clips, audio, and scripted sequences of events. Such a system diverges completely from the mainstream development of the web as a publishing mechanism, by converting it into something resembling an advertising tool: sophisticated, proprietary software is required to build such presentations, and while their use may appeal to the advertising and marketing community on the web, they are not central to its development.

That other language: scripting

Not only is the web a babble of distinct hypertext languages, the scripts and programs used for controlling it are also written in a multitude of dialects.

There are several levels in the web at which it becomes necessary to program in a traditional programming language. Forms support, for example, presupposes the presence of a script on the HTTP server system that can respond to a POST or GET request by generating a document. Query support presupposes the presence of a search tool on the server system. The HTTP server and browser (or other client) are themselves programs written in some appropriate language. It is possible to write automated web exploration programs (called knowbots – knowledge robots – or 'spiders'), which probe web sites and retrieve information; or to write other programs that analyse web documents for consistency, completeness and broken links. Finally, there are tools that help the user create and maintain HTML documents, such as syntax-directed editors and HTML syntax checkers.

Many of these levels of programmatic intervention are irrelevent for our purposes. (If you want to write your own web server, you are probably running on a rather non-standard computer ... or you are a serious TCP/IP network programmer.) However, the day-to-day tasks of writing server-side scripts, running or maintaining a spider, or automatically checking documents for validity demands a knowledge of programming.

Today (1996), the commonest languages in use on the web are:

- C/C++

- Perl

- Tcl

- Java

(plus a little Python, awk, UNIX shell and other specialized systems like Userland Frontier).

There's a fairly good reason for the prominence of C and C++; they are the keystone of modern software engineering practice, used for everything from accounting systems to the UNIX kernel. Whether it is appropriate to write a web client in C++, as opposed to Tcl, is a moot point – clients have been written in both languages. Nevertheless, C is best categorized as a portable assembly language; powerful, fast, and rather difficult to learn. C++ is similar, only much bigger and rendered more usable at higher levels of abstraction by the addition of object-oriented extensions.

I would argue (and a true C/C++ aficionado would doubtless object) that these are not the ideal languages for writing quick scripts to support a web server. C forces the programmer to address a lot of low-level issues, to the detriment of focusing on the purpose of their software; for example, a UNIX filter to count the number of words in a text file takes approximately four lines of Perl, but runs to well over a hundred lines of C. A C solution might run faster, but there is a trade-off between the investment of programmer time and the saving of user time. While it makes sense for a primary application (such as a word processor or an operating system) to be written in a language as close to the bare metal as possible, a quick form server which will be invoked a couple of hundred times at most should not demand an excessive input of programmer time. It's always necessary to choose the right tools for the job in hand, and for most ancilliary web support purposes, a Very-High Level Language (VHLL) is probably the best solution.

VHLLs have graduated relatively recently, to the point where seminars about them are held at Usenix conferences. During the 1970s and 1980s a number of so-called fourth-generation languages were developed in an attempt to replace COBOL as the database mangling solution of choice. These languages typically added database addressing commands to a high-level syntax reminiscent of Pascal (or, in the case of xBase, of the old Business Basic languages). Modern VHLLs, however, are not dedicated database construction tools. Although VHLLs share many of the characteristics of Fourth-Generation Languages (4GLs), they are typically designed for different tasks, notably:

- client–server application development

- rapid prototyping

- scripting

- system administration

A language like Perl, Tcl or Python typically has:

- high-level flow-control constructs

- embedded text pattern (regular expression) matching commands

- embedded operating system access commands (making it suitable for existence in a multi-user, multi-tasking environment)

- embedded networking services (for communications across a TCP/IP network)

- very rich string handling semantics

- the ability to evaluate internally stored data as commands (recursive execution)

In addition, they usually have one or more of:

- a built-in database handler

- auto-loading external libraries containing language extensions

- object orientation

- a report generator

- an application generator

- GUI extensions (typically, access to the Tk widget set)

- the ability to be embedded within an application (to give it a precanned scripting language)

- a compiler

In addition to the VHLLs, another choice for scripting is a true scripting language, such as REXX, or the UNIX Bourne shell (in conjunction with UNIX string-handling languages such as sed or awk). Such languages are designed for job control in an interactive environment, that is, for launching and controlling other programs. They are typically slow interpreted systems, but they have the advantage of being able to take the output from one program and feed it to another. Used in conjunction with awk and a TCP/IP tool, the Bourne shell can achieve most of the functions of Perl or Tcl. However, this solution is relatively slow and inelegant, and can present side-issues of security and performance. In general, starting up extra language interpreters or compiled programs carries a certain overhead; using a language that forces you to run loads of external programs to accomplish a single task is possibly erring too far on the side of simplicity.

A special case can be made for two Macintosh scripting languages: AppleScript and Frontier. Macintoshes are a minority interest, but a fully configured Power Macintosh with a WebStar server installed can make a very cost-effective alternative to a high-specification UNIX workstation. The Macintosh system, since System 7.0, has been built around an event-driven model that permits Object Scripting Applications (OSAs) to be dropped in. OSA languages are effectively interpreters that can control properly written, scriptable, Macintosh applications as if they are complex data objects. WebStar is capable of executing AppleScript or Frontier objects, which in turn can be used to extract and format data from any scriptable Macintosh application (and a compatability box exists to enable WebStar and MacPerl to execute standard UNIX CGI scripts). Thus, a Macintosh with properly written scripts (in AppleScript or the previously commercial but now public domain Frontier language) can be configured as a web gateway to repositories of data in proprietary application formats (for example, collections of Microsoft Excel spreadsheets, or a FoxPro database).

AppleScript is a component of the Apple MacOS product, included with release 7.5. Userland Frontier was previously a commercial product but is now being freely distributed, along with a most excellent toolkit for embedding Frontier scripts in HTML pages. While these active documents are useful only on Macintoshes at present, the philosophy behind them is similar to that of Java, discussed below. Frontier is perhaps the most useful tool on the Macintosh for developing active web documents and scripts right now (although MacPerl is the most generally useful CGI scripting language for text processing applications). See

```
http://www.hotwired.com/Staff/userland/
```

for details.

Let's have a look at the VHLLs of (current) choice. These languages are spreading on the back of the web; for example, something like 80% of the spiders running over Christmas 1994 were written in Perl, and most common CGI scripts use that language.

Python

From the abstract of the Python programming tutorial:

> Python is a simple, yet powerful programming language that bridges the gap between C and shell programming, and is thus ideally suited for 'throw-away programming' and rapid prototyping. Its syntax is put together from constructs borrowed from a variety of other languages; most prominent are influences from ABC, C, Modula-3, and Icon.
>
> The Python interpreter is easily extended with new functions and data types implemented in C. Python is also suitable as an

extension language for highly customizable C applications such as editors or window managers.

Python was developed during the late 1980s and early 1990s by Guido van Rossum, of CWI Amsterdam. It inherited its string handling characteristics from SNOBOL by way of Icon, a language designed to combine pattern matching with modern programming constructs. Python is object-oriented, so that it is relatively easy to encapsulate a new task in a library module; it can also be embedded within another application, to provide it with a control language.

Embedded languages are most useful when you have something like a library of database routines and want to 'glue' them together in a usable form – you add a language interpreter, give it hooks into the library, and then use its own language to write scripts that drive your database back-end.

The development of embeddable languages was triggered by the arrival (during the 1970s) of programs that were too complex to operate manually. Today, virtually all 'serious' applications have a internal macro language. However, it isn't desirable to have to learn a new language for every new program. Consequently, portable embedded languages are now being developed. The idea is that if every complex application has the same macro language (albeit modified by adding special extensions to the core syntax), it will be a lot easier for end-users to develop scripts that 'glue' the programs together and accomplish some useful task.

Tcl

Tcl (Tool Command Language) is the canonical portable embedded language. Initially Tcl was seen by its author, Dr John Ousterhout (of the University of California at Berkeley) as being no more than a general-purpose embeddable language. Tcl was designed to have a simple core grammar, to be easy to extend, and to be compiled into other applications. For example, a text editor with Tcl compiled into it would then be a text editor with a scripting language. (The text editor the manuscript for this book was written in, Pete Keleher's Alpha editor for the Macintosh, is in fact a Tcl-scriptable text editor – the entire menu structure is accessible and modifiable from inside the editor, and it is possible to automate complex formatting operations by using Tcl scripts to drive the programs text-editing extensions.) Tcl could be used to facilitate communications between graphical applications, by sending streams of Tcl commands from one program to another. For example, a debugger (running a compiled program) could send Tcl commands to the text editor session used by a programmer, causing the editor to highlight each line of source code as it was executed; the programmer, meanwhile, could drive commands in the debugger from within the editor, while having the illusion that the debugger and the editor were an integrated programming development environment. (Again, Alpha interoperates very tightly with MacPerl at this level, to the extent that it is possible to develop Perl scripts within Alpha and execute or debug them without leaving the editor.)

However, Tcl didn't stay small and portable for long. Rather than embedding Tcl in other applications, a lot of programmers decided they rather liked it and wanted to use it as a language in its own right. Extended command libraries (notably the TclX extensions) were written and spliced into Tcl to give it operating system interaction capabilities; the ability to search for regular expressions in files, to spawn child processes and so on. Meanwhile, Ousterhout's research interests led him to develop Tk, a modular toolkit for building software under the X windowing system.

X is notoriously difficult to program in C, but Tcl and Tk between them make it possible to build complex applications very rapidly. For example, a minimal 'Hello World' program for X Windows and Motif, written in C, takes about 150 lines of source code to create a button labelled 'Hello', and exit when the button is pressed. The same program takes a single line of Tcl/Tk code. Thus, Tcl and Tk allow programmers to try out new ideas for graphical applications far faster than they could manage using conventional tools.

For example, the TkWWW web browser is written in Tcl/Tk; although a C version exists, it is not much faster or more useful than the original Tcl implementation, and the Tcl version is far easier to customize or extend.

At the time of writing, Sun Microsystems is funding development of Tcl and Tk, including efforts to port the environment to Microsoft Windows and MacOS. Initial beta releases for MacOS and Windows are already available (see http://www.smli.com/ for details). The significance of this development, which would result in a portable, high-level language for rapid prototyping of GUIs, cannot be overemphasized.

Java

Announced in late 1994, Java is perhaps the most exciting of the new languages on the web. (Details can be found at http://java.sun.com/.) It differs fundamentally in its application from the other languages described here.

Java is being developed by an engineering group within Sun. It is an object-oriented language, fairly close in style to C++. However, unlike C++, Java is not compiled to machine code for direct execution on a target machine. Instead, it is compiled to a byte code, which can be interpreted by a Java microkernel on any target platform. Unlike C++, Java does not give direct access to memory; it has built-in garbage collection, and high-level interprocess communication mechanisms. (The microkernel itself is fairly small, and is being actively ported to non-UNIX systems; although at the time of writing it is available only on Solaris 2.3, it is being ported to Windows, MacOS, and other flavours of UNIX.) It was designed this way because the original goal of the Java project was to develop a language for controlling networks of embedded controllers – the invisible computers that run our cars, washing machines and airliners.

The Java microkernel is designed to be embedded. The goal of the Java project is to embed Java interpreters in web browsers, so that documents containing precompiled Java programs can be downloaded and executed on the client machine with reasonable security. Thus, rather than relying on servers to carry the entire computational burden of the web, clients could execute programs and take actions. The primary purpose for this is to permit a much richer array of interface objects to be embedded in HTML, but other applications can be envisaged; for example, active web 'worm' documents that execute on remote machines and pass only useful information back to their home, removing much of the bandwidth burden imposed by current worms (as described in Chapter 8).

Early examples of Java 'applets' for the web include background generators – programs that generate a moving picture for the background of a web page – and small 'toy' programs such as calculators.

However, Java is designed to encourage code reuse, and the programming interface between Java and a host web browser is designed to make it possible to add new protocol methods for handling new protocols specified in URIs. For example, most web browsers can handle ftp: URLs in addition to http: and gopher: URLs, even though these require a completely different protocol (formal specification for information interchange between a client and a server). A Java compatible browser can learn how to handle new information protocols, new types of data and new kinds of file, on the fly: by downloading the protocol handler, it becomes able to handle information transmitted via that protocol. Thus, Java makes web browsers flexible and extensible.

The implications of Java are extremely exciting. For example, some preliminary work is going on (Iced Java) towards the production of a three-dimensional graphics package, written in Java, hosted within a web browser, that will support VRML (Virtual Reality Modelling Language, which promises to be to virtual reality what HTML is to the web). If this effort succeeds, any Java-aware browser will acquire the ability to handle VRML files. Alternatively, if you need to design a specialized version of HTML with extension tags to match your own requirements, you can write handlers for your tags in Java and be fairly certain that any user with a Java-compatible browser will be able to read your files.

Netscape 2.0 incorporates a Java interpreter. While it is too early to predict how successful this implementation will be, it appears likely that this software release (or one like it) will catapult Java into the public eye and change the web incalculably over the next two years.

Perl

Perl, the Practical Extraction and Report Language (alternatively known as the Pathologically Eclectic Rubbish Lister, according to its inventor), seems to have become the language of choice for web maintenance work. There are several reasons for this. Developed by Larry Wall of Netlabs, Perl is not an exercise in academic language design: it is a programmer's Swiss Army chainsaw, designed initially to extricate its designer from an impossible task, then extended to enable him to tackle any number of even more difficult problems.

Perl superficially resembles both C and awk. It is a functional superset of awk, and it is possible to convert automatically any awk program into Perl code (using the a2p converter). It is also possible to do in Perl most things which are normally programmed in C, although Perl is comparatively poor at very low level tasks that require access to the hardware and software below the operating system level. Unlike C, it is interpreted; unlike awk, it is not interpreted one line at a time, but is compiled to an intermediate format by the interpreter, then executed rapidly. The result is a combination of compiled-language speed with interpreted-language convenience.

Most of the flow-of-control operators in Perl are classical C, while most of the pattern-matching operators are classical awk (except for the bits that Larry chose to copy from **sed** and **grep**). Virtually all the standard UNIX library functions are built into Perl as commands, making a listing of its syntax rather complex. But Perl really shines at handling variables. Variables can be scalar (individual) strings (which can be treated as numeric types when you need to do arithmetic), or vectors (an array of scalars), or associative arrays (essentially hash tables). Using the built-in data types, the pack() and unpack() functions (which convert scalars into packed arrays of bits), and some imagination, it is possible to emulate any complex data structure that you might need to handle in a C program. And because Perl doesn't force the programmer to allocate memory and handle addressing issues directly, it is usually possible to take a C program, rewrite it in Perl, and wind up with something smaller and easier to maintain.

Perl is by no means a purist's language. The underlying philosophy of its design was not 'make it simple and elegant' – it was 'get the job done as efficiently as possible'. It is a rich language, insofar as it has very complex semantics and a plethora of operators and constructs; these sometimes make it hard to deal with. For example, it is possible to use Perl 5.0 to write programs in several styles: procedural, functional, object-oriented, or even (with a few contortions) declarative. It is at its best when used to write report generators for databases, to churn through huge piles of text files and carry out complex search/replace operations on them, to connect to a remote server on the world wide web and to slurp all the documents off the server and to carry out routine file maintenance tasks – but these are by no means the only things it is suited for. The arrival of Tk/Perl in early 1995 added true GUI construction capabilities to the language. More to the point, the combination of Perl 5 (with object-oriented programming extensions) and the web means that Perl is likely to make significant inroads into the rapid prototyping field, as a serious commercial client–server programming environment. However, Perl is not notably good at is being embedded in another application (although Perl 5 is supposedly easier to embed than previous versions). Therefore, it is reasonable to view the use of Perl and Tcl as complementary.

This book, by its very nature, must include some code examples. I have chosen to write them in Perl for several reasons:

- Perl is available on most platforms (including UNIX, VAX/VMS, MS-DOS, and Macintosh).

- Perl is available free of charge.

- Perl is already widely used on the web.

- Perl programs are generally smaller and more readable than their C equivalents.

There are some objections to using Perl. Notably, many people object to the use of any server-side program that is not written in C for security reasons. Programs executing in the UNIX environment inherit access permissions from their parents. Many tasks must be carried out with 'root' (superuser) privileges; sometimes it is necessary to write a program that non-root users can use for a specific authorized task, which runs with root permissions. It is not uncommon for intruders to attempt to gain access to a system by causing such a program to crash in such a way that they are left with a program that they can execute with root privileges. A common objection to the use of scripting languages for sensitive server-side tasks is that they are insecure, easy to crash and may accidentally grant a child process excessive access permissions.

Perl has been designed specifically to address some of these concerns – notably by keeping track of inherited permissions and locking out certain types of access (by means of a variant program called taintperl, that tracks access permissions and warns of security violations), and by reducing the number of child programs that need to be executed by a given script. (Each external program is a potential security hole to a UNIX system, because UNIX has a per-file or per-process permission system rather than using access control lists.)

One objection to Perl is that under some circumstances, buggy caching proxy servers (notably early versions of the CERN httpd) may fetch a copy of the executed program and store it in their local cache. If this happens, your Perl CGI script might be exposed to users who could search it for security holes. This is not a design feature, but a failure on the part of some HTTP servers; you should check the documentation for any Web server scrupulously to see how it handles CGI scripts, and then test it with a browser to ensure that it does what it says it does.

In the next chapter I will give a rather abbreviated overview of Perl, and show some examples of how it can be used to make a Web administrator's life easier.

5

INTRODUCING PERL

● ● ● ●

Perl was developed from 1987 onwards, and began to surface on the Internet in 1989. The main version in use today is the (stable) Perl 4.036; although Perl 5 came out in November 1994, it is still under development. This chapter covers Perl 4.036, but makes mention of some Perl 5 extensions.

Perl is an interpreted language. When the Perl interpreter first runs it parses the specified program, builds a data structure representing it, then executes the program without having to pause and reinterpret each line as it reaches it. Perl programs therefore run faster than those written in a typical interpreted language; rough tests suggest that an awk program, converted to Perl (using the `a2p` automatic converter) runs roughly 50% faster.

Perl is available free of charge via the Internet. UNIX Perl, and some example programs, can be obtained from:

```
ftp.demon.co.uk:/pub/perl
```

Macintosh Perl can be obtained by FTP from:

```
ftp://ftp.switch.ch/software/mac/perl/
```

(and elsewhere). DOS Perl can be obtained from any Simtel20 ftp mirror: for example:

```
ftp://ftp.cis.ufl.edu/pub/perl/src
```

UNIX Perl can be found in many places, notably via:

```
http://www.perl.com/
```

Documentation on Perl, in the form of a UNIX man page, is available with the program. Alternatively, see Wall and Schwartz (1990).

Perl is a large, complex language. This introduction attempts to provide a broad overview of the language's features, along with some brief notes on what can be done with them. If you intend to get heavily into Perl, you might want to start with Schwartz (1992), then get a copy of Wall and Schwartz (1991) – the official book of the language.

A quick overview of Perl

Perl has most of the standard C operators and control constructs, with the exception of address dereferencing (&var) and pointers (*var). It takes a similar approach to variables to the UNIX shells (Bourne, Korn, or Bash, to be precise); a simple variable name is indicated by a preceding $ sign, and references to $variable are replaced by the value of $variable. The dollar symbol can be escaped (that is, its special meaning removed) by preceding it with a backslash.

Variables can contain strings (sequences of characters) or numbers. The two are interconverted freely, depending on the context in which they are encountered. Strings are identified in a program by surrounding them with double or single quote marks. For example:

```
$myvar = 6;
print $myvar;
```

assigns the numerical value 6 to the variable $myvar, then prints:

```
6
```

You can do the same with strings of text as well as numbers:

```
$myvar = "fred";
print $myvar;
```

assigns the string fred to the variable $myvar, then prints:

```
fred
```

Strings can contain references to variables. If the string is enclosed in double quotes, any variable names within the string are replaced by the contents of the variable. Single quotes prevent variable substitution. For example:

```
$myvar = "fred";
print "Hello, $myvar";
print 'and hello, $myvar';
```

produces:

```
Hello, fred, and hello, $myvar
```

The C arithmetic and relational operators apply:

```
$variable = 4;      # set $variable to 4
$variable++;        # increment the value of $variable
```

```
if ($variable >= 5) {
    print "Variable is \"$variable\"\n";
}
$variable -=7;     # decrement the value of $variable
print "but now it's $variable\n";
```

This prints:

```
Variable is "5"
but now it's -2
```

Note the use of a preceding backslash to escape the special meaning of the double quote, so that it prints as a literal character. The \n symbol has the same meaning as in C, that is, a new line.

The lines containing a hash sign, #, preceded by whitespace are comments, and everything from the hash to the end of the line is ignored.

The flow of control operators should look very familiar to a C or awk programmer:

```
if (EXPR) BLOCK
if (EXPR) BLOCK else BLOCK
if (EXPR) BLOCK elsif (EXPR) BLOCK ... else BLOCK
LABEL while (EXPR) BLOCK
LABEL while (EXPR) BLOCK continue BLOCK
LABEL for (EXPR; EXPR; EXPR) BLOCK
LABEL foreach VAR (ARRAY) BLOCK
LABEL BLOCK continue BLOCK
```

where BLOCK is a set of commands enclosed in curly braces, and EXPR is some valid expression that can be evaluated to true (zero) or false (non-zero). Perl is more traditional than C in its willingness to use labels for blocks of code; goto is also available, although its usage is deprecated.

Perl provides several different ways to accomplish any task. For example:

```
open(INPUT, "<$myfile") || die "Could not open $myfile!\n";
```

takes the file named by the variable $myfile, associates it with the filehandle INPUT, and attempts to open it for reading. (Note the input redirection operator, <, in front of the filename; this specifies that data is going to be read from the file. If it were a >, it would be open for writing; if it were +>$myfile it would be open for reading and writing.) If this statement fails, the subsequent command (die "Could not open $myfile!\n") is executed – the logical-OR operator, ||, is used to execute commands on the basis of the returned value of the preceding command. (Logical-AND, &&, is also available; the following command is executed only if the preceding command succeeded.)

This rather terse line is equivalent to:

```
if ( open(INPUT,"<$myfile") == 0) {
    die "Could not open $myfile\n";
}
```

(a style which might be more familiar to C programmers) or:

```
$result = open(INPUT, "<$myfile");
if ($result == 0) {
    die "Could not open $myfile\n";
}
```

(a style more familiar to Pascal programmers).

Perl provides a couple of built-in filehandles; STDIN, STDOUT and STDERR, the standard input, output and error streams. STDIN is read from by default if no files are specified on the command line, and STDOUT is written to by default if no filehandle is selected. You can read from a filehandle by assigning to a variable from <FILEHANDLE>; for example:

```
$line = <FILE>
```

This reads a line of text from FILE into the string $line, and advances the filehandle FILE to the next line. By default, if no handle is specified the standard input is used; so it is common to see notation like:

```
$_ = (<>);
```

which means 'read a line from standard input into the variable $_'.

The built-in variable called $_ stores the result of the most recent operation. When you read from a filehandle using a loop, $_ is set in sequence to the value of each line in a file. Consequently the explicit reference to $_ can often be omitted. Perl exhibits a lot of default behaviour, for example:

```
while (<>) {
    print ;
}
```

Because no filehandle or input variable is specified, Perl reads from the standard input and while it contains something, reads it into $_; by default, the print command prints $_, so this filter simply prints the standard input to the standard output.

Perl can handle three data types:

- scalars ($fred)

- arrays (@fred)

- associative arrays (%fred)

A scalar is a simple variable, of the kind we have already seen; it holds a string or a number. An array consists of a list of scalars, which are grouped under a common name. (We'll deal with associative arrays later.)

Individual scalars in an array can be identified by their position in the array. For example:

```
$fred[4]
```

refers to the fourth item in the array @fred.

Note that $fred[4] and @fred[4] both refer to item 4 in fred, but do so in different ways. The $ prefix means that $fred[4] is a scalar, the fourth item in the array. The @ prefix means that @fred[4] is an array 'slice', a chunk of @fred containing a single element. In general, Perl lets you freely transfer data between arrays and scalars, but you've got to keep track of the context in which you refer to the variables. You can't directly change arrays, scalars and associative arrays. For example, although it is perfectly legitimate to assign one scalar to another, or one array to another, if you assign an array to a scalar the scalar ends up holding the not the contents of the array, but the size of the array :

```
$fred = "hello";
$joe = $fred;
print $joe;
@fred = ("Fred", "Joe", "Margaret", "Hilda");
$joe = @fred;
print $joe;
```

will result in:

```
hello4
```

Note that by default, Perl numbers array elements from 0, so although there are three items in @fred, the items are numbered 0 .. 2. (If necessary, you can change the array base.) You can refer to a slice, or range of elements in an array, using the two-dot ellipsis:

```
foreach (@fred[1..3]) {
    print "$_ ";
}
Fred Joe Margaret
```

To convert an array into a scalar, use the join() function:

```
$joe = join(" ",@fred);
print $joe;
Fred Joe Margaret
```

join() takes two arguments; a spacer string to interpolate between array elements, and an array. It converts the array to a string, with the spacer string between each item. (Otherwise the elements in the array are all concatenated.)

The converse function is called split(); this takes a pattern and a target string, and splits the string into array elements wherever the pattern occurs:

```
@fred = split(":","Fred:Joe:Margaret");
foreach (@fred) {
    print "$_ ";
}
```

prints:

```
Fred Joe Margaret
```

You can grow arrays dynamically; the subscript of the highest element in an array @array is represented by the variable $#array, and the index of the base element of an array is set by the global variable $[(which is normally 0 but can be 1, or can be reset to anything you like). $array[n] is the *n*th element of @array. You can refer to a range of variables in an array, for example:

```
@array2 = @array1[1 .. 4]
```

assigns elements 1 through 4 of @array1 to @array2. And:

```
@array2 = (@array1[($#array1-4) .. $#array1]);
```

assigns the last five elements of @array1 to @array2.

For a really useful shorthand:

```
open (INPUT, "<$file") || die "couldn't digest $file\n";
@file = (<INPUT>);
```

reads everything from the file named $file into the array @file, one line per array entry.

Much of the beauty of Perl lies in its brevity and flexibility. Both solutions are valid – but there is a short, elegant one, and a long one (that may be more appropriate under some circumstances). Perl is not a straitjacket.

Data types

We've seen simple, scalar variables like $newline; these are simply strings by any other name, although if they contain numeric data they can be treated as numbers. We have also seen simple arrays (vectors) like @line; these are simply arrays of scalars. $line[n] is the *n*th element of @line, and @line[1..4] is an array slice containing the 1st through 4th elements of @line.

Associative arrays are arrays where the subscript is not a number, increasing in sequential order, but a string. Associative arrays are named something like %array, while their elements are referred to as $array{"key"} – this refers to the value associated with the subscript "key". (Note that the subscript here is a string, not an array position.)

You can use associative arrays to store a variety of information:

```
$dog{"small"} = "chihuahua";
$dog{"large"} = "rottweiler" ;
$dog{"medium"} = "labrador";
$bite{"chihuahua"} = "itsy";
$bite{"rottweiler"} = "grievous"
$bite{"labrador"} = "medium"
```

You can then find out how nasty the bite of a medium dog is by looking up the value of $dog{"medium"} and using it as a key in %bite:

```
foreach $fang ("small","medium","large") {
    $breed = $dog{$fang};
    # work out the dog's breed from its teeth
    $pain = $bite{$dog_size};
    # from the size of the dog, derive its bite
    print "A $breed has a $pain bite\n";
    }
```

prints:

```
A chihuahua has a itsy bite
A labrador has a medium bite
A rottweiler has a grievous bite
```

You can use associative array entries as keys to other arrays. The following is a more compact but less readable version of the same program:

```
foreach $fang ("small","medium","large") {
    print "A $dog{$fang} has a $bite{$dog{$fang}} bite\n";
    }
```

This is an example of using an associative array to store pointers. In effect, you can emulate complex data structures (trees, directed graphs, linked lists and so on) using an associative array. Each element of an associative array has a key and a value. The key is the subscript; the value is the value associated with it. This example uses the value in the array %dog as a key into the array %bite.

Associative arrays can be interconverted with ordinary arrays, and initialized in the program. To all intents and purposes, they can be treated like arrays with an even number of entries grouped in "key","value" pairs:

```
%dog = ( # initialize an associative array
    "small","chihuahua",
    "medium","labrador",
    "large","rottweiler",
};
```

In fact, associative arrays are extremely useful; they can be used to emulate databases, and indeed they can be bound to a disk file and retained for use in future sessions. UNIX pioneered the use of dbm files, hash tables on disk where a key:value tuple could be stored and retrieved efficiently. Perl permits you to associate a file with an associative array:

```
dbmopen(%dog, "dog-data",$permiss)
```

opens a file, */usr/filename*, with permissions $permiss (something of a UNIXism), and associates it with %dog. Thereafter, you can read the contents of dog-data as if they are an associative array, and data assigned to %dog is stashed in dog-data. If you execute a dbmclose(%dog) the file is closed (and %dog becomes useless). For example, suppose we want to store our array of canine attributes for use by another program at a later date:

```
#!/bin/perl
%dog = ( # initialize an associative array
    "small","chihuahua",
    "medium","labrador",
    "large","rottweiler",
};
# open the dbm file, or quit with an error message
dbmopen(%dog,"dog-data",0700) ||
    die "Couldn't open dog-data!\n";
# store data in dog-data
%dog = (
    "small","chihuahua",
    "medium","labrador",
    "large","rottweiler",
};
# close the dbm file
dbmclose (%dog);
exit 0;
```

Now a separate program reads the database file:

```
#!/bin/perl
# open the file, for reading
dbmopen(%dog,"dog-data",0400) ||
    die "Couldn't open dog-data!\n";
# now print its contents; note that keys(%assoc)
# fetches all the keys to the associative array %assoc
foreach $size (keys (%dog)) {
    print "My $size dog is a $dog{$size}\n";
}
dbmclose %dog;
```

The first program creates a DBM file called dog-data. The second file reads from it and prints:

```
My small dog is a chihuahua
My medium dog is a labrador
My large dog is a rottweiler
```

The main use of this is to allow programs to retain a 'memory' of what a user is doing. You can store state-specific information from a CGI script in a dbm file, then take its name, and a key for the file, and pass them to a browser as a 'cookie' embedded in an HTML form. On presenting the cookie back to a subsequent run of the CGI script, the script can retrieve its previous state information and generate some more output, giving users the illusion that they are participating in a continuous interactive session rather than a disjoint series of transactions.

We will see some useful examples of associative arrays later.

Regular expressions

Perl lets you do just about everything to an input line that you can do in awk, and a few extra things besides. It does this by using regular expressions, a compact notation for representing patterns of characters. Several functions are provided for working on regular expressions:

```
tr//      Translates character ranges
s///      Performs sed-like string editing
=~        Binds a pattern to a variable
```

By default, everything happens to $_, although you can specify operations on other variables. For example:

```
$fred = "This is a sample line of text";
$fred =~ s/of text/of green elephants/;
print $fred;
```

prints:

```
This is a sample line of green elephants
```

The command s/of text/of green elephants/ replaces each occurrence of the expression of text with the expression of green elephants. Both of these regular expressions simply represent the characters they consist of.

By default, the s/// command is applied to $_, but by using $fred =~ (command) we have bound the effects of the pattern-matching command to $fred.

We can do more than apply simple string operations. Perl recognizes UNIX-style regular expressions. A regular expression is a pattern that matches a string of characters, rather than a literal string of characters. That is, it is a kind of template for text; it describes the form the text must take, rather than the exact content. A simple text search, such as s/food/, must match the letters food, in that order. But a regular expression can specify something like the letter 'f', followed by one to three 'o's, then some other terminating letter (other than a 'z'). For this reason, regular expressions make it easier to search for something where you don't know precisely what the word is, but know part of it (or how it is formed).

Regular expressions are formed using ordinary letters, some of which are given special meanings. Thus, the string 'food' can be used to make an exact text search, matching the letters 'f','o','o','d', even though it is interpreted as a regular expression. The letters simply represent themselves. However, a number of punctuation characters have special meanings: you can override the special meaning by 'escaping' them with a preceding backslash, \, if you really want to search for a literal asterisk, for example.

Regular expressions in a nutshell

In the beginning, a special meaning was assigned to the full stop '.'. It meant 'any character goes here'. For example, sh.t can stand for shot or shut (or a couple of other words that don't belong in a reference book).

Because this wasn't much use for matching a real full stop, a convention was agreed: the backslash '\' would henceforth mean 'remove the special meaning of the next character'. So \. means 'remove the special meaning of the following ".". metacharacter', in other words, match a '.'.

So sh\.t can stand only for the literal text sh.t. \\ means 'match a literal backslash'.

The * was next to be picked on. It meant, 'zero or more of the preceding character'. So .* is short for 'zero or more of anything'. For example, sh.t can only match one random character (shot and so on), but sh.*t can match sht or shot, or shoot, or even shoooooot.

Because you need to type ..* to match 'one or more of anything', an abbreviation was added – +, which means 'match one or more of anything'. (So ..* is roughly equivalent to .+, although there are some subtle differences I won't go into here.) For example, fo+d matches fod, food, foood, and so on, but fo*d can also match fd (by matching 'f', 'no o's', 'd').

You can specify a precise number of matches. {n} means 'match precisely *n* occurrences of the preceding expression', while {m,n} means 'match from *m* to *n* of the preceding expression'. For example:

    e{1}

matches a single 'e', on its own, while:

    e{1,3}

matches one to three e's.

Expressions can be grouped by putting them in parentheses, ( ). You can match any of a set of grouped expressions by separating them with a vertical bar character, | (which means 'or'):

```
(red)|(blue)|(green)
```

matches any of those subexpressions.

Finally, the idea of matching one of a set of characters seemed handy – so the square brackets, [..], were co-opted. Put some characters in square brackets, and they will match any one character (as long as it's one of them). For example:

```
[abdef]
```

matches 'a' or 'f' but not 'c'.

A range of characters can be represented in brackets, for example:

```
[a-ds]
```

means 'match any character from "a" to "d" inclusive, and "s", but nothing else'.

By putting a ^ at the start of a character set, you can negate its meaning. For example:

```
[^a-ds]
```

matches any character not in [a-ds].

In addition, Perl recognizes the following extra expressions:

\w	Any alphanumeric character (including _)
\W	Any non-alphanumeric character
\b	Any word boundary character (within a character class, \b represents a backspace character rather than a word boundary)
\B	Any non-boundary character
\s	Any whitespace character
\S	Any non-whitespace character
\d	Any digit
\D	Any non-digit
^	Matches the beginning of a line (if it occurs unescaped or outside square brackets)
$	Matches the end of a line (if it appears unescaped)

Built-in variables

Perl has a huge number of built-in variables, like awk. Some of these are useful for setting up the internal configuration of a Perl program, for example, it is possible to use $[to set the base subscript of an array. Normally, $[is 0, but for compatibility with some systems it is useful to be able to set $[to 1. Alternatively, $/ specifies the input record separator. When reading from a file, Perl reads in a record delimited by the character specified by $/. Normally this is a new line character, but it can be reset to a different value if the file being read is not a UNIX text file. Similarly, $\ sets the output record delimiter. Normally this variable is unset – Perl does not automatically print a new line after each print statement – but if you set it to \n Perl will automatically add a new line after each print (or other output).

Here are some of the other, more commonly used built-in variables:

$.   The current input line number of the current filehandle. For example:

```
foreach (<>) {
    print $_;
}
print $.;
```

prints the standard input, then the number of lines read from it.

$_   The current workspace. By default, if you don't specify a variable most Perl commands are applied to $_.

$'   The string preceding whatever was matched by the last pattern search.

$'   The string following whatever was matched by the last pattern search.

$/   The input record separator. Normally a newline \n character.

$\   The output record separator. By default, this is undefined. It is printed after every output record.

$,   The output field separator. Normally this is undefined. If you set it to some value, that value will be printed between each output field. For example:

```
$, = ":";
$a = $b = $c = $d = 1;
print $a, $b, $c, $d;
```

results in:

```
1:1:1:1
```

$#   Controls the output format for numbers. Perl can handle C's printf() function – there is an exact equivalent – and by default the simpler print function formats numbers as %.20g. You can reset this by assigning a printf-style format specifier, to change the precision with which numbers are printed.

$0   Contains the name of the script being executed.

$@ The error status returned by the last eval command. If set, it indicates that the eval failed. (eval($foo) executes $foo as a Perl script in its own right. You can use this as a way of trapping errors in your programs.)

@ARGV An array containing the command-line arguments to the script. For example, if the script test.pl contains:

```
foreach (@ARGV) {
print "$_ ";
}
```

then if you run it by typing:

```
test.pl 1 2 3
```

it will print:

```
1 2 3
```

Note that ARGV does not contain the name of the script itself; that's $0.

%ENV An associative array containing the environment for the running program. You can create new environment variables by assigning a new value in %ENV. For example, $ENV{"REQUEST_METHOD"} returns the HTTP method used to run a CGI script from the environment (either GET or PUT).

Operating systems

One of the original design goals of Perl was to replace the UNIX shells – specifically the Bourne and Korn shells – as the tool of choice for writing a certain kind of application. Typically, large shell scripts tend to run slowly because they rely on external programs (UNIX tools) to do most of their work.

A lot of the standard UNIX tools were written to give access to a specific low-level feature of the UNIX operating system. For example, **ls** lists files by reading a directory file, identifying the inodes (index nodes) associated with each filename in the directory, then executing a stat() function call to obtain information about the inode for each file. (stat() returns information about a file, such as its length, creation time and so on.)

Perl has all the necessary functions to implement **ls** built-in; it has a suite of functions (opendir(), readdir(), closedir() and so on) for reading directories, and it has its own version of stat() for obtaining information about files. (This is useful, because Perl can run on platforms other than UNIX, including some which don't have inodes or anything similar; stat() in Perl on these programs simply returns the equivalent information about a file.)

In fact, Perl has a whole plethora of low-level commands for interfacing with operating system services. Using system(), Perl can execute other programs (assuming the operating system it is running under knows how to do this). Using `sysread()` and `syswrite()` it can read and write raw data from a file, controlling the number of bytes read. Just about the entire UNIX library of function calls for handling shared memory, semaphores, locks on files and so forth, are implemented – as are sockets, for Perl can handle pipes and Internet domain sockets. (One particular library shipped with the Perl runtime, *chat2.pl*, comes in handy here: it allows us to write easy text-level TCP/IP applications that connect to a port and chat with the server on that port. We'll see more of this later.)

Perl's operating system interaction hooks are somewhat daunting; there are over a hundred such commands built-in. They do confer a major advantage: any file, process, or memory management operation that you would normally accomplish in a shell script by invoking an external program can probably be accomplished within Perl by a judicious use of the more obscure language features.

Functions, libraries, extensibility

No programming language is complete without the ability to define extensions such as user specified functions. Arguably, it also helps to be able to bundle up frequently used extensions into a library file that can be loaded on demand. Perl is fairly unexceptional in that it provides these facilities (and a little bit more besides).

You can define a subroutine in Perl quite easily:

```
sub myfunc {
    local ($arg1, $arg2) = @_;
    local ($result);
    # do something or other with $arg1 and $arg2
    # then place the results in $result
    return $result;
}
```

This declares &myfunc, a user subroutine.

&myfunc makes use of two arguments; these are passed to it in the array @_, which is allocated locally when &myfunc is called. (There might be more than two arguments, in which case the extra ones are discarded.)

The function `local()` takes a variable as its parameter and makes a copy of it locally, that is, $arg1, $arg2 and $result are local to &myfunc, and are expunged when &myfunc finishes.

Finally, after doing something with the arguments, a result is assigned to the local variable $result. The return command returns the value of its parameter; so when &myfunc finishes, it returns whatever was in $result:

```
$answer = &myfunc("1","2");
```

Note that in Perl, variables are global by default, and must be specifically identified as local if you want their scope to be restricted. This is the opposite behaviour to languages like Pascal or, to a lesser extent, C. It is less of an issue in Perl 5, which can handle persistent, encapsulated data objects.

The reason for the odd variable scope rule takes some explaining. Perl keeps all its variables in a central symbol table (called `main`). When you define a variable within a subroutine as being local, a local symbol table is created; thus, references outside that subroutine don't see an entry for a variable of that name in the main symbol table.

Perl can load libraries of external functions by using the require statement. `require "filename"` makes Perl load and interpret `"filename"` as a sequence of Perl commands. If the commands are preceded by a package declaration, like:

```
package myfuncs;
```

a new symbol table is created (called `myfuncs`). You can refer (within the scope of main) to symbols in myfuncs by using a quote-mark, ', to qualify the reference. For example, suppose we have a file called *otherstuff.pl*, that contains a package called `otherstuff`:

```
# otherstuff.pl
#
package otherstuff;
@myarray = ("sweet","sour","salty");
1;
#
# note that all packages must return "1" when exiting
```

Now let's create a program that loads the package `otherstuff` and does something with it:

```
# main program
#
# define an array, @myarray

@myarray = ("red","green","blue");

#let's load package otherstuff from file otherstuff.pl
#
require "otherstuff.pl";
#
# now let's print the contents of the array @myarray,
# first in the scope of the main symbol table, then
# in the scope of otherstuff;
```

```
foreach $thing (@mystuff) {      # main symbol table
    print "$thing\n";
}

foreach $thing (@otherstuff'mystuff) {   # otherstuff
    print "$thing\n";
}
```

This will result in the output:

```
red
green
blue
sweet
sour
salty
```

If a variable is defined in a package, you can refer to it in the main program by specifying the package name. This makes Perl check the package's symbol table rather than the main one. Subroutines with local variables also have symbol tables, and you can access them from the main program (and vice versa).

If you don't add a symbol table specifier in front of a variable name, the main symbol table is assumed; so `$fred` is identical to `$main'fred`.

A large number of packages are available to Perl users; many of them are specifically designed for the world wide web. First and foremost, for serious work on the web it is useful to get hold of a copy of libwww-perl. This library (which can be obtained from `http://www.ics.uci.edu/`) provides an extensive set of tools for handling HTTP queries and parsing HREF tags.

This library enables you to do things like:

- get files from remote servers using Perl scripts

- automatically convert relative URLs (like *mydir/thisfile.html*) into absolute URLs

- handle dates (as formatted by most web servers)

- read and manipulate HTML documents

- correctly handle MIME content-types

While it's not essential for writing CGI scripts, it comes in very useful in advanced work.

It's also useful to have a library to hand for handling CGI stuff; notably for getting requests, decoding them and giving access to the variables in them through an associative array. (Routines for doing this are included later in this chapter. Alternatively, check

```
http://www.yahoo.com/text/world_wide_web/CGI/
```

for the latest popular ones.)

If you are willing to learn, it may be worth looking into Perl 5. While there is still a shortage of tutorial texts on this language, Perl 5 is strictly speaking a superset of Perl 4; the most significant addition is object orientation. Various object libraries are available, including:

CGI.pm   For creating forms and handling CGI queries. Includes 'persistence' – you can reload a form and view the state of a query at a later date.

GD.pm   For creating GIF images on the fly. Using GD (which requires some external compiled code) you can specify arcs, lines, fill regions and colours, then output a GIF containing a diagram composed to your specifications.

HTML.pm For generating HTML programatically. This is most useful in conjunction with a database library, for automatically producing the HTML text around a database report.

DBI.pm   For interfacing to databases. Currently supports a range of databases including mSQL (a popular free SQL database), Oracle, Informix and most of the heavyweight commercial SQL databases. You can compose queries in SQL, and receive the results in a neatly formatted Perl array (which you can then print using HTML.pm).

To learn about Perl 5, the best starting point is the usenet newsgroup:

```
comp.lang.perl.announce
```

FAQ (frequently asked question) files are posted there on a weekly basis. These include a list of all available Perl 5 modules, and their current status. You can also find more information about Perl, and pointers to Perl information, on

```
http://www.perl.com/
```

Once you have read the FAQs, you can read the newsgroups

```
comp.infosystems.www.authoring.cgi
```

(general CGI-related questions – a FAQ is also posted there, every week) and

```
comp.lang.perl.misc
```

(miscellaneous Perl-related discussion).

Be advised that, before you even think about posting a question, it's a good idea to read the FAQ; FAQs contain the most frequently asked questions and their answers, and there's a good chance that someone has asked the question before you. (Asking a question which is answered in the FAQ is a good way to get shouted at.)

Perl on different platforms

Perl is available for most common operating systems. However, if you intend to use a Perl script on more than one platform there are certain things to bear in mind.

UNIX

Perl is written in C and is usually provided in compiled form for those platforms that don't usually come with a C compiler. Most flavours of UNIX come with a C compiler; furthermore, as UNIX systems are not normally binary compatible, you may have to roll your own Perl binary.

Luckily, Perl comes with a complex shell script called Configure. When you run it, it checks your system for various options which may (or may not) be present, asks you some technical questions, then writes a Makefile. You then run the UNIX utility make, which interprets the Makefile and drives the C compiler. Assuming Configure did its job properly, make will build a version of Perl customized to the facilities available on your system. Those services that your operating system does not support are simply not compiled into your copy of Perl.

A test suite is included with the standard Perl distribution. Running the test suite executes a series of Perl scripts which exercise the interpreter and check that the output from it conforms to what is expected of the language.

To make matters a bit easier, if you have a common UNIX system (say, SunOS 4.1, Solaris 2.3, or SCO UNIX) you can probably obtain a precompiled copy of Perl. Indeed, although Perl is not part of UNIX (and is not listed for inclusion in the definitive SPEC1170 standard), many vendors are now shipping Perl with their systems as unsupported software.

Perl was originally designed for UNIX. If you have a good UNIX implementation, you can use all Perl's features. Perl knows no obvious memory limits, can fork() and exec() child programs, can connect to servers across a TCP/IP network, and can take advantage of most of the system's facilities. One of the advantages of Perl on UNIX is that as long as the Perl binary is reasonably well put together, it removes all the usual issues of memory management from the programmer. Writing C source code on a UNIX system condemns the programmer to a life of drudgery, hunting for obscure memory leaks.

MS-DOS

Perl suffers under MS-DOS for a simple reason: DOS cannot provide many of the features Perl requires. There is no standard TCP/IP stack for DOS, DOS doesn't understand multitasking, and DOS has very primitive memory management. For this reason, a pure DOS version of Perl is a sorry beast.

Luckily the PC architecture has outgrown its humble origins. Windows takes over memory management from DOS and allows properly written Windows applications to access all the memory on a PC. At the same time, memory-management utilities called DOS extenders provide access to blocks of memory above 1 Mb for ordinary DOS applications. BigPerl for DOS can execute under Windows 3.1's DPMI-compatible memory manager. It still doesn't understand TCP/IP, and can execute only one child process at a time, but gives a full 16 Mb of virtual memory for messing around in.

Note also that Perl on DOS suffers from problems associated with file-name semantics. The DOS filename separator is a backslash, \, but Perl views a backslash as an escape character, you must therefore use an escaped back-slash, \ \, to separate elements in a pathname.

BigPerl is currently available only for Perl 4.036. A Perl 5.0 port is under development.

Macintosh

The Macintosh is an alien beast. However, MacPerl is much friendlier than you might expect. MacPerl is currently available as an integrated environment (a text editor which can execute Perl programs) and a standalone interpreter (that runs under Apple's MPW command-line shell). MacPerl is bound by memory limitations, but these are somewhat less extreme than those for DOS Perl; you can allocate memory up to the maximum amount of virtual memory available on your Macintosh and Perl will use it. MacPerl also has a rather interesting socket-handling package. Unlike standard Perl, MacPerl uses a custom set of socket interfaces called GUSI – the Grand Unified Socket Interface. GUSI provides a Berkeley sockets interface and supports TCP/IP and the Macintosh networking protocols. Using GUSI you can do most of the TCP/IP stuff that a UNIX Perl program can do.

The eccentricities of MacPerl should be obvious if you think for a moment about the eccentricities of the Macintosh environment. Firstly, Macintosh filename semantics are sufficiently different from DOS or UNIX to make it necessary to modify scripts that open files. Secondly, MacPerl can't execute external programs in the same way as UNIX Perl – although it has an interface to the AppleScript scripting mechanism, so that it can drive script-able Macintosh applications (and communicate with them), and can interoperate with the MPW ToolServer. Thirdly, there is a package of external commands for MacPerl which you should use with any Macintosh Perl scripts. This lets you prompt for input and display simple dialogues, and load external compiled code fragments (XCMDs and XFCNs). It's essential, because Macintosh programs don't have a runtime environment to pass vari-ables in (like UNIX or DOS).

MacPerl can interoperate tightly with the WebStar web server, thus allowing CGI scripts in Perl to be ported between Macintosh and UNIX fairly easily. A package to allow emulation of standard CGI scripts is available.

Currently, MacPerl is stable at the level of Perl 4.036 for UNIX. However, work on MacPerl 5.0 is in progress. A version of MacPerl that is usable as an Apple OSAX (native scripting language) may become available in the near future, and support for the Macintosh port of the Tk widget toolkit (currently being carried out by Sun Microsystems) has been suggested.

This small library interconverts Macintosh and UNIX pathnames. If you need to write a Perl script that can run in either environment, it may prove indispensible. Note that these routines rely on regular expressions to do the conversion, so they may look a little opaque at first. A 'better' way would be to build a pushdown stack of pathname elements, remove the parents of .. elements, and then pop all the elements off the stack – but that's a complex solution to code, and a little slower to execute.

Macintosh pathnames consist of a series of folder names separated by colons, followed by a filename. A leading colon means that the path is 'relative' to the current folder. Two colons in a row mean 'go up a level'; three in a row mean 'go up two levels', and so on.

UNIX pathnames consist of a series of directory names separated by slashes, followed by a filename. A leading slash means that the path is 'absolute', from the top of the filesystem. Two dots in a row mean 'go up a level'; three in a row is a mistake.

```perl
#!/usr/local/bin/perl

sub mac2ux {
    #
    # takes a macintosh pathname and reformats it as a UNIX pathname
    #
    local ($inpath) = @_[$[];          # first argument to &mac2ux
    $inpath = &eat_parents($inpath);   # convert "::" refs
    $inpath =~ s#:#/#g;

                                       # change all ":"to"/" in $inpath

    while ($inpath =~ m#//#) {         # while $inpath matches "//"
        $inpath =~ s#//#/../#g;        # replace "//" with "/../"
    }

    if (substr($inpath,$[,1) eq "/") { # if the first character of $inpath
                                       # is already a "/", remove it
        $inpath = substr($inpath, $[+1);
    } else {                           # otherwise, insert a leading "/"
        $inpath = "/" . $inpath;
    }
    return $inpath;                    # return the value of $inpath
}
```

```perl
sub ux2mac {
    #
    # takes a UNIX pathname and reformats it as a Macintosh pathname
    #
    local ($inpath) = @_[$[];
    $inpath =~ s#/#:#g;                    # change all "/" to ":"
    if (substr($inpath,$[,1) eq ":") {     # if $inpath begins with a ":"
                                           # remove the leading colon
        $inpath = substr($inpath, $[+1);
    } else {                               # otherwise, insert a leading colon
        $inpath = ":" . $inpath;
    }
    # the next substitution is particularly complex. It means:
    # look for matches of two periods and a colon (unless they are preceded
    # by another colon), and replace them with ":..:"
    #
    $inpath =~ s#[^:]\.\..:#:...:#;
    while ($inpath =~ m#:\.\..:#) {         # while the string contains ":..:"
        $inpath =~ s#:\.\..:#::#g;          # replace it with "::"
    }
    $inpath = &eat_parents($inpath);       # now remove "::" pairs and their
                                           # parent directories
    return $inpath;                        # return the value of $inpath
}

sub eat_parents {
    #
    # this subroutine looks for patterns like (directory1:)(directory2)::
    # and replaces them with (directory1:)
    #
    local ($line) = @_[$[];
    #
    # let's eat our parent directories wherever we see "::"
    #
    WHILE:                                 # a loop identifier
    while ($line =~ m#::#) {               # while there are "::" constructs ...
        last WHILE if ($line =~ /^:(:)+[^:]+/);
                                           # quit the loop if there are no
                                           # directories to discard left in $line
                                           # - something's probably gone wrong
        if ($line =~ /(.*:)([^:]+::)(.*)/) {
                                           # if the line contains the target
                                           # pattern
```

```
                    ($prefix,$target,$suffix) = ($line =~ /(.*:)([^:]+::)(.*)/);
                                        # apply the pattern to the line and
                                        # split the chunks into prefix, bit
                                        # to get rid of, and suffix
            $line = $prefix . $suffix;
        } else {
            if ($line =~ /[^:]*::[^:].*/) {
                                        # if the line consists of
                                        # (directory::)filename
                ($target,$suffix) = ($line =~ /([^:]*:)(.*)/);
                                        # get the filename, and return that
            $line = $suffix;
                                        # then exit the loop because there
                                        # are obviously no more directories to
                                        # discard
            last WHILE;
        }
    }
    return $line;
}

# test script: running the following script (on UNIX) tests
# the routines above. Type the script's name to start it, then type unix
# pathnames followed by a carriage return. It will convert them to mac, then
# back to UNIX, and tell you if they match.

# Note that it can't handle multiple "../" operators on one line.

#!/usr/local/bin/perl
while (<>) {
    chop;                               # chop() dumps last character in a line
    $inp = $_;
    $res = &ux2mac($inp);               # unix filename -> mac
    print "ux2mac($inp) ==> $res\n";    # print results
    $cmp = &mac2ux($res);               # turn mac filename back into unix
    print "mac2ux($res) ==> $cmp\n";    # print results
    if ($cmp eq $inp) {                 # say if the back-conversion got back
                                        # to the original pathname
        print "functions are orthogonal\n";
    } else {
        print "Warning: input not identical to output!\n";
    }
    if ($inp =~ /\.\./) {
        print "This may be because your input contained\n";
        print "the \"..\" operator.\n";
    }
}
```

CGI scripting in Perl

Perl can be used to implement CGI scripts to automate form handling. In this section, we will see a simple CGI handler written in Perl. (This version is specific to UNIX; the WebStar server uses a rather different mechanism for communicating with scripts, although bindings for MacPerl are available.)

To recap: an HTTP server that supports the Common Gateway Interface exports several environment variables that can be read by scripts executed under it. Scripts usually reside in a designated directory (often called *cgi-bin*) under the server's home directory, although they can be located elsewhere. They can be invoked by HTTP requests; usually either a GET request, with an appended query string, or a POST request, with the body of the query in the body of the request. (Note that you can also trigger a script by sending a HEAD request, or using some other non-typical request method – this frequently causes badly written scripts to fall over.)

The first thing a CGI script in Perl needs to do is to establish what query method is being used, and to obtain the query text. As we have seen, Perl can read the UNIX environment as if it is an associative array. For example, $ENV{"foo"} contains the value of the variable named "foo". The CGI specification requires that several environment variables be set; the main ones are:

REQUEST_METHOD Either GET or POST – the method used to submit the request. (Might also be a HEAD request, but such requests do not usually require any additional processing.)

QUERY_STRING If a GET request is submitted, this variable contains the text of the URL following the initial ?. (The part before the ? points to the CGI script; the part following it consists of a query.)

CONTENT_LENGTH If a POST request is submitted, this variable contains the length (in characters) of the query. The CGI script can then read the query from standard input. (Note that the script might hang if it tries to read beyond the extent of CONTENT_LENGTH.)

CONTENT_TYPE If a POST request is submitted and this variable is set, it contains the MIME content-type of the data in the request.

These are the important variables. There are some others that might be used: notably REMOTE_HOST (the host making the request), REMOTE_ADDR (the IP address of the remote host) REMOTE_USER (the authenticated user ID of the user making the request) and AUTH_TYPE (the authentication method used to validate the user). However, we will see some discussion of these variables later; they are not necessary in this example.

```
if ($ENV{'REQUEST_METHOD'} eq "GET") {
    $request = $ENV{'QUERY_STRING'};
} elsif ($ENV{'REQUEST_METHOD'} eq "POST") {
    read(STDIN, $request,$ENV{'CONTENT_LENGTH'})
        || die "Could not get query\n";
}
```

To get the query, the code fragment shown first checks to see if the environment variable REQUEST_METHOD is GET.

If it is, it obtains the query string from the variable QUERY_STRING and stashes it in $request.

If it is not a GET request, then a check is made for a POST method. If the query has been posted, the script needs to read CONTENT_LENGTH bytes into the variable $request, from the standard input (STDIN); this is carried out by the read() function.

There is a die() call which is executed only if the read() fails.

Now we have the query, what can we do with it?

A typical complete query URL looks something like this:

```
/cgi-bin/dog-bite-report.pl?size=medium&bite=bad
```

This can be divided into two parts. The CGI script itself:

```
/cgi-bin/dog-bite-report.pl
```

and its parameters, the query:

```
size=medium&bite=bad
```

Variable=Value pairs are separated by ampersands, &. Non-alphanumeric characters are represented by their hexadecimal value (as %nn) in the Latin-1 codeset; for example, %20 for space (ASCII/Latin-1 character 32 in decimal, 20 in hex). Note that the (obsolescent) ISINDEX tag encodes a space as a plus sign, +.

So we need to:

● translate the characters that have been modified

● split up the variable=value tuples

● put them into a convenient format

Typically, Perl scripts use an associative array to store the parameters to a CGI script; it's a convenient format, because you can store an arbitrary range of named values and check to see if they exist, and if so, what their value is.

```
@parameter_list = split (/&/,$result);   # split string on '&' characters
foreach (@parameter_list) {              # foreach variable=value pair
    s/\+/ /g;                            # replace "+" with a space
    s/%([0-9A-F][0-9][A-F])/pack("c",hex($1))/ge;
                                         # COMPLEX: replace any two
                                         # characters preceded by a per
                                         # cent sign with their own packed
                                         # hex value. See the perl "pack()"
                                         # function for details

}
```

Firstly, we chop the query string up, dividing it on each &, and placing the results in an array of strings called @parameter_list.

Secondly, we loop over the array. Each element in the array is in turn implicitly assigned to $_ (the current workspace), and the substitution commands in the loop are applied to $_.

The first substitution is relatively simple. s/\+/ /g means 'substitute all literal + signs, replacing them with a space. Repeat globally.' The g parameter ensures that if there is more than one + in the workspace, all of them will be processed. The backslash escape before the + is required because the + symbol is normally a regular expression; its special meaning must be removed in order to make the s/// command look for it as a literal character.

The second substitution is a lot more ambitious. Let's look at it again:

```
s/%([0-9A-F][0-9A-F])/pack("c",hex($1))/ge;
```

The first part, the string we are searching for, is a regular expression consisting of a percentage sign followed by two hexadecimal digits (the numerals 0–9 and the letters A–F). The parentheses group the two characters following the % sign, and they can be referred to later in the same search/replace operation as $1, because it is the first regular expression group to be encountered in this process. (If we had the search expression /%([0-9A-F])([0-9A-F])/, the first character would be $1 and the second would be $2.)

The 'replace' part of the substitution is more complex. In this case, the pack() function is called, taking as an argument the hexadecimal value of the two characters matched in the search expression. hex() converts a hexadecimal number to a hexadecimal string; pack() is used to take a value and pack it into some sort of data structure. In this example, the c parameter to pack() tells it to put the hexadecimal number into an unsigned char variable – a character.

The /ge at the end of the expression tells Perl to apply the substitution globally (g) to the string, rather than stopping at the first match, and to evaluate (e) the replacement expression as if it is a Perl expression, rather than just a regular expression.

This is about as hairy as Perl regular expressions ever get. If you understand it, consider yourself an expert.

Now we have an array, @parameter_list, containing name=value pairs for each parameter passed in the GET or POST request. How do we turn that into a neat, handy, associative array?

```
foreach (@parameter_list) {
    ($name, $value) = split(/=/);
    $passed{$name} = $value;
}
```

This little bit of code iterates over the variable=value pairs in @parameter_list. Each entry in @parameter_list is loaded into $_ in turn. It then splits the entry on the = sign, stashing the two halves in $name and $value. Finally, we add the entry to the associative array %passed.

If we check the value of $passed{"something"}, it will either contain nothing (indicating that no variable called something was passed in the HTTP request), or it will return the value associated with something. So the array %passed is effectively an index to the variables passed to our script.

Of course, there are some potential pitfalls in this code. For another thing, the split(/=/) command runs the risk of going awry if one of those hexademical numbers encoded in the value being split is itself an 'equal to' sign – there would be an item like foo=bar=quux in @parameter_list, and this would not fit neatly into our final associative array. Therefore, it makes sense to do the splitting before we expand the characters. Putting it all together we get something like this:

```
if ($ENV{'REQUEST_METHOD'} eq "GET") {     # if we're receiving a GET
    $request = $ENV{'QUERY_STRING'};       # the request is passed in the
                                           # environment variable QUERY_STRING
                                           # else ...
} elsif ($ENV{'REQUEST_METHOD'} eq "POST") {# if receiving a POST request the
                                           # length of the posted data is
                                           # passed in CONTENT_LENGTH, and it
                                           # is read from stdin
    read(STDIN, $request,$ENV{'CONTENT_LENGTH'})
        || die "Could not get query\n";
}
@parameter_list = split(/&/,$request);     # split the parameters up

foreach (@parameter_list) {                # split each variable=value pair
    ($name, $value) = split(/=/);
    $name =~ s/\+/ /g;                      # replace "+" with spaces
    $name =~ s/%([0-9A-F][0-9A-F])/pack("c",hex($1))/ge;
                                           # replace %nn with characters
    $value =~ s/\+/ /g;                     # repeat for the value ...
    $name =~ s/%([0-9A-F][0-9A-F])/pack("c",hex($1))/ge;
    if !(defined $passed{$name}) {
        $passed{$name} = $value;
    } else {
        $value =~ s/:/\\:/g;.
        $passed{$name} .= ":$value";
    }
}
```

This has the advantage of saving us an extra loop iteration, although it would have to be a remarkably huge CGI request for this to impact the performance of the average server.

Note the final loop:

```
if !(defined $passed{$name}) {
    $passed{$name} = $value;
} else {
    $value =~ s/:/\\:/g;
    $passed{$name} .= ":$value";
}
```

This covers the possibility that our query string includes several values for one variable. For example, a multiple selection list might return something like:

```
files=first.txt&files=third.txt&files=fourth.txt
```

In this code fragment, if the %passed array doesn't contain a value for the key files, one is created; if the variable already exists, the new value is tagged onto the end of it, separated by a colon. (If $value contains a colon, the colon is replaced by \:, to prevent confusion. It also covers backslash-escaped colons by additionally escaping them, like \\:). To get the list of values out of a variable (named by $key) such as this and into an array, you do something like:

```
@parameters = split(/[^\\]:/, $passed{$key});
foreach (@parameters) {
    s/\\:/:/g;
}
```

Providing some feedback

Now we've figured out how to get query information into a Perl script, it's time to consider how to deliver the output of the script back to the server.

CGI scripts simply print their output to the standard output; the HTTP server reads the output and sends it back down to the client in the form of an HTTP body. First, it writes a brief header – usually not a full HTTP header. The header consists of a line containing some server directives, or a full HTTP response followed by a blank line. (Server directives are interpreted by the server, which generates an appropriate HTTP header.) Next, the script writes to standard output whatever text needs to be returned to the client. The server digests the standard output from the CGI script and sends the appropriate portion of it back to the client. For example:

```
Content-type: text/html

<HTML>
<!-- stuff goes here >
</HTML>
```

This tells the server to send the script output as HTML, then sends the output from the script. (The HTML is presumably generated by print statements or some equivalent mechanism.)

Note the blank line between `Content-type` and `<HTML>`. If there isn't one, you'll get a `500 Server Error` message, and the server error logfile will contain a message like 'Malformed header from script'. This is because your neatly printed HTML will be mistaken by the server for part of the HTTP response header, rather than the body of the message.

Alternatively, the client can return a pointer to some other document. Instead of the normal header (containing a `Content-type:` line, and optional additional information), it contains a reference:

```
Location: /pub/myfile.txt
```

The `Location:` header is sent to the client, which then tells the server to send */pub/myfile.txt* instead. The location can also be a full URL, for example:

```
Location: http//www.tardis.ed.ac.uk/~charlie/index.html
```

tells the client to go look at that file instead of the URL, that was initially looked at.

The CGI environment

CGI scripts receive a fair amount of information about their execution environment from the web server. Not all this information is standardized; some servers and some clients pass extra information.

You can examine the contents of the environment of a CGI script by checking the keys to the associative array `%ENV`. `%ENV` contains environment variables; their names are the keys to the array. For example, `$ENV {'QUERY_STRING'}` contains the HTTP query that was passed to a CGI script.

When developing scripts it's often useful to have a simple, dumb CGI script kicking around that prints out your environment. In conjunction with a couple of different browsers, you can work out ways of finding out information about your users. Here's a simple script which doesn't actually read a GET or POST query, but prints out everything it finds in its runtime environment (using a neatly formatted table):

```
#!/bin/perl
#
#
print "Content-type: text/html\n\n";

print "<HEAD><TITLE>Environment dumper</TITLE></HEAD>\n";
print "<BODY><P>\n";
print "<TABLE BORDER=\"4\">\n";
```

```
print "<TR><TD><B>Variable</B><TD><B>Value</B>\n";
foreach (keys (%ENV)) {
    print "<TR><TD>$_<TD>$ENV{$_}\n";
}
if ($ENV{'REQUEST_METHOD'} eq "POST") {
    $stdin = <STDIN>;
    print "<TR><TD COLSPAN=\"2\"><B>Uploaded file follows</B>
    (raw MIME data)\n";
    print "<TR><TD COLSPAN=\"2\">$stdin\n";
}
print "</TABLE>\n</BODY>\n";
exit 0;
```

It produces output like Figure 5.1. This tells us a lot about the web browser making the request, even though it doesn't actually parse the query. (Note that if the REQUEST_METHOD variable is set to POST, it reads in the query and prints it in a cell in the table without performing any substitutions on it.)

For example, we can see that the HTTP_USER_AGENT (the web browser) is a beta copy of Netscape 2.0, and it's coming from the machine (REMOTE_HOST) fma0.demon.co.uk, at network address 158.152.6.20. The browser is willing to accept the following MIME types:

Variable	Value
HTTP_USER_AGENT	Mozilla/2.0b1 (Macintosh; I; 68K)
SERVER_NAME	server.demon.co.uk
HTTP_HOST	www.demon.co.uk
QUERY_PRAGMA	no-cache
QUERY_STRING	
SERVER_PORT	80
HTTP_ACCEPT	image/gif, image/x-xbitmap, image/jpeg, image/pjpeg, */*
SERVER_PROTOCOL	HTTP/1.0
REMOTE_ADDR	158.152.6.20
HTTP_CONNECTION	Keep-Alive
PATH	/bin:/usr/bin:/usr/ucb:/usr/bsd:/usr/local/bin
GATEWAY_INTERFACE	CGI/1.1
REQUEST_METHOD	GET
SCRIPT_NAME	/cgi-bin/dumper.pl
SERVER_SOFTWARE	NCSA/1.3
REMOTE_HOST	fma0.demon.co.uk

Figure 5.1

```
image/gif, image/x-bitmap, image/x-jpeg, image/pjpeg, */*.
```

If additional information is available, it will show up in this listing, for example, the undigested HTTP query will appear here, as will security information passed using HTACCESS and `HTTP_COOKIE` data in the HTTP header. (We will cover HTACCESS authorization and cookies later, in Chapter 9, see 'Security', p. 247.)

Putting it together

Now we've covered the basics, it's possible to examine some working CGI scripts. Here are two:

- a simple reflector that prints out whatever variables you pass it in the form of an HTML page,

- a simple search script that looks for text in a set of HTML files, and returns a page containing links to those files that match the search criteria.

A reflector script

Here's a simple reflector script. All it does is reflect back to the client everything that the client sends to the server. It does so by encapsulating the query strings in a definition list. You can use it to get a feel for the way forms work, create forms, make sure that their ACTION invokes this script, and it will tell you exactly what the form sent to the server.

```perl
#
# first get the query
#
if ($ENV{'REQUEST_METHOD'} eq "GET") {          # get input for GET requests
    $request = $ENV{'QUERY_STRING'};
} elsif ($ENV{'REQUEST_METHOD'} eq "POST") {    # get input for POST requests
    read(STDIN, $request,$ENV{'CONTENT_LENGTH'})
        || die "Content-type: text/html\n\n<HTML>\n<H1>Fatal Error</H1> \
        Could not get query\n</HTML>\n";
}

#
# print a generic header to standard output, to send back to the client
#
print "Content-type: text/html \n\n";
#
# from now on, our output is in HTML, because that's what we've said we're
# sending
#
```

```perl
print "<HTML\n";
print "<H1>Query reflector</H1>\n";

#
# sanity check; return an error if the query is empty
#
if (length($request) = 0) {
    print "<B>No</B> query was detected. Did you send a request?\n";
    print "</HTML>\n";
    exit 0;
}

#
# now parse the query
#

@parameter_list = split(/&/,$request);          # split name=value pairs
foreach (@parameter_list) {                      # for each parameter ...
    ($name, $value) = split(/=/);                # get the name and value
    $name =~ s/\+/ /g;                           # convert characters
    $name =~ s/%(..)/pack("c",hex($1))/ge;
    $value =~ s/\+/ /g;
    $value =~ s/%(..)/pack("c",hex($1))/ge;
    $passed{$name} = $value;                     # put them in %passed
}

#
# now return the query embedded in an HTML document
#
print "I received the following variables and values:\n";
print "<HR>\n<DL>\n";                            # we're sending back a
                                                 # definition list of variables

foreach $key (keys %passed) {                    # loop through %passed
    print "<DT>$key\n";                          # printing key, value pairs
    print "<DD>$passed{$key}\n";
}
print "</DL><HR>\n";                             # be nice and close the list
print "</HTML>\n";

exit 0;                                          # exit in good order
```

Although this script is trivial, it is quite useful. As it is, it returns the entered values to the user. However, with minor modifications it can be used to take more complex actions, for example, to email the variables to a specified mail address.

A simple mail feedback form

To make this send email to a given address, using the UNIX sendmail
system, add the following lines at the top of the file, where variables are
being declared:

```
$recipient = 'user@host';
$mailer_binary = "/usr/lib/sendmail";
$mailer_flags = " -odi -t";
```

(making sure to set user@host to your email address). Then replace the last 14
lines of the file with this:

```
$message = "\nContent Feedback Report\n";
$message .= "=======================\n";
foreach $key (keys %passed) {                    # loop through %passed
    $message .= "$key: $passed{$key}\n";         # printing key, value pairs
}                                                # the following stuff is
                                                 # all put in the environment
                                                 # by the web server
$message .= "Protocol:       $ENV{'SERVER_PROTOCOL'}\n";
$message .= "Remote Host:    $ENV{'REMOTE_HOST'}\n";
$message .= "Remote IP addr: $ENV{'REMOTE_ADDR'}\n";
#
# Now send mail to $recipient
#
open (MAIL, "|$mailer_binary $mailer_flags $recipient")
    || die "Can't open $mailprog!\n";            # open a pipe to sendmail
print MAIL "Subject: Content Feedback\n";        # print $message into sendmail
print MAIL "From: daemon\n";                     # remember the From line
print MAIL "$message";
close (MAIL);                                     # close the pipe and quit
return 0;
```

This script does exactly the same – except that instead of printing its output to
the standard output, where it is captured by the HTTP server and sent back to
the user, it sends it to the **sendmail** mail daemon via a pipe. **sendmail** is a
mail transport agent; it handles the process of taking mail from a mail application and sending it to an SMTP server, and the process of receiving mail and
storing it in user's mail folders. (Note that invoking a mail tool such as pine
or elm from within a CGI script is potentially hazardous, as these programs
have the ability to execute shell commands and it is not impossible for a
hacker to sneak some instructions in via an odd set of form arguments, which
are then executed on the server and open up a security hole. Security issues
are discussed in more detail in Chapter 9.)

A simple search script

This script is a bit more complex. It searches files in a directory hierarchy for a regular expression, and returns a bulleted list of URLs, the clickable text of which is the TITLE string for the matching file. To use it, create a form like this:

```
<HR>
<FORM ACTION="/cgi-bin/scan.pl" METHOD="GET">
<PRE>Enter search text:  <INPUT NAME="search">
Press here to start: <INPUT TYPE="Submit" VALUE="Start
search">
</PRE>
</FORM>
This form permits you to enter a Perl regular expression.
It searches all the files in directories under public_html,
and returns a bullet-list of files that contain the expres-
sion.
<HR>
```

The form's ACTION should point to the following CGI script:

```
#!/bin/perl


# read a GET request; quit if method is not GET
# take first argument
# search for it in all .html files below $basedir
# return URLs for all files containing matches, formatted as bulletlist,
# with <H1>..</H1> string contents as clickable link text

$basedir = '/apache/docs/public_html';    # root directory for HTML files
$serverroot = '/apache/docs';              # server root directory
$exclude = '/graphics';                    # pathname component to ignore
$dirsep = '/';                             # directory separator character
$searchform = "search.html";               # name of search form
# $DEBUG = 1;                              # debugging output toggle
                                           # if $DEBUG = 1 is set, print
                                           # lots of debugging messages

print "Content-type: text/html\n\n";
print "<head><title>Search Results</title></head>\n";
print "<body>\n";

if ($ENV{'REQUEST_METHOD'} ne "GET") {     # we only process get requests
    print "<H1><i>Error</i></H1>\n";
    print "Malformed or incorrect request detected\n</body>";
    exit 0;
}
```

```perl
$request = $ENV{'QUERY_STRING'};
@parameter_list = split(/&/,$request);    # split name=value pairs
foreach (@parameter_list) {               # for each parameter ...
    ($name, $value) = split(/=/);         # get the name and value
    $name =~ s/\+/ /g;                     # convert characters
    $name =~ s/%(..)/pack("c",hex($1))/ge;
    $value =~ s/\+/ /g;
    $value =~ s/%(..)/pack("c",hex($1))/ge;
    $args{$name} = $value;                # put them in %args
}

if ($args{'search'} eq '') {              # check for a search argument
    print "\n<H1><i>Error</i></H1>\n";
    print "No search string was entered\n</body>";
    exit 0;
}
#
#---------------------------------------------------------------------------
#
# Now we have acquired the query, we can start looking for files.
# To do this, we will open the directory $basedir using opendir(), get a
# list of the files in it, and save them. Then, for every entry in $basedir
# that is a directory, we will push it onto a stack.Then we pop the next
# directory off the stack and repeat the process, until the stack contains
# no more directories.
#
# Note that this script explicitly avoids the "." and ".." directories, and
# refuses to follow symbolic links. This ensures that the search goes down,
# rather than up or sideways, in the directory structure.
#
# ASSUMPTIONS:
#
# That files contain lines like <TITLE>file's title</TITLE>, with no line breaks
#
# That it's a bad idea to invoke Perl's glob() built-in, because it relies on
# invoking the C shell
#
#---------------------------------------------------------------------------
#
$pattrn = '^[^.]{1,2}.+';                 # pattern for files to avoid
                                          # -- one or two dots at
                                          # beginning of name
push(@dirstack, $basedir);                # initialize stack of dirs to
                                          # visit
# now we are ready to walk recursively the directories below our starting point
```

```
while ($#dirstack >= $[ ) {              # while @dirstack is not empty
    $path = pop(@dirstack);              # take the first directory on it
    next if ($path =~ /$exclude/);       # ignore dirs matching $exclude
    @result = &glob($path,$pattrn);      # call glob() to get file list
    foreach $dir (@result) {
        $path =~ s/(^.*)$\/$/$1/;        # strip trailing "/" from file
        if ( -d "$path\/$dir") {         # process directories ...
            $location = "$path/$dir";
            $DEBUG && print "$location [DIRECTORY]\n";
            push (@dirstack, $location);  # put newly discovered dirs on
                                          # the stack
            $visited++;                   # keep count of dirs visited
        }
    }
    #
    # now we've processed the directories in $path, let's have a look
    # at the HTML files in $path
    #
    @htmlfiles = &glob($path,'(^.*\.[Hh][Tt][Mm][Ll]$)|(^.*\.HTM$)');
    foreach $target (@htmlfiles) {        # foreach HTML file
        if (! -l $target) {               # ignore symlinks
            $DEBUG && print ".";
            push(@targetfiles,"$path/$target");
        }                                 # @targetfiles holds the list
    }                                     # of HTML files we've found
}

$DEBUG && print "\n\nFound $#targetfiles matching files in ",
    "$visited directories\n<P>\n";

# now search (using grep()) through @targetfiles for $args{'search'}

print "<H1>Search Results</H1>\nThe following files were found to ",
    "contain [<CODE>$args{search}</CODE>]:\n<P><HR><P>";

print "<UL>\n";                          # start listing results
$catches = 0;
foreach $filename (@targetfiles) {        # loop through the HTML files
    #
    # read in the file. Search it using grep(). If the target is found,
    # get the file's TITLE and use that, plus the file's pathname, to
    # create a URL for it.
    #
    undef @hits;                          # clear these variables
    undef $hits;
    undef @fil;
```

```perl
        open (FIL,"<$filename") || die "Could not open $filename,read-only\n";
        @fil = <FIL>;                       # read in the file into @fil
        close FIL;
        $hits = grep (/$args{'search'}/i,@fil);look for $args{'search"}in @fil
        $DEBUG && print "Found $hitz matches for $args{search} in $filename\n";
        if ($hitz > 0) {                    # if we found any results ...
            @hits = grep(/<TITLE>/i,@fil);  # get all lines containing
                                            # <TITLE> tags and save in @hits
            $tag = @hits[$[];               # we use the first <TITLE> line
            chop $tag;                      # get rid of trailing carriage
                                            # returns
            $tag =~ s/(<TITLE>)(.*)(<\/TITLE>)/$2/i;
                                            # get rid of <TITLE>..</TITLE>
            $tag =~ s/^(\s+)(.*)/$2/i;      # get rid of leading whitespace
            $tag =~ s/(.*)([\s]+)$/$1/i;    # get rid of trailing whitespace
            $target = $filename;            # begin building pathname
            $target =~ s/$serverroot//i;    # remove leading server root
                                            # directory from pathname
            next if ($target =~/$searchform/i);# we don't want to include the
                                            # searchform in the search
                                            # output, do we?
            $output = "<LI><A HREF=\"$target\">" . $tag . "</A>\n";
            print $output;                  # print the URL
            $catches++;                     # total of the number of hits
        }
}

if ($catches == 0) {                        # what to do if we didn't find
    print "<LI><I>No matches found</I>\n";  # any matching files
}

print "</UL>\n";

print "<br><hr></body>";                    # tidy up and quit
exit 0;
#
#-------------------------------------------------------------------------
#
sub glob {

    # usage: @files = &glob(directory,pattern);
    # returns all filenames in directory that match pattern
    # without making use of Perl's ability to call on the C shell's
    # globbing -- we might be running in a chroot'd environment where
    # C shell is not available(!)
    #
```

```
     local ($dir) = @_[$[];                   # get the directory
     $DEBUG && print "glob(): dir is $dir\n";
     local ($patt) = @_[$[+1] ;                # get the pattern to match
     $DEBUG && print "glob(): patt is $patt\n";
     if (( -e $dir ) && ( -d $dir)) {          # if dir exists, is directory
        opendir (DIR, $dir) || warn "could not open $dir\n";
        @files = readdir (DIR);               # get all the files in $dir
         $DEBUG && print "directory contains \n@files\n\n";
        closedir (DIR);                       # close $dir
        eval (@globhits = grep(/$patt/,@files));
                                              # search for $patt in the
                                              # filenames we found in $dir
                                              # do this inside an eval()
         $DEBUG && print "returning \n@globhits\n\n";
        return @globhits;                     # return the array of filenames
                                              # that matched
     } else {                                 # if $dir isn't usable
                                              # directory is bogus!
        die "$dir nonexistent\n";            # program exits abruptly. This
        return;                               # should never happen.
     }
  }
```

A few points are worth noting about this program. Firstly, Perl has a built-in glob mechanism, but this program doesn't use it. glob derives from the name of an obsolete UNIX utility that was used to match regular expressions for filenames. The UNIX shells perform globbing, taking patterns and returning all the files that match the patterns (which are simple regular expressions). Perl can quite easily glob files, but it does so sneakily, by using the UNIX C shell.

Normally this would not be a problem, but very often CGI scripts have to execute in environments where other programs (such as the C shell) are inaccessible. This is a common security procedure, and if this script relied on C shell globbing it would fail to work.

Secondly, the program is designed to avoid certain files. It uses a variable, $exclude, to flag directories to avoid. If you follow the convention of keeping all your graphics files in directories called graphics, set $exclude to graphics and the search script will not waste time exploring directories that contain nothing of interest.

In addition to avoiding directories with $exclude in their pathname, the program avoids directories and files that begin with a period '.'. This ensures that it doesn't start climbing up to parent directories, fanning out into the filesystem at large. It also avoids symbolic links – pointers to other directories and files outside of the current directory – for the same reason. We want the search to be restricted to a hierarchy of directories, not to the entire filesystem on the server.

6

UNDERSTANDING SERVER AND WEB STRUCTURE

● ● ● ●

In the preceding chapters we've looked at the world wide web from a fairly low-level viewpoint; how to write HTML, how HTTP works, the various languages used on the web and so on. We've dipped a toe in the murky waters of Perl programming and seen how a CGI script works. But all of these considerations are peripheral to the more fundamental concerns of administering large webs. While they are essential tools that need to be mastered before we can do much on the web, they don't help us write better hypertext.

A hypertext web, at the simplest level, can be viewed as a collection of documents stored on a computer. What distinguishes them from any other collection of documents is not their content, but their overall structure; the fact that they can contain links pointing to one another.

In this chapter we're going to discuss various design issues surrounding hypertext. We'll start by examining the structure of a typical web server, and how files are stored by it. I'll then examine the web, with a look at how documents rely on each other, then move on to style issues, with some suggestions about good authoring practice, and maintenance issues, with a few words about how to design for maintainability.

Web server structure

A web server is a collection of programs and data that provide access to a hierarchical arrangement of files. There are no hard and fast rules defining where the suite of software that makes up a web server lies on any given computer, and it is quite easy to customize most server layouts. However, the commonest servers tend to share a similar structure: in this example we shall discuss the layout of an NCSA httpd 1.4 server running under UNIX, as a fairly typical example of probably the commonest server in current usage. (NCSA httpd is also the basis for Apache, which may in due course replace it as the publicly available server of choice.)

The NCSA HTTP server was developed for the National Center for Supercomputing Applications by Rob McCool and other members of the team who founded Netscape Communications Corporation. It is still under development, and can be found at http://www.ncsa.uiuc.edu/. Related material (including the HTACCESS authentication tutorial) can be found at http://hoohoo.ncsa.uiuc.edu/, and a derivative server, Apache, can be found at http://www.apache.org/apache/. As the NCSA server is an ancestor of the Netscape Commerce Servers and Apache – the most popular commercial and non-commercial servers – it repays examination.

The NCSA server, by default, is installed on a UNIX system below */usr/local/etc*. Within this directory, the server software lives in *httpd*. This directory contains the following:

cgi-bin   Home directory for the CGI script area. This directory, and its subdirectories, contain files which the server is configured to execute as programs.

conf   Configuration files (see below).

htdocs   Root directory for files published to the web. Anything above
(or docs) this directory is invisible, unless it is specifically targeted by a symbolic link from below this area (and symbolic link tracking is switched on in a configuration file).

icons   Directory where various system icon graphics are stored.

logs   Logfiles (*error_log* and *access_log*) are stored here; every access generates an *access_log* record, and every error generates an *error_log* entry. Logfiles are stored in common logfile format (described shortly).

and, as part of the distribution package:

support   Contains supporting programs (htpasswd, for generating password files, and inc2shtml, for server-side includes, among other things).

cgi-src   Source code for various CGI scripts (mostly in C).

The *conf* directory is the most important: the files in here govern the way the server operates, including the names and nature of all the other directories. Failure to set up the server's configuration files correctly can result in a system which doesn't work, which is insecure (permitting intruders to run hostile programs), or which errs in the opposite direction and doesn't let authenticated users read files.

In general, you need to be aware of (and possibly change) the following files:

httpd.conf   The central configuration file. This determines what the other configuration files and directories in the server suite are called, what TCP/IP port number the server runs on, what effective user ID the server executes with (important for security reasons in the UNIX environment) and who the administrator is.

access.conf   The access control file. This determines who can access which directories and files, using which HTTP methods. Access can be limited on the basis of hostname or authorization group, and can be restricted so that certain hosts cannot access an area, or so that none but some trusted hosts can access it. Note that HTACCESS authentication side-steps this mechanism and is effectively subordinate to it; you can grant access to a directory in the *access.conf* file, and then impose a password-protected authorization using HTACCESS.

mime.types   The MIME file type mapping file. This file maps file suffixes (the common UNIX way of indicating the type of a file) onto MIME content-types, so that the server can indicate to a browser the type of a named file.

srm.conf   The server namespace definition file. Using this file, you indicate how pathnames on the web site are mapped to pathnames on the actual UNIX system underlying the site. You can specify a common directory name to be picked up, so that users can publish files from their home directories; you can also specify whether symbolic links are to be followed, where script files live, what icons are used to represent directories and files (when looking at a directory with no default HTML file) and so on.

Full guidelines for the syntax of these files can be found on the hoohoo server (`http://hoohoo.ncsa.uiuc.edu/`), including a tutorial on many of the server's features. It is not appropriate to cover the specifics of NCSA HTTPD administration in this book, but if you want to go further and find the NCSA documentation inadequate you may want to consult Stein (1996).

Pathnames on the server

It is important to note that pathnames on an HTTP server do not work in exactly the same way as pathnames on a normal UNIX system. By convention, the root directory, /, is at the top of the filesystem, and absolute pathnames are specified by listing the directories you must traverse from / to get to a given file. Web servers, in contrast, designate a subdirectory as being their notional root directory. A file in this subdirectory called index.html would be retrieved by requesting the path */index.html* from the HTTP server, even though its real location in the UNIX filesystem might be something like *usr/local/lib/http/docs/index.html*. The server operates a chroot (change root) environment, mapping absolute pathnames so that they refer to the designated directory as if it were the root. This is a useful security feature (it prevents strangers from examining any of your computer's files that lie outside the server area), but it can cause problems for CGI scripts. CGI scripts may well see file pathnames correctly, and therefore have to perform the same mapping themselves.

Server script execution facilities

Programs written to use the common gateway interface (as described in Chapters 3 and 5) can be executed by the server from the *cgi-bin* directory, and any nominated CGI directories.

In addition to straightforward CGI scripts, the NCSA server supports an alternate script-execution facility, called Server-Side Includes (SSI). This may well be turned off – it is commonly viewed as a major security hole – but if not, it provides useful facilities to a user.

SSIs make use of a simple feature of any web server: in order to function, the server daemon must somehow load the data in a requested file before sending it to the client's browser. When SSI processing is switched on, the server watches for certain key strings in all files with the suffix *.shtml*: these are embedded in comment strings.

If the server sees an *include* directive in an SHTML file, it reads in the designated file and interpolates it at the current point. For example, it is not uncommon to see something like the following at the end of all documents on a well-maintained server:

```
<P>
<HR>
<P>
<!--#include file="footer.html" -->
</BODY>
</HTML>
```

The #include directive means 'read in the file *footer.html* and interpolate it at this point'. (footer.html is a standard document footer, in this case, indicating the author's name and institution, along with a link to the home page of the site – see 'Indexing and entrypoint provision' later in this chapter.)

More to the point, a second SSI mechanism is provided: #exec. This directive causes the web server to execute the named program and interpolate its output at the current point. For example:

```
<P>
The date and time is: <!--#exec cmd="/bin/date" -->
<P>
```

This is replaced by something like:

```
The date and time is: 10/10/95 20:12:03
```

(The **date** command on UNIX prints the date and time by default.)
The server-side directives are:

`#config errmsg="SSI parse error string"` `#config sizefmt="file size format"` `#config timefmt="time display format"`	Configure the way output from parsed commands are represented.
`#echo var="varname"`	Includes the value of a named environment variable called *varname* in the text. In addition to the normal environment variables, SSIs recognize the following: `DOCUMENT_NAME,` `DOCUMENT_ URI,` `LAST_MODIFIED,` `DATE _LOCAL.`
`#exec cmd="command"`	Execute the indicated command under the Bourne shell (**/bin/sh**). Note that if this mechanism is used to execute a CGI script, any specified arguments to the file containing this SSI are accessible to the script.
`#fsize file="filename"` `#fsize virtual="filename"`	Prints the size, in bytes, of the specified file.
`#flastmod file="filename"` `#flastmod virtual="filename"`	Prints the last modification time of the specified file.
`#include file="filename"` `#include virtual="virtual_file"`	Includes the specified document at the current point in the file. If `file=` is specified, the pathname is relative to the current document. If `virtual=` is specified, the pathname is relative to the server document directory.

It is worth noting that there are some functions for which SSIs are better suited than ordinary CGI scripts.

Hit counters

One case in point is the 'hit counter'. A hit counter is a display indicating how many times a web page has been accessed by readers. They are implemented by a CGI script that, given the name of a page (as a parameter) keeps a logfile indicating how often it has been executed. Every time the page is loaded, the CGI script is executed. The script:

● consults a logfile, looking for a number associated with the current page,

● increases the count it finds in the file by one,

● saves the logfile,

● prints out the number.

If invoked via SSI, a hit counter can simply print some text which is integrated into the page. But if SSIs are disabled, the only ways to run a hit counter are to invoke it within a <FRAME> tag (recognized only by Netscape 2.0; see 'Framesets', p. 202 for details), or as an IMG SRC tag. If invoked as an image, it must not return a numerical count, but a GIF (or similar) image depicting the number of hits.

Hit counters should really be deprecated, because they entail lots of extra processing and disk accesses – usually on the home page of a site, which receives a lot of hits. But it should be noted that an SSI hit counter at least doesn't have to download a bundle of GIF files; and the things are sufficiently popular that they aren't going to go away in a hurry. If you really need one, you can find a slew of publicly available hit counters on

```
http://www.yahoo.com/text/world_wide_web/cgi/hit_counters/
```

Imagemaps

Imagemaps are a curiosity of web navigation. They consist of a graphic (usually a GIF file) and a map which contains coordinates describing areas on the image and URLs associated with each area. Usually an image is tagged as being a map using ISMAP, and the coordinates the user clicks the mouse in are sent back to the web server for interpretation by an **imagemap** program (typically called */cgi-bin/imagemap*). The format of the mapfile varies depending on the precise imagemap program being used. For the NCSA imagemap program a simple mapfile might look something like this:

```
rect help.html 0,0 39,109
rect /author/about.html 40,0 79,109
rect /archive/archived.html 80,0 119,109
```

147

The first item in each line is a type of object: **rect** (rectangle), **circle** (circle), **default**, or **poly** (polygon). Each item is followed by the URL associated with it. Finally, each item (except for **default**) is followed by a series of (x,y) coordinate pairs, indicating the coordinates occupied by the object when it is superimposed on the image (in pixels).

The HTML file contains something like this:

```
<A HREF="/cgi-bin/imagemap/mapfilename">
<IMG SRC="map.gif" ISMAP>
</A>
```

This URL invokes the imagemap program. The pathname component following */cgi-bin/imagemap* is passed to the CGI program as a parameter and indicates the location of the mapfile. Meanwhile, the IMG SRC tag inside the URL is flagged as ISMAP, meaning that when it is clicked on the coordinates of the mouseclick are sent as options to the HTTP request for */cgi-bin/imagemap*.

When the mouse coordinates are received by the imagemap program, it opens the mapfile, works out which (if any) of the areas in it the mouse coordinates lie in, and returns a Location: command to the user's browser. If a **default** URL is specified, this will be returned if the user clicks outside any of the other regions in the map.

Imagemaps are useful insofar as they can replace collections of GIF-tagged URLs (buttons) with a single clickable image, reducing the number of HTTP transactions required to pull in a graphical site navigation diagram, though they're quite handy for all sorts of purposes. (For example, atlases can have clickable cities or regions, anatomy webs can have clickable organs and so on.)

Netscape 2.0 provides support for 'client-side' imagemaps. A client-side imagemap uses essentially the same principle, except that the map is contained in the HTML. It uses a mutant version of the imagemap syntax. For example, in a file called *mymap.html*:

```
<IMG SRC="mapfile.gif" USEMAP= "mymap.html#map">
```

This designates *mapfile.gif* as being an imagemap; the map itself is located somewhere in the same file, below the MAP tag "map". (It can, of course, be located in another file entirely.) The map area looks like this:

```
<MAP NAME="map">
<AREA SHAPE="rect" COORDS="0,0,40,40" HREF="index.html">
</MAP>
```

This specifies a map. It contains a single area, of shape **rect**, with the given coordinates; it points to the file *index.html*.

Note that the Netscape client-side imagemap syntax is not identical to the NCSA imagemap program syntax. Nor is either of them identical to other imagemap programs that run on other servers. Indeed, there is no standard specification for a universal imagemap syntax.

Logfiles

The server logs all requests and errors in two files. These are not intended to be humanly readable, but they do follow a regular pattern and can be used for debugging purposes, or fed to logfile analysers (programs which produce a digest of server activity).

Most web servers – including NCSA HTTPD – produce logs in the common logfile format. This is a simple text file, consisting of one-line records. Each line represents a transaction. For example:

```
158.152.6.20 - - [21/Oct/1995:09:56:00 +0100] "GET / HTTP/1.0" 200 684
```

From left to right, the fields in this query are:

IP address of requester	158.152.6.20
Client authorization type	(or — if not applicable)
Client authorization value	(or — if not applicable)
Date and time stamp	(Note inclusion of time zone info.)
HTTP request	GET / HTTP/1.0
HTTP response status	200
Number of bytes sent	684

The client authorization information is used by the HTACCESS system to determine whether the user is permitted to carry out the requested transaction.

In general, logfile analysers digest files containing these records and can report lots of useful information – notably, which files are most popular, which hosts request the most files and so on. (Links to a large number of log-file analysers can be found at http://www.yahoo.com/.)

The *error_log* file contains errors generated by bad HTTP requests. It looks like this:

```
[Sun Oct 15 11:35:07 1995] httpd: caught SIGTERM, shutting
    down
[Sun Oct 22 15:21:30 1995] httpd: malformed header from
    script
```

In general, *error_log* records consist of the time the error occurred, followed by a message; in the first instance a routine server shutdown, and in the latter case a 'malformed header from script' error. 'Malformed header from script' is a common bedevilment for CGI programmers. It means that at a minimum, a CGI script failed to print a proper Content-type: line; more likely, the Perl interpreter spotted a bug and printed an error message. (The HTTPD cannot distinguish between Perl error messages – where it expects to read a MIME header line – and a malformed MIME header.)

If you suspect a script isn't working, checking the error log is the first indicator that something has gone wrong. (The next step is to see what sort of output it's writing, by setting the REQUEST_METHOD and QUERY_STRING environment variables to something it could reasonably expect to see, and running it from the UNIX shell prompt, but that's another story.)

Security and the NCSA server

SSIs that use exec to execute arbitrary programs are usually discouraged by administrators who have to support large numbers of users because they permit users to place just about anything in a web document. Security is a contentious issue on the Internet, and especially in the UNIX world, because UNIX systems that are badly configured are extremely vulnerable to hackers.

UNIX has a generic security mechanism based on the idea of user and group identity. Everyone with access to the system is assigned a name, and membership of one or more user groups. Permission to read from, write to, or execute a file is determined on the basis of your user ID or the group to which you belong. In addition, privileged users may be allowed to 'change' their ID, adopting an 'effective user ID' for certain tasks. As users are trusted by the owner or administrator of the system, they may be assigned greater and greater freedom of access; at the top of the pyramid of UNIX permissions is *root*, the super-user, who is allowed to do pretty much anything.

Restricting root access to a server is paramount, because a malicious user with root privileges can wreak much harm. While an ordinary user probably cannot delete or damage anything critical to the running of a server, the root user can type a 7-character command and delete everything on the computer. Because there is no telling who might be reading your web documents – or triggering CGI programs, which can in turn execute other software on the server – it is normal to assign the HTTP server minimal privileges. That way, if hostile users figure out a means of subverting a badly written CGI script, they may not be able to accomplish much. A CGI script which executes as *root*, in contrast, can deliver control of the entire system to a malicious user.

A secondary consideration is that programs executed on a UNIX server inherit the access permissions of the owner who spawned them. Thus, a program owned by *root* runs with *root*'s privileges, while a program owned by *charlie* has only those access privileges that user *charlie* owns.

This may seem like an irrelevancy, but the complex web of interdependent language environments which make up a UNIX system makes even the most unlikely security holes potentially hazardous.

For example, it is a major security breach to allow *any* unfiltered characters typed by a user to be passed to a UNIX program. Consider the following UNIX shell script (set of commands executed as a batch job):

```ksh
#!/bin/ksh
echo "Content-type: text/html"
echo
echo "<H1>Search results</H1>"
```

```
echo "<PRE>"
grep $(echo $QUERY_STRING | sed -e 's/search=//g' ) *.html
echo "</PRE>"
```

This fragment is actually a very short CGI search script, similar to the one described in 'A simple search script' (p.137), except that it runs under the Korn shell and prints the names of matching files in the current directory rather than generating URLs pointing to them. It is intended to be used with a simple query form that passes a query field named *search* to the script. The command echoes the QUERY_STRING environment variable into a pipeline, where the line editor **sed** removes the field name; the resulting string is used as an argument to **grep**, the search program. This is fairly standard for first attempts at CGI programming.

It is also completely poisonous. A knowledgeable UNIX hacker can bolt together a script that sends an HTTP GET request containing the following:

```
foo bar ; cat >>myprog
. . .
some unauthorized programs go here
. . . .
^D
chmod +x myprog
./myprog
```

The first chunk of this, foo bar;, subverts the CGI script. The two parameters satisfy **grep** that it has the right material to munch on – a search string and a filename. But then comes the semi-colon, a command separator; and from there on, the search script ventures into hacking territory. The **cat** command is used to write some text into a file called *myprog*; the write is ended by the ^D (control-D) character, and the rest of the input attempts to make this file executable and run it.

If you pass unfiltered text from a user's input through to a program executed by a UNIX shell (the Korn shell being no more insecure than any of the others) you are taking a gamble: namely that none of the users will attempt to insert UNIX commands into the stream of text. This is one of the reasons for preferring scripts written in Perl; they are not automatically safer, but it is easier to make them so. (And they run much faster in any event.)

The degree of risk is to some extent dependent on the permissions the HTTP daemon runs scripts with. If (as is usually the case) it runs with the user ID *nobody* and membership of no user groups, it has minimal access to files on the server. In particular, if some hacker succeeds in subverting it, the hacker won't be able to get very far.

Some general principles of server security:

- Never run CGI scripts or web server daemons accessible to the public as *root*. Ideally, run everything as *nobody* and ensure that *nobody* is denied permission to do anything to files outside */usr/local/etc/httpd/htdocs*.

- Only permit SSIs and symbolic link following if you are sure your users (the people who place documents on the server) can be trusted not to misuse the facilities (by #execing dangerous programs or by linking private directories into the web server's domain).

- Ensure that CGI scripts on your server don't allow user input to go direct to any UNIX program or shell without at least some cursory checks within a 'safe' environment (such as a Perl program).

- Keep an eye on the usenet newsgroups relevent to your server, for example:

  comp.infosystems.www.servers.unix

  If security holes are discovered, they're announced here first.

- Don't assume that you are immune from a specific avenue of attack because virtually nobody has heard of it; 'security through obscurity' is simply an efficient way of letting the bad guys do whatever they like unchecked.

- Regularly check the *error_log* file. If somebody is trying to hack into your system, the odds are that they will make mistakes – and the errors will show up here. (If they have already succeeded, look for signs that the *error_log* file has been tampered with.)

A detailed analysis of web server security can be found in the World Wide Web Security FAQ, maintained by Lincoln Stein (see http://www-genome.mit.edu/). His book also goes into considerably greater detail on this issue.

Collaborative systems and HyperNews

One particularly important area where security concerns are an issue is that of collaborative (or conferencing) systems (such as HyperNews – see http://union.ncsa.uiuc.edu/ for details of HyperNews and links to other collaborative systems).

The web was designed from the outset to support collaborative working, and even the publishing-oriented form in which it has caught on has extensive potential in that area. A conferencing system is a web, with supporting CGI scripts, that is set up to allow users to hold discussions on a range of topics, bulletin-board style. (No example source code for a conferencing system is given in this book because unfortunately they tend to be among the largest CGI scripts out there – the smallest I am aware of is twice the size of the largest script in this book.)

There are a lot of uses for collaborative systems: some businesses use them to service user support enquiries; user groups use them to discuss common issues; there are recreational ones; and some academic organizations use them for peer review of papers. Discussions consist of a series of articles (or 'postings') which users create using a form. Articles can follow one another, or start new topics; they are usually grouped hierarchically in a context determined by their subject.

In general, all collaborative systems have at least two components: a file browser that lets users read articles in the discussion, and a message posting form, that lets users reply to previously posted articles or start new discussions. (Other components, such as search and mail facilities, may also be provided.) Behind the message posting form lies a CGI script that must actually create a publicly viewable document inside the web space on the server.

It should go without saying that it is foolhardy to permit users to post an article on a public collaborative system without authenticating their identity. Unrestricted use of anonymous upload facilities on the Internet is a major problem, insofar as it is prone to abuse – notably by software pirates (or 'warez d00dz' as many of them prefer to be known), but also by anyone else who is too unscrupulous to turn down a free lunch at somebody else's expense. Space on your server, if freely obtainable, is space that somebody will try to fill.

Consequently, unless you are running a server on a secure private network, it is pretty important to ensure that when installing a conferencing system, you *make users register their name and identity* before you let them post articles. (See 'HTACCESS', p. 247 for a basic introduction to placing directories on your server under password-protected control.)

How web document structure relates to the server

A web is, trivially, a set of documents (typically HTML files) stored on a computer running an HTTP daemon. The documents contain cross-references to each other. One or more documents is designated as a root document – an initial point of entry into the web. In addition to documents there may be supporting files (such as GIF images that can be imported into the text) and programs (search scripts, form handlers and database interfaces). The programs typically generate 'virtual documents' – programmatic output that resembles a document but which is actually a snapshot of the internal state of the program.

Web servers are designed to provide numerous aids to the web architect. Several mechanisms exist to make it easier for multiple users to put files on the server, most notably:

Directory aliasing   An alias is a predefined alternative name for a directory. For example, the NCSA HTTPD configuration is set up (by default) to 'pick up' any directory called *public_html* that is in a user's home directory, and alias it to *~username.*

Server-side includes SSIs permit files to be included in other files as they are served up to the browser.

Symbolic links A symbolic link is a UNIX operating system feature that can be used by a server configured to recognize them; a small file that points to another file or directory, so that when you specify the pathname of the symbolic link the file you get back is somewhere else on the system.

Default documents If no file is specified in a GET request, the NCSA server looks in the current directory for a default document – conventionally called *index.html*. This isn't a mandatory name – the web administrator can redefine the default document name – and it's not the only kind of default behaviour permitted.

These features let you configure a web in such a way that the *logical* structure of the documents does not directly depend on their physical layout in the computer's filesystem. But there are pitfalls in this sort of design; in addition to making it convenient for people to add files to the server, they can make it hard to see what the global effect will be of making changes at any given point in the local web.

In the next sections, we're going to discuss some of the basic principles of web structure, and some of the design considerations that go into building a web hosted on a specific server.

A simple web design

For the sake of simplicity, I'm going to steer around the more complex webs. Multiserver systems, systems based entirely on dynamic or virtual documents and systems that have complex access control systems all superimpose an additional layer of complexity on top of the basic principles of web design. While they are discussed in Chapters 7 and 9, for the time being we will consider a simple web stored on a single server, with one entrypoint (the file *index.html*) as shown in Figure 6.1.

This figure represents a simple web. It contains three different types of file; document text (in HTML), graphics and server scripts. The main *index.html* file sits on top of the five directories that store the graphics, scripts and three batches of HTML files. It's a generic structure insofar as you can use it for just about any web that divides into three sections. For example, a manual for a computer system might be split into a tutorial, a user's guide and a command reference: these might be mapped onto *part1*, *part2* and *part3*. Images sourced into the manual might all be held in */images*, while the search scripts for accessing an online index of the manual might be held in */cgi-bin*.

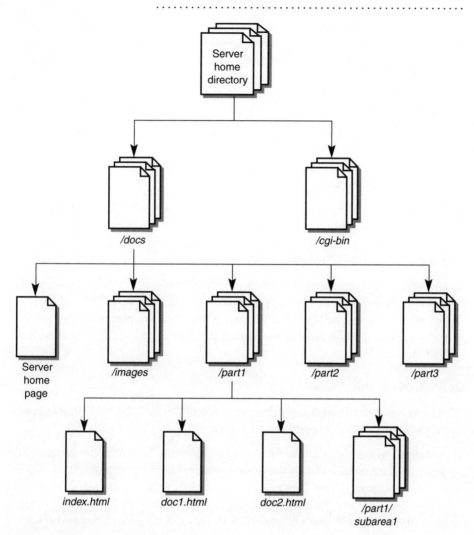

Figure 6.1

Let's suppose that all the files in this web are well-formed HTML, written like this:

```
<HTML>
<HEAD>
<TITLE>Chapter 1</TITLE>
<LINK NEXT="chapter2.html" PREVIOUS="index.html"
PARENT="index.html">
<NEXTID N="z004">
</HEAD>
<BODY>
```

```
<H1>This is a chapter in the Tutorial</H1>
<HR>
And this is some text.<P>
This is a cross-reference to the
<A HREF="http://myhost.com/part3/index.html">
Command Reference index page</A>.
<HR>
</BODY>
</HTML>
```

Some points are worth noting:

1 The `<LINK>` tag in the document header indicates the relationship between this file and the others in the web. (The implication is fairly obvious; by declaring `NEXT="chapter2.html"`, the document informs the web browser of the next document to select in the sequence.)

2 The `NEXTID` tag uniquely identifies a web document. The ID is in a format that is not intended for human use; rather, it is for use by HTML editors, to permit them to associate IDs with named destination points on the server, and so avoid reusing old pathnames (even after the file at that location has been deleted).

Deficiencies in this design

Although a web built on these principles is 'well formed' in an abstract sense, there are several problems with its structure.

1 Although the information in the `LINK` and `NEXTID` tags is enough to describe the position of this document within the web, neither of the tags is human-readable. These tags are correct according to the HTML 2.0 specification, but they are ignored by virtually all current web browsers. Indeed, the only navigable link information in this document as it stands is the HREF near the bottom.

2 There are various stylistic issues which make the web less than navigable; these are discussed in 'Web style' below.

3 The web is hard-wired; the HREF points to

`http://myhost.com/part3/index.html`

Suppose that the owners of `myhost.com` wish to rename it `www.myhost.com`: what then? Every single document in the hierarchy will have to be edited, and all URLs containing the string `myhost.com` changed to `www.myhost.com`. Although this is a tedious project, it is quite easy to automate; later on, I'll demonstrate a Perl script that can make changes to all the files in a directory in one pass. Moreover, the problem can be sidestepped by using either relative URLs, or a complex system based on more abstract link information (as explained below).

Relative and absolute URLs

It is almost invariably better to use relative URLs rather than absolute URLs. A relative URL is simply the pathname to a file, starting from the current host and directory. If we are looking at a file in the *part1* directory, a relative URL that replaces the one in the example file is: *../part3/index.html*. If we had written it that way to begin with, the major search/replace operation above would not have been necessary.

Neverthless, the same problem arises if, for example, we want to move the file being addressed by the cross-reference into the *part2* directory. The difference now is that we must search for all URLs pointing to that file, and change only them (rather than a general search for all URLs everywhere).

This is symptomatic of a fundamental problem of the world wide web: URLs are brittle. They break! If you move the file that a cross-reference points to, it will fail. If you change the cross-reference without moving the file, it will fail. And if you need to make (n) changes (renamings or movements) to the files in a web, then in the worst case you might have to make as many as n^2 file edits.

Web style

When writing a chapter in a book, for example, you usually map out an outline of what you want to say – then you say it. Heading leads to introductory paragraph, then subheading and text, subheading and text and so on. You can be reasonably confident that your readers can get to the informational content of your chapter in only three ways;

- by reading the entire book from front cover to back cover,

- by looking for a known keyword in the index, then referring to the page it is indexed on,

- by browsing the table of contents for a conceptual match (that is, for a topic that appears to match their interest), then referring to the page the section starts on.

You can therefore make certain assumptions about the level of prior knowledge a reader of your chapter will have. You must have followed one of these three entrypoints to have arrived at this point in this book. (Other entry methods are possible, for example, opening a page at random, but I'm making the assumption that nobody really reads a technical document in such a manner; although in the case of some badly written user manuals this might be as productive a strategy as any.)

A hypertext system adds many additional entrypoints to a document. You cannot write an effective hypertext by starting at the beginning with an introduction, introducing concepts linearly and ending with a conclusion. It doesn't work, because your reader has as many possible entrypoints into the text as there are links into it from outside – and, more importantly, because the reader might have reached any given point in the text by following a variety of possible paths through the web:

- by finding the index page, and following it to *document1*, then following linear links from *document1* to *document2*, *document2* to *document3* and so on;

- by finding the index page and reading the first section of each chapter in turn, until finding a chapter with some interesting contents;

- by finding a link to some random low-level file in the web, and following a link from that file to the index page or the next document;

- by finding a link to some random chapter's first section from elsewhere on the web, and following a link from that chapter section;

- by conducting a free-text search (via an interface like Lycos, `http://www.lycos.com/`) and discovering one of the files in the web at random.

Consequently, the process of writing a web, and of maintaining and editing a web, is different from the process of writing a traditional linear text. Broadly speaking, any writing task requires that the author first knows their audience.

Knowing the audience can be split into two areas: who are they, and what are they reading your web with? The latter question is a technical one, but no less important than the former – not all web browsers are born equal, and not all users will be able to access all the features of your web. The presentation of graphical, multimedia and ancilliary information in your documents is particularly vulnerable to such considerations.

On top of this, the web requires you to orient your audience. A reader can enter your web at any point. Therefore every document really should have a button in it marked 'home', unless it is intended to be totally self-contained and self-explanatory. The example file in 'A simple web design' is hopelessly inadequate – you can navigate from there to the next document, but that's all.

Next, there is the issue of designing the information content in the web. Several designs are available; you can mirror an old-fashioned linear text by forcing users to plough through an introductory node before you allow them to browse the web, and by funnelling them into a concluding section, or you can design a more free-form structure. There are relatively few formal methodologies for designing hypertexts, and they are not widely known yet.

Then there are issues of indexing and providing access to the web. A conventional document has only three real entrypoints; a web may have many, including in-text cross-references, in-head LINK declarations, a text searching engine, a free-text lookup engine, a table of contents and the traditional subject index.

Finally, there are issues of web management: tracking revisions, checking the HTML for syntax errors, controlling 'brittle' cross-references and editing files.

Coping with the readers' requirements

Before writing a book, it is a good idea to know who you are writing for. It is then necessary to be clear on how your audience will absorb the information in the book. For example, consider this text. You are obviously interested in the web. You may have flicked through a few pages in a bookshop or library, and now you are reading it – probably from cover to cover, unless you have already done so and are referring back to this chapter for some reason. As each chapter in this book builds on the preceding chapters, it would be unwise for a total web-novice to dive in at this point.

The world wide web is different. If you place your web on a public server, there is nothing to prevent anyone in the world from adding a link to your web from their home page. There is nothing to stop anyone from following that link – from a totally inappropriate starting point – to some document buried deep in your tree of text. In fact, you must work on the assumption that the information in your documents is atomic, that is, the reader may encounter it in the absence of an appropriate framing context. So all the good work you put into structuring your web may come to naught unless you work on the assumption that a reader may have entered your web from literally anywhere.

You can do several things to make your web more visitor-friendly. One is to provide cross-references to a compass page. A compass page is basically a device to help new readers orient themselves. It should combine some of the functions of a table of contents in a book – notably, a list of references to related documents – with a brief introduction explaining anything the reader needs to know in order to use the web. There is no reason why your compass page should not be the initial entrypoint to a web. However, documents are not all equal. For example, consider a hypothetical user manual. The HTML files in it might follow the general structure shown in Figure 6.2.

A subsection's compass page should not point at all the chapter files in the book; it is more appropriate for it to point to all the other subsections in that section, along with a pointer to the section and chapter pages and the table of contents. In other words, information about other branches of the document tree should be 'hidden'; when examining a document a reader should be able to go to its peers and its parents, but it is relatively unlikely that a reader will want to go to a same-level subheading in a completely different chapter.

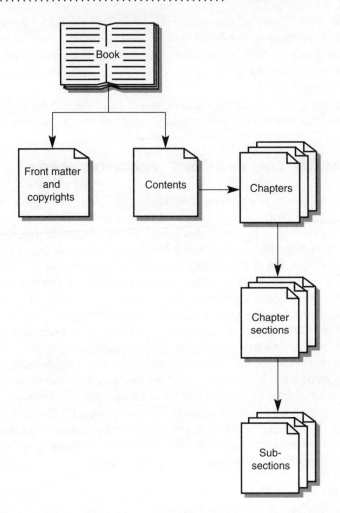

Figure 6.2

For example, in a book it makes sense to have a compass page for each chapter, and to have each separate file (containing a subsection of the chapter) contain a cross-reference to the compass page (Figure 6.3). Note that at any given level, the files all point to a compass page for that level.

Another thing you can do is to provide a panic button on each page. A panic button leads to a help page, not to a compass page. Help pages don't contain context information about a small chunk of a web; they contain help for the perplexed. If someone has just jumped into Chapter 4 of your textbook on widget manufacture when they were expecting the sales catalogue for a skateboard shop, they don't want a link to the compass page for Chapter 4 (Quality assurance metrics in widget validation processes), they want to know how to

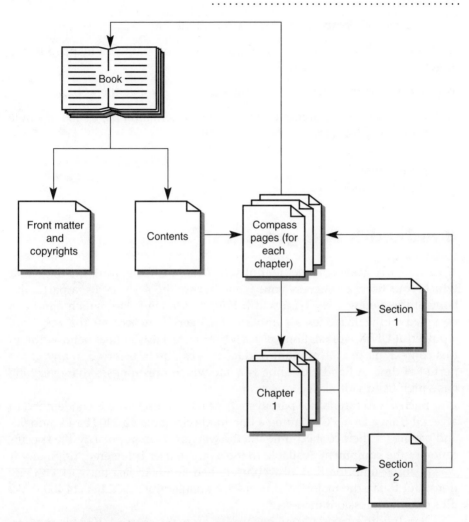

Figure 6.3 Book with per-chapter compass pages.

get where they were going to begin with. A help page should therefore provide a brief synopsis of what your web is about, along with some options for getting to the top-level compass page or out of it altogether (perhaps by pointing to one of the central web indexing and search mechanisms).

Finally, you can provide search access. Not all web structures suit all users. Suppose someone is trying to use the generic user manual described at the beginning of this chapter. If they have blundered into the tutorial by mistake (despite being an expert user), they don't want to mess around backtracking: the most useful thing you can give them is a searchable index. Ideally this should be only a single hot-spot away from any document in your web, although it can occupy a page of its own.

The general points to take away from all this are:

- Don't assume your reader has followed the entry path you mapped out to get to the page they are reading.

- Don't assume readers want to follow your path through the web.

- Always give readers access to one or more orientation pages, just a single hot-link away from the current document:
  - compass page
  - panic button
  - searchable index page.

Bandwidth and graphics

A particularly gruesome element of web design is estimating the degree to which your users can access your web. During the early 1990s, a particular bane of the web was the bandwidth hog; an academic site which had been designed on the unspoken assumption that everybody accesses the web from a powerful UNIX workstation, over a T1 (or faster) leased line. Bandwidth, in this context, means the amount of data that can be transferred in any given period of time. A bandwidth hog is a site which presupposes that everyone has a high-bandwidth fast connection.

Such a web can induce paroxysms of fury in a user who is condemned to access it from a DOS PC, running a line-mode client over a 2400 baud modem, and paying for their connect time. As the web grows in popularity, the specification of the equipment available to the average user is lowered; originally it was a fair assumption that all web users had access to fast network connections, but today the majority of users are hobbled by a V32.bis (14 400 baud plus data compression) modem.

Bandwidth places a huge constraint on web access. A V32.bis modem can download between 1.1 kb and 2 kb of data per second over a SLIP or PPP dialup connection (depending on how efficiently it is set up). A 10BaseT Ethernet connection, in contrast, can pull in between 30 kb and 250 kb per second in practice, while a serious FDDI network can pull in more data than most workstations can digest. Thus, a user's mode of connection to the Internet puts an absolute upper limit on the speed with which new (uncached) documents can be delivered to them.

It is not the case, however, that maximum throughput is achieved in real life. Users with modems capable of pulling in 1.6 kbps of data may in practice pull in files from your web site at a far lower average speed, because unless they are directly connected to your local network backbone the packets of data which they receive will have to cross between networks. The total bandwidth of a network connection may be high, but when it is shared between several thousand users it can slow communications to a crawl. And the more network exchanges that must be passed through, the lower the effective bandwidth of the connection.

As a rule of thumb, it seems that hops from one network to another cut the available bandwidth by something between 10% and 20%. So a 10-network route is going to leave you with a bare fraction of your initial bandwidth – and such routes are extremely common between, for example, UK-based dialup service users and commercial servers in California. (If you have login access to a UNIX system, you can trace the number of network hops to a given server using the `traceroute` command. The results are frequently enlightening.)

As another rule of thumb, readers are impatient. Web browsing users tend to be male, with an average age in the 18–35 range, and above-average income and education. They browse the web either for entertainment or for work. If they're there to be entertained, they're probably paying for the privilege or expect something other than glacial slowness. If they're trying to drill down and find some information, they're also likely to be in a hurry. Thus, it's sensible to ensure that when a new user visits your web it takes less than about 30 seconds for something to show up on screen, or you will lose some users before they even see your material.

As the average home connection seems to run at about 14 400 baud at present, this suggests that if you are running a commercial web server, if you provide a published link to a page containing more than 30 kb of data you should indicate that it is large and may take some time to download. If your target audience is academic or corporate you might assume that their connection is at least a 64 kbps leased line, and that they'll be able to pull in 2–5 kbps; therefore the threshold can be raised to 50–100 kb before you need to apply a warning. Of course, you can't apply this rule to every page on your site, but it's pretty important that the 'front door' page consumes as little bandwidth and loads as rapidly as possible.

Of all the contentious issues that hinge upon bandwidth, graphics are the most serious.

As noted in Chapter 2, an image may take up to one bit of data to represent a single pixel in black or white. The more colours, the more bits per pixel: to represent a range of 256 colours takes 8 bits per pixel, while 16 million or so colours can be handled using 24 bits per pixel. A fairly typical high-resolution monitor displays 72 pixels per inch; a PC's VGA display (the lowest common denominator of web design, because it is the minimum specification for virtually any computer capable of running a graphical user interface) displays 640 × 480 pixels in 8-bit colour. Thus, a screen-filling colour picture for a PC can take up to 307 kb of data.

In practice, the compression built into the GIF and JPEG file formats squeezes this down immensely. But even with 90% data compression, a screen-filling JPEG takes up to 30 kb. In contrast, English text contains an average of approximately 6.5 characters per word (including punctuation and whitespace). Thus, a thousand words (two to three pages of this book) occupies only 6.5 kb.

It appears that the old adage that 'a picture tells a thousand words' should be replaced, on the web, with 'you can shoehorn two or three books into the space of a single reel of holiday snapshots'.

Presenting images

Images are popular on the world wide web for several reasons:

- You can use them to add graphical navigation tools (imagemaps).

- They make a document more attractive.

- You may be representing visual data.

They are disadvantageous for other reasons:

- Not all browsers can display graphics.

- Even those which can may not be able to represent the same number of colours or display the same size of image.

- Images soak up far more bandwidth than text.

For example, suppose you want to write a page that is a gallery of large images. You have a bunch of GIF files, called *image1.gif*, *image2.gif* and so on. You have a collection of thumbnails, *img1-t.gif*, *img2-t.gif* and so on. (The thumbnails contain the same images, reduced to, say, 64 × 64 pixels from the original 640 × 480 images.) If you are running a graphical browser, you might instinctively write:

```
<HTML>
<HEAD>
<TITLE>Image Gallery</TITLE>
</HEAD>
<BODY>
<H1>Cool Pictures</H1>
Here's my art gallery!
<HR>
<A HREF="giger.gif"><IMG SRC="giger-thumbnail.gif"></A>
<A HREF="kahlo.gif"><IMG SRC="kahlo-thumbnail.gif"></A>
<HR>
</BODY>
</HTML>
```

This is, of course, valid HTML – but it will not be much use to a character browser! Nor is it the most sensible solution for some graphical browsers. A large number of web users (80%, at the time of writing) use Netscape. This browser recognizes a range of non-standard HTML tags, including additional parameters to the IMG tag. Most notable among these are the WIDTH and HEIGHT attributes. For example:

```
<IMG SRC="giger-thumbnail.gif" WIDTH="64" HEIGHT="64">
```

tells Netscape that the image giger-thumbnail.gif is 64 pixels high and 64 pixels wide. This means Netscape can display the rest of the page of text while the image is loading, leaving enough space for it to fit into – thus giving the impression of great speed. (These attributes are ignored by most other browsers with a few notable exceptions, like Microsoft's. Thus, it's safe to use them routinely – unless you are concerned with making your web documents future-proof, as discussed in Chapter 7.)

An alternative use of the WIDTH and HEIGHT attributes deserves mention. If you use a percentage value, for example WIDTH="64%", Netscape tries to scale the image to that percentage of its original size. However, this notation is incompatible with SGML.

Also worth noting is Netscape's ability to render inline JPEG images (a feature being copied by some other browsers), and the LOWRES HIRES tags, which specify two alternative renditions of an image (in low-resolution form, to be loaded first, and in high resolution form, to be overlaid on top of the low-res version). In addition, Netscape provides any number of ways of aligning images relative to text, not all of them pleasing to the eye, and none of them part of the HTML specifications.

This leads us neatly to the conclusion that not everyone supports the same level of HTML. In general, most browsers in use in late 1995 supported HTML 2.0, to at least level 0 (and preferably to level 1). However, character mode browsers will always be incapable of viewing graphics or playing audio tracks; and some browsers support HTML 3.0, or parts thereof (the standard not yet having been finalized). Some browsers come with non-standard HTML extensions that may become part of the standard (such as the <FRAMESET> syntax of Netscape 2.0), while others come with non-standard extensions that seem designed to place them beyond the pale of all other web users. It pays to adopt a cautious approach to using new features in your pages.

A more sensible move would be to use the optional text in the <IMG> tag, with the ALT= option. For example:

```
<HTML>
<HEAD>
<TITLE>Friendly Image Gallery</TITLE>
</HEAD>
<BODY>
<H1>Cool Pictures</H1>
Here's my art gallery!
```

```
<HR>
<A HREF="giger.gif">
<IMG SRC="giger-thumbnail.gif" HEIGHT="64" WIDTH="64"
ALT="H. R. Giger: mutation 3(34 kb)"></A>
<A HREF="kahlo.gif"><IMG SRC="kahlo-thumbnail.gif" HEIGHT=
"64" WIDTH="64"
ALT="Frita Kahlo: Portrait of Dorothy Hale (129 kb)"></A>
<HR>
</BODY>
</HTML>
```

If the browser can handle graphics, it should render the thumbnail image as a hot-spot that can be clicked on to download the main image. If the browser can't handle graphics, it should show the ALT text instead. If the browser is Netscape (or recognizes the Netscape additions to IMG) it will render the page containing the thumbnails particularly rapidly. This way, at least the non-graphical reader can get some kind of idea of what they're missing – and most browsers provide an option to load and save the next file to disk.

As an aside, forms support is becoming ubiquitous. However, table support (as specified in HTML 3.0 and implemented, in a slightly different way, in Mosaic and Netscape) is not yet universal; mathematical notation is still probably best handled by inline images or downloadable Postscript documents (although it is an important part of the HTML 3.0 specification).

You have no direct control over the font and character size that your readers use on their browsers; you can't even specify that a given font should be used if it is available. And there are no real standards yet for integrating audio, video, or embeddable application code into HTML, whatever Netscape or Microsoft might want the world to believe.

Backgrounds

Backgrounds deserve a small note in and of themselves. The ability to add an attribute to the <BODY> tag of a document, specifying how its background should appear, is part of HTML 3.0. However, you can do this in two ways: by giving an example image, or by specifying a background colour and/or texture to use.

HTML 3.0 lets you specify a GIF file, which will be tiled across the background of the HTML file you are reading. For example:

```
<BODY BACKGROUND="gifs/brown_paper.gif">
```

Typically, background GIFs are small (64 × 64 pixel) images, because the trade-off between bandwidth (image size) and processor overheads (tiling the image repeatedly instead of simply filling the screen with it) comes down heavily in favour of tiling.

However, Netscape (and some other browsers) have adopted an alternative solution. This is to specify a colour value in an RGB colour space. This is a hash sign followed by a triplet of two-byte colour values, specified in hexadecimal, which represent the 'brightness' (actually, the saturation) of red, blue and green, respectively. The numbers vary from 00 (none) to FF (fully saturated), equivalent to a decimal range of zero to 255. So we can represent the colour white by specifying #FFFFFF – a colour fully saturated in red, blue and green – black by #000000, pure red by #FF0000, pure blue by #00FF00 and so on.

This colour-space model is inconsistent. There's no guarantee that an RGB colour value on one computer monitor is identical to the equivalent RGB value on a monitor with a different temperature spectrum. But it *is* very bandwidth-efficient – you can set a colour without the need for an image map – and it can be applied to other elements. Netscape lets you assign colours to text, unvisited HREF links, highlighted links and visited links. And for these reasons it is worth using.

Most web browsers display text as black on a pale grey background. This is an historical accident with little planning behind it; Mosaic just happened that way, and a plethora of imitators slavishly followed suit. Black on grey looks fairly 'cool', but there's a low contrast ratio between the text and background. Computer-visible text is hard enough on the eye as it is. It helps, therefore, to set a background colour that is as near to white as possible without being *quite* there. Pure white on a computer screen is not like pure white on paper; paper doesn't emit light. So rather than setting your background to #FFFFFF it makes sense to experiment with levels like #FFF0F0 (slightly pinkish tint), #F0FFF0 (slightly more green), or #F0F0FF (blue-dominated). A number of web pages serve the sole purpose of letting you pick a colour from a map and printing its RGB triplet value.

Alternatively, you might experiment with using tiny, fixed-colour GIF images as background maps, or with textured images. But be advised that textured backgrounds are generally a bad idea for these reasons:

- Firstly, you have no idea what kind of hardware your reader is reading your file on. Using a many-hued background can really distract a reader who is trying to view your text on a machine that can display only 16 colours at the same time.

- More significantly, the dithering model that Windows uses to represent colours it cannot directly display differs so radically from that used by the Macintosh that a background that looks great on one system may look unreadable on the other – even if both systems use exactly the same number of colours per pixel.

- Finally, background colours should, so far as is possible, be clustered around the opposite corner of the RGB colour space from the text colour; a strong background can render the text of your page illegible.

So if you want to use a background texture, it makes sense to make it very subtle – perhaps by placing some heavy paper in a colour scanner then using PhotoShop or a similar tool to compress its range of frequencies, or by using a texture provided by an expert who specializes in providing such images. Certainly, for beginners a near-white background specified using Netscape's RGB values may be the lesser of two evils, unless strict conformance to the appropriate HTML DTD is mandatory.

Designing content and cross-references

At this point, it is not possible to lay down any hard and fast rules governing how to provide content in hypertext; what you are writing will affect the way you write it, and vice versa. If you are trying to use the web to create a new art form (a hypertext novel?) your concerns will be very different from those of someone writing an online user manual for a computer program or a history textbook.

In general, it is worth noting that the content of a web, and the cross-reference structure of the web, are disjoint. You can often change the cross-references completely without rewriting a word of the text – and vice versa (although to do so might not be productive).

A second point to note is that reading text on a display is tiring. Human factors testing suggests that reading comprehension falls when text must be read on screen as opposed to paper. (This is not so surprising when you consider that the contrast ratio of black ink on white paper in sunlight is higher than most monitors are capable of achieving, that a high-resolution monitor displays perhaps 72 dots per inch, compared to the 1200 dots per inch considered acceptable for typeset text, and that monitors emit light while paper simply scatters and reflects it.)

Thus, good practice suggests:

- separating document structure from document content (that is, keeping URLs out of textual material wherever possible, or at least distinct enough to be easy to see);
- minimizing eyestrain by not forcing readers to scan long passages of unbroken text;
- paying attention to ergonomics where it's possible to alter the visual appearance of the text to make it readable without compromising compatibility (for example, by setting background and text colours to something easier on the eye than the default values).

The least sensible way to write HTML is the way that virtually everybody starts out (Figure 6.4). (Problems with this page include, but are not limited to: missing TITLE tag, random header hierarchy, uninformative link text, URLs scattered throughout the text with neither rhyme nor reason, a gigantic inlined self-portrait with no warning and no ALT tag, and some egregious typos ... in short, a beginner-level attempt at writing a world wide web home page.)

The first thread most people weave in the web is a learning document. They experiment with URLs, adding them to the text to see if it works. If they are ambitious, they write a couple of interconnected documents, with URLs to other places (typically including a photograph and their hotlist of recently visited links). This is a good learning exercise. However, it is not a particularly good way of structuring a 'live' web site that exists for some purpose (even if that purpose is just personal amusement or a public biography with contact details).

A more sensible way to work is to establish the type of information you want to provide, in the form of an outline. Using the classical hierarchical outline for putting together a linear text, your outline should list headings, chunks of information and related headings to which they may refer. Once you have assembled such an outline you can write the nodes; once you have the nodes you can experiment with various strategies for interconnecting them.

The important point to grasp is that for the purposes of the web, the actual cross-references are not informational content that changes what the reader can learn from the web; they are meta-information that imposes a structure on the way the web is used.

In a nutshell: they don't affect *what* you learn, they affect *how* you learn it.

Some software tools are becoming available for just this purpose. For example, on the Macintosh platform it is worth getting hold of a copy of Clay

```
<H6>Is this a heding?</H6>
<H2>HIIYA D00DZ!
<BR></H2>
<H1>I'M B1FF! WELCOME TO MY WEB SITE!</H1>
IVE BEEN ON THE NET FOR 2 DAYZ AND 1 WANT TO SHARE MY
K0LLECTION OF URLS WITH U:
<A HREF="http://web.nexor.co.uk/places/satelite.html">HERES
</A> THE UK WEATHER MAPS. OR YU COULD G0
<A HREF="http://english-server.hss.cmu.edu/Journals. html"
>HERE </ A> FOR THE
JOURNALS AND GNUSPAPER HOME PAGE. (OH, ITS MOVED AGAIN.)
<P>
HERE'S A GIF OF G00D 0LE B1FF:
<IMG SRC="B1FF-huge.gif">
<P>
B C N U!
```

Figure 6.4 Biff's home page.

Basket by Userland (`http://www.wired.com/staff/Userland/`). This is an outline processor that works on a Netscape hotlist – or on any outline structure expressed in HTML. It has the ability to save an outline as a series of interconnected HTML pages; each heading in the outline becomes a separate file, the text under it becomes the body of the file; and it has links to its parent heading, the next item in the outline and the top level. Other companies have announced equivalent programs. SiteMill (from Aldus) promises similar capabilities, while Netscape have announced WebForce, a graphical web manager that maintains and changes the links between documents as you move them. While it *is* possible to produce a web with broken links using these tools, they do try to make it harder.

There are other strategies for organizing outlines of HTML. I have a personal obsession with removing URLs from inside the body of HTML files – or at least, with minimizing the damage a broken URL can do. In the next chapter, we'll see two mechanisms for dynamically binding the connection between documents; a small-scale URN mechanism and a dynamic, graphical indexer.

Indexing and entrypoint provision

As noted above, in a conventional linear text there are usually only three ways of getting to a subsection: via the index, via the table of contents, and by reading from the beginning. Hypertext is inherently more flexible, and consequently you can be much more creative in your provision of entrypoints.

For example, you may want to provide internal entrypoints in the form of compass pages, panic button pages and a free-text search page. The traditional index is not obsolescent in hypertext, despite the availability of free-text searching (which allows you to locate all occurrences of a given word or words in a set of documents); it indicates where a term is introduced in context, while free-text searching indicates only the usage of the term. You may also want to provide external entrypoints in the form of a top-level table of contents, or navigation pages which are imposed on the raw informational content of a web after the web itself has been assembled. And you need to bear in mind the possibility that the web is being entered at random by confused visitors who may not know where they are or what they are looking at, and who need panic buttons pointing to compass pages or to the front cover page.

In general, a web of any size should have an index. Simple CGI scripts that search a web for text using a program like **grep** (the UNIX string-searching tool) are fairly easy to whip together. However, as the size of the web increases, the speed of a linear string search decreases. It is best to use purpose-built search engines for scanning large webs. Different environments have different search tools.

Macintosh

The Macintosh system can search huge volumes of text very fast by using the (commercial) AppleSearch server. AppleSearch is a full implementation of the Z39.50 networked text search protocol; WAIS is an implementation of an earlier draft of the standard. The WebStar server can interface to AppleSearch via AppleScript; using an AppleSearch engine therefore permits you to index a large document set and provide rapid access (as with WAIS) based on any word in the text.

UNIX

Several search engines are available for UNIX. For huge sets of files, the FreeWAIS implementation of WAIS is probably a sensible choice. WAIS is designed to build an inverted index, storing every word in its file set in conjunction with a set of pointers to every location of that word in the files. By submitting a multiword query, WAIS can check for those files that have the highest number of congruent matches and return a sorted list of the most probable 'hits'. (Bear in mind, however, that WAIS – or AppleSearch – indexes can be up to the same size as the original set of documents.) WAIS (like AppleSearch) is at its best relative to the other systems when indexing huge file sets containing over 50 Mb (and possibly over 1 Gb) of textual data.

For medium to large document sets (up to about 100 Mb), glimpse (from the University of Arizona Computer Science Department) comes in on top. glimpse is another text indexing system. Unlike WAIS, glimpse doesn't store pointers to the exact location of every word in its file set – it stores pointers to the block the word lies in, then uses a rapid text search mechanism to find the exact location. As a consequence, glimpse is slightly slower at searching large file sets, but creates much smaller indices (between 5% and 50% of the size of the original documents). glimpse is at its best when handling archives of 10–100 Mb of text data. Other points to note are that glimpse comes with a set of scripts for integrating it on a web server, and that it's free.

For small document sets, a simple CGI script based around **grep** usually suffices. Above about 10 Mb, however, the serious index search engines begin to show their muscle. A noteworthy option is to use **agrep** instead of **grep**. **agrep** was developed by the same team as glimpse; it is a fast string search program that can recognize regular expressions and which can also handle approximate matching. For example, an **agrep** search can be told to tolerate up to three spelling errors in the word it is looking for.

PCs

HTTP servers, and a port of Perl, are available for NT: as far as I know these are up to the same standard as the normal UNIX varieties. (I am not aware of the status of free-text searching engines on the various PC operating systems, but I would be extremely surprised if they did not equal the peformance and availability of the UNIX-based systems. As a lowest common denominator, public domain versions of GNU **egrep** and **agrep** have been made available on MS-DOS; these should be usable under the other operating environments.) OS/2 2.3 is also a viable HTTP server platform with an implementation of Perl that understands sockets.

Managing the web

Once you have worked out how to go about structuring your web, both in terms of content and in terms of cross-referencing, there is a final constraint to be dealt with before you can begin writing it. How are you going to provide access to your files? And how are you going to maintain them?

Cataloguing webs

Providing access to all the documents in a web is a non-trivial problem. A large single-person web, written by hand, can easily grow to over a hundred files. A program-generated web based on a database can run into thousands of files extremely easily. And the job of webmaster for a university site cannot be easy; if the institution provides web space for everybody, there could be several thousand undergraduates clamouring for access to the server, with demands ranging from a single page to a hugely elaborate online dissertation project.

A common way around this problem is to use a hierarchical filesystem, with directories and subdirectories grouped on the basis of some affinity; for example, staff and student directories, department subdirectories, and year subsubdirectories for the students. The link structure imposed on top of such a hierarchical organization does not have to reflect the underlying structure, but can impose a parallel – or alternative – structure. For example, a top-level index page might list all senior faculty members and all departments; the department indices might list all staff members, and then provide access (via 26 alphabet pages) to an index of students. In this case, pages are made accessible in accordance with their perceived importance within the organization.

Alternatively, what if the web is something like a book catalogue? A publisher's database probably contains hundreds if not thousands of titles. Each book has a unique key, in the form of the author's name and the book's title: it is also quite likely that the database (if it has been designed properly) has a key field containing some unique identifier string for each record. However, an obvious problem arises in deciding how to arrange the files. Do you access them:

- in alphabetical order by title?

- in alphabetical order by author name?

- in order of publication?

- in some hierarchical order based on subject (for example, the Dewey decimal system)?

- in all of the above, using a search script to present the titles in accordance with a selected sorting order?

It all depends on what information is already in the database. If it contains the Dewey number of the titles, then you are in luck – you can write a script that, given a list of Dewey catalogue categories and the database, will assign books to index pages and index pages to catalogue categories. Each book can reside anonymously in a single large directory, yet a hierarchical index can distinguish them clearly (Figure 6.5).

One example of such a hierarchical index is the massively successful Yahoo site (`http://www.yahoo.com/`). Yahoo started life as an experiment in collaborative hotlist. Two researchers put together a simple hierarchical index structure, and added a form to it so that readers could propose URLs to be filed under each heading, or new headings to be created.

Yahoo rapidly snowballed. As it gained links, users found it more useful; after a while, web authors began to provide references to their pages routinely, so that Yahoo rapidly swelled into the tens of thousands of entries in hundreds of categories. Because it follows a catalogue structure like this it is infinitely extensible; if a new subject appears, space can be found for it below or between the nearest existing topics, and a new category is born. (In fact, Yahoo is one of this author's favourite resources for web-related references; the section on the world wide web holds literally thousands of sources ranging from the trivial to the astonishing.)

Maintaining the web

Another concern of web administration is configuration management. There are two parts to the configuration management of webs: management of changes to the text of files, and management of the link structure. Configuration management is the art of keeping track of changes. For example, if you are writing a web by hand, you may add to, delete from, or modify a file. You may want to keep track of what changes you made, and when, so that if some critic later tells you to change it back you can do so mechanically (rather than by rewriting everything).

Programs have existed for some time to aid software developers in the job of managing source code configuration. Many of these tools are also directly applicable to the world wide web, because HTML files can be handled just like source code; they have complex internal interdependencies, and they take the form of structured text.

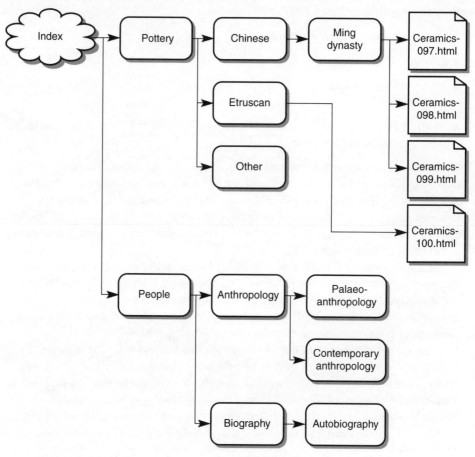

Figure 6.5 A hierarchical index and flat file storage.

Most configuration management tools work by maintaining two parallel directory hierarchies: a 'work' directory and a 'freeze' directory. (The subdirectories beneath these two should mirror each other exactly.) A file is edited in the work directory; whenever it is time to log a change, a copy is stored in a database in the freeze directory.

The configuration management tools typically track the ownership of files to ensure that only one person is editing a file at any given time, to prevent deadlock situations from destroying work in progress. At any time, the owner of a file can make a 'delta', using the tool to store their recent changes (since the last delta) in the freeze directory. (The term 'delta' comes from the fact that configuration management tools don't make an exact copy of the entire file; they simply store a compact representation of the *difference* between the current state of the file and its previous stored state. 'Delta' seems like a natural mnemonic for this process if you spend too much time studying differential calculus.)

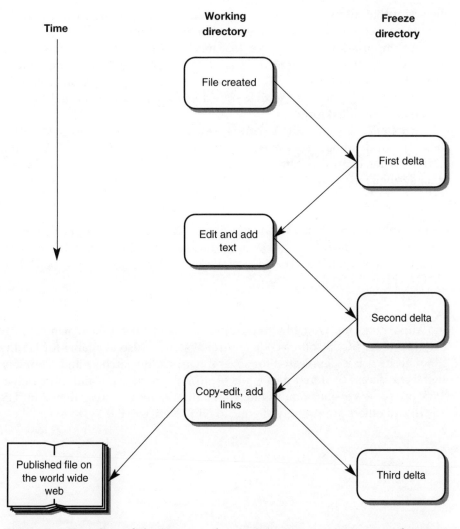

Time

Working directory

Freeze directory

Figure 6.6 Time line of changes to a document using a revision control system.

Using a configuration management tool, it is possible to extract any given version of a file for which a delta exists. So if you make some changes to a document and later discover that they're inappropriate, you can roll back to the earlier version.

Most configuration management tools also let you 'merge' divergent 'forks', where two or more sets of disjoint changes have been made to a file. For example, a CGI script might be written to act as a search tool on a particular web server. To port it to a different server, some changes may be needed, so the stored file is 'forked' into two distinct series of deltas, each of which tracks revisions to a different version of the file. Later, changes are made to

175

the script that allow it to work on either server; the different version series need to be merged back into a single stream at this point.

An important point to note is that most revision control systems permit the user to 'split' a file, that is, to create two different versions that are maintained for different purposes. Thus, you can use a configuration management tool to customize your web so that your documents can be exported to other servers in a modified form.

A detailed introduction to configuration management tools lies outside the scope of this book. However, it is worth noting that free versions of the UNIX revision control systems RCS and CVS are available for DOS, UNIX and other systems; see:

```
http://src.doc.ic.ac.uk/packages/gnu/
```

for example. (CVS is considered superior to RCS because it supports hierarchies of related files; RCS works on individual files.) Commercial revision control systems (such as Voodoo, available in demo form from the INFO-MAC archive:

```
http://www.mid.net/INFO-MAC/
```

and MPW Projector, available from Apple) are available for the Macintosh.

The older SCCS source code control system is also available for UNIX, although its use is deprecated for several reasons: it is archaic and relatively inefficient; access to stored files tends to slow down as more and more deltas stack up; some versions don't understand any file format other than 7-bit US ASCII; and others are strongly allergic to NFS (Network File System).

## 7

BUILDING A PORTABLE WEB

• • • •

If you write a web, then you might expect it to be readable months or years from now. In this chapter, we'll see some tools, techniques and ideas for building a truly portable web, and look at some of the things that make webs date. Despite the problems highlighted earlier, there are ways to address the problem of 'brittle' URLs. We'll take a look at a set of Perl programs that effectively implement a simple local URN-like scheme via CGI scripts, and another Perl program that uses some Netscape-specific features to make a totally link-free web.

Why make it portable?

A first point: some categories of web are intentionally ephemeral. They're designed as throwaways, advertisements or flyers to publicize some time-bound event or offer. This chapter isn't about that kind of web. If you know your documents will go in the bin after the product is sold or the conference is over, you don't need to worry about permanence or portability.

However, it's often the case that complex, content-rich sites are not time-bound. They're intended to stand on their own, as magazines or books do; publications that will at the very least be archived for future readers to refer to. In some cases (published scientific papers, for example) they constitute a vital legacy of information that you want to preserve for the future.

If you're writing such a web, you probably want to see that it's durable. Hardcopy documents last as long as the paper they are printed on, but electronic media are much less secure and may have to migrate to new storage devices or new operating systems from time to time. A web might easily become a 'difficult' legacy format if its usability is intimately linked to its file storage structure.

Portability is another issue. There are several occasions when you might want your web to be portable. By portable, I mean movable – either to another server, or to another directory structure, or to another operating system.

For example, your web may have grown large, with the addition of files over time. There may come a point when you need to reorganize the files in it, to make it fit your filesystem a bit better or to speed up access to files in a large directory.

Alternatively, you might be writing a web that is not intended for a single point of publication on the Internet. For example, the world wide web provides a whole new way of distributing information on CD-ROM. CD-ROMs tend to sprout notoriously huge filesystems, and the ability to bind the files together with a wrapper of hypertext is a major boon. Unlike proprietary multimedia solutions, the web standard is free – it is fairly easy to blast a huge mass of files onto a CD-ROM, in such a form that they can be mounted under a web server for local browser access. Alternatively, Java applets can be spliced into documents in the CD-ROM to control navigation and provide indexing for the files.

For another example, you might want to have your web supported on several different servers (perhaps one on a high-speed LAN behind a corporate firewall, and an edited version on a low-speed WAN connection for public consumption).

What does portability require?

To be deemed portable, a web needs to have the following characteristics:

- standard file format (browser independent)
- no hardware dependencies
- no software dependencies

The file format requirement should be obvious; if the web can be read only by specialized software, then it may not be maintainable. Future availability might depend on your ability (or that of whoever acquires responsibility for the archive) to write a program to convert it into a readable format.

This is a big problem in some cases. Standard HTML documents written for portability tend to be visually boring because they consist mostly of text and images, with no neat tricks to capture the eye. Browser-specific HTML extensions are a big no. So are some other typographical tricks that make the semantic content of the document harder to index and extract – inserting GIFs of symbols in the flow of text, for example. Indeed, it's probably stating the obvious to say that there's a trade-off between graphical sophistication and permanence on the web.

Hardware dependencies are a less obvious source of portability woes, but they're still lurking in the background. It's dangerous to make assumptions about the hardware your readers have access to, even in the present day; to make predictions about the equipment available in ten years' time is even more foolhardy. For example, a lot of software written during the 1960s was designed to run on large batch-mode mainframe computers that used punched cards and tape streamers for local file storage and I/O. Such software can still be run on modern hardware, using an appropriate emulator, but it is hardly likely to make full use of the resources of the newer computer. And the software may prove difficult to load and run if, for example, it is stored on paper tape or a punched card deck and expects to read information off such a medium.

In general, proprietary solutions are dangerous insofar as they require specialized equipment that may become obsolete or unavailable. This has become a major problem for the US government, which is now discovering that large amounts of important – or even unique – data from the 1960s and early 1970s is now unavailable because tape drives capable of retrieving the information no longer exist and the magnetic particles are delaminating from the tapes.

Software dependencies are probably the most pernicious problem of all. What might appear to be a portable solution today is not necessarily going to look that way next year. And in the software marketing world, nothing seems to be quite as popular at present as declaring that some piece of equipment is an open system that will be forever accessible. During the 1980s, the C programming language was hyped as being portable and efficient – as was the UNIX operating system. Both claims are true to some extent; a C compiler can be customized (or already exists) for just about every microprocessor ever designed, and a variant of UNIX runs on just about every significant computer system. However, recompiling a program written in C that runs on one flavour of UNIX for another is not always an easy job – and trying to take the C source code for, say, a Windows program, and compiling it on a Macintosh, is not a task for the inexperienced.

Clouds on the horizon

It is extremely difficult to make predictions about the usability of an electronic document or program more than a few years in the future. Webbed text may be more akin to traditional literature than software in terms of life expectancy; it is not impossible that your web may be useful 20 years from now, if it is a scholarly document. However, although books may remain in print for years, the standard software development cycle is around 18 months between revisions, and up to 36 months between operating system releases. Therefore some of today's web documents may have to outlast contemporary software by a factor of 10.

A web document is fundamentally a distributed information system; it is not tied to any single processor. Some experts in the networking area expect the next twenty years to bring gains that will make Moore's law pale in comparison.

How much change takes place in twenty years?

We can't predict the future, but we can get an idea of the changes twenty years will bring to the computer industry by looking back to 1975.

In 1975, the first personal computer (the Altair) was just a twinkling in its inventor's eyes. Intel were producing the 4004, a 4-bit microcontroller, and were working on the 8008, an 8-bit microprocessor (that would later be developed into the famous 8080 and its 16-bit sibling, the 8086). The state of the art in mainframe storage relied on hard disk drives with a capacity of the order of 30 Mb, and might have as much as 256 kb of core storage. Minicomputers like the PDP-11 were in widespread use, with capacities in the range 8 kb to 64 kb; such departmental systems would serve a number of users on dumb terminals or teletypewriters. The first releases of UNIX were percolating out into the offices of AT&T; and a professor of computer science called Gary Kildall was considering writing an operating system for the 8008-based minicomputers that everybody expected to see in the next year or two. (That operating system was to become CP/M, the indirect ancestor of MS-DOS.)

Between 1975 and 1995, microprocessor performance increased by a factor of two every eighteen months. This is explained by Moore's law (Gordon Moore being the chairman of Intel): as the size of components decreases, so does their power consumption – and they can switch faster. Smaller equals faster and more efficient. Microprocessor speed doubles on a regular basis.

Economist and telecommunications specialist George Gilder suggests that we can expect the available network bandwidth to double every twelve months (not every eighteen) for at least the next decade. Economic and technical progress suggests that Gilder is hardly a rosy-eyed dreamer. And the growth in network availability and access is certainly going to impact the maintainability of web documents as much as the vast increase in microprocessor performance has impacted the maintainability of software.

The difference, to repeat once again, is critical: a web is a publication, not a piece of software. Software is usually written to interact with a specific application, which sooner or later is a function of the computer itself. A web may have nothing to do with the computer system that delivers it – it is a piece of literature (in the broadest sense). Consequently, it is rarely necessary for a piece of software to outlast the computer architecture that gave birth to it. The world wide web may be another matter. Even the mechanisms used to locate data on the web may change.

The uncertain future

Given the pace with which the web is growing, and the speed at which standards are appearing and falling into obsolescence, how can you best go about protecting your information?

Perhaps the most important thing you can do is to be clear about the net's tendency to render existing standards obsolete with bewildering speed. Only two or three years ago, UUCP was considered a viable long-haul network protocol for most purposes. Today it has been left behind. Likewise, HTML has almost been designed to be a legacy file format (one which is obsolescent but still in use because a huge body of legacy information is encoded in it).

The idea that HTML 3.0 (1995–96) might be a permanent standard is a dangerous one, although it is superficially attractive. HTML 3.0 is an outgrowth of HTML 2.0, but remains a relatively limited application of SGML. In the long term other more flexible or powerful document types will come along and supersede HTML. In all probability, DSSSL-based translators will be used to parse HTML into these new formats; because HTML is an SGML application, and DSSSL offers an unprecedented ability to interchange data between SGML applications, it is possible that HTML will vanish from the web almost overnight (if a suitably attractive new SGML application emerges). Just as browsers are subject to fits of fashion (witness the replacement of Mosaic with Netscape, as soon as that product appeared), so too is the medium.

Another alternative is Java. Java holds out the possibility that every data type on the web will 'know' where to find an applet that can render, translate or otherwise make use of it. The act of loading the document will itself load the tools to make use of it. Thus, HTML 3.0 documents – years down the line – will come with a mini-HTML viewer that runs as an applet inside the display of some monumental application descended from today's browsers.

A third possibility is that the web will be neutered and turned into a publication-only medium through the use of complex proprietary presentation media; not just portable document formatting languages like Acrobat, or multimedia formats, but literally read-only documents that are difficult to produce without specialized tools. (This possibility, that the web will effectively turn into another branch of the industrial publishing industry, is somewhat depressing to contemplate from today's perspective.)

In summary, there is more to the world wide web than HTML and HTTP. The web can be viewed as an abstract structure of information linkages (the link structure) that spans a collection of information containers (the resources available on the web). This view is implicit in the concept of the URL, which breaks down into a protocol, a site and a target resource; it is being made explicit in the move towards URCs and URNs.

Flexible references: URLs, URIs, URCs and URNs

In the beginning, the world wide web was a simpler place. It consisted of a relatively small number of documents. These documents could be viewed as resources – entities that could be made use of by one another. However, as the web grew, the problem of tracking resources became critical. A new, somewhat more rigorous vocabulary for discussing resources had to be developed: in fact, it's so important to the focus of this chapter than the terms need defining right now.

Resource	An object, service, or piece of information that can be made use of by an application on the world wide web. (A web may itself be an application.) For example:
	`http://myhost.com/part1/index.html`
	Note that most computer filesystems insist on file path/name combinations being unique. As hostnames are also unique, a hostname:pathname combination should also be unique, within the scope of the Internet.
Universal Resource Characteristic (URC) (alt: Universal Resource Citation)	Resource meta-information that describes a resource, for purposes of making it available (published) on the web, and which binds its name (URN) to its actual location (URL).
Universal Resource Indicator (URI)	A mechanism (URL, URN, URC, or some other as-yet unspecified process) for providing access to a resource.
Uniform Resource Locator (URL)	The access protocol to use, and the host/pathname to access, in retrieving a resource. For example:
	`http://myhost.com/part1/index.html`
	(Note that if the file were accessible by FTP or Gopher instead of HTTP, the resource name would be the same – but the URL would be different.)
Uniform Resource Name (URN)	The name (in principle, unique) by which a resource is known on the web. For example:
	`<URN:dns:path.net:mitra1234>`
	Given a URN, it is possible (or will be possible) to derive a URL to retrieve the resource, without initially knowing where it is stored.

(*Note:* the 'universal' in these acronyms was slowly replaced by 'uniform' when it became obvious that the web was growing so heterogeneous that there was scant hope of making anything on it universal.)

What do all these acronyms signify? In a nutshell, the existing URL mechanism is so brittle that there is a major effort under way to replace it with a flexible referencing scheme.

A URL points to an actual location on the web. A URN, the reference that will replace it in everyday use, is no more than a unique name. The name contains several pieces of information, including the address of an authority that holds a URC describing the resource the name refers to. Using the URC, the authority can always derive a URL for the resource. So when you insert a URN into a document, you can be certain that if the resource is properly registered then any and every reference to the URN will work, even if the file is moved. The principle is:

- Browser reads document containing URN.

- User tells browser to fetch URN.

- Browser uses URN to work out appropriate registration mechanism to consult and sends a query containing the URN.

- Registration server reads URN, finds the URC for that URN, and returns the URL of the actual resource to the browser.

- Browser uses URL to send a request.

All of this is intended to take place in the background. You shouldn't notice the additional query taking place at all. Meanwhile, the owner of the resource is free to give it a different name, move it, even put it on another web server; all the owner has to do is to create a new URC and forward it to a registration server.

By introducing an intermediate stage in the process – by changing over from 'hard' pointers to documents to 'soft' indirect addressing, the URN/URC scheme promises to make the web much more manageable (Figures 7.1 and 7.2).

At the time of writing, this scheme is somewhat vague; requirements and discussion documents have been submitted, but no official RFCs have been issued and no servers or clients yet support the process. However, given the speed with which the web has grown it will become essential within the near future to have such a dereferenced addressing mechanism.

There is some question over the likely registration scheme. However, the IETF Draft URN resource schema (expired in April 1995) sheds some light on

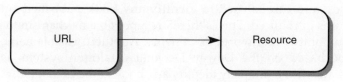

Figure 7.1 Hard pointers: resource moves, link breaks.

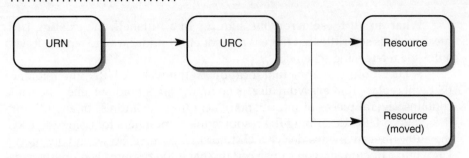

Figure 7.2 Resource can move: URC tracks it, and document containing URN doesn't even know about it.

its probable implementation. According to the draft, a URN will consist of four parts: its header URN, a namespace identifier, a naming authority and an opaque string. The naming authority ID is assigned by a distributed process and the opaque string is assigned by the owner of the naming authority ID. A typical URN (according to the draft) might look like this:

```
<URN:dns:path.net:mitra1234>
```

The namespace identifier (dns) indicates the domain within which to search for the URN. (Other name spaces are possible.)

What is a name space?

A name space is essentially a system that can be used to assign unique names to entities; a cataloguing system. For example, when we talk about the UNIX filesystem name space, we are referring to the set of all possible valid filenames permitted by the UNIX filesystem's naming rules.

   The web uses a name space based on the Internet domain name conventions, and the UNIX filesystem conventions. That is, a URL consists of one or both of a host's domain name and a file's pathname. However, this is not the only possible unique way of identifying a textual object on the Internet, or in the real world for that matter.

   The draft URN document permits 'isbn' as a legitimate name space. The International Serial Book Number is a mechanism established by international treaty to give every published work of literature a unique identifier; ISBNs are assigned in a manner somewhat akin to IP addresses, and can be used to identify any book published since the scheme was introduced. This is therefore a possible mechanism to permit URNs to point to real-world documents. Another possible name space could be based on the Dewey Decimal catalogue system used by libraries, which can uniquely identify any book in the catalogue.

The domain name (path.net) indicates that a naming authority is available at uri.path.net. The naming authority is a TCP/IP server daemon, which uses a syntax modelled on the whois++ service. It can accept queries for a URN, in which case it returns the URC; it can also accept commands to update the URC. A URC contains information about a file, along with a URN and a URL.

The URN name (mitra1234) is a name assigned to some resource by its author, who sends it in a URC to the server. Once a URN is registered with some server, it can be tested by querying other servers; the goal is for URNs to be propagated via a caching distributed database mechanism similar to the internet DNS (Domain Name System).

A comment about URNs

Don't bet the house on URNs becoming available during 1996, or even 1997. This scheme is still under discussion, and chunks of it exist only as a tentative sketch. Although everyone agrees that such a scheme is essential to the long-term future of the web, it is not a cut-and-dried proposal!

Later in this chapter, I'll discuss a coding practice that gives the benefits of a URN scheme to a local web, using some short Perl scripts to update a central cross-reference database. It's by no means an alternative to the full-blown URN mechanism, but it's available today.

Strategy for the future

The web is not simply the combination of information linkages and resources, but the methods that mediate those links. Some 'documents' on the web are actually programs, front-ends to databases or other applications. In this case, the programs that give access to the data are as much a part of the web as the data itself.

This suggests that there is a sensible strategy for the long-term future of the web, which we can adopt right now: to keep the information as separate from the storage mechanism as possible.

HTML documents have a limited life expectancy. If they are prepared in conformance with the SGML DTD for HTML, their content can in principle be modified to conform with new document types, as they are developed. However, we can (and should) ensure that any non-standard mechanisms we use to provide access to data are written in as transparent a manner as possible – so that in the absence of the access mechanism, the data remains usable.

To expect something as seemingly universal as a C compiler or a UNIX operating system platform capable of running CGI scripts to be available in ten years' time is to make a dangerous assumption. However, SGML is likely to be at least a usable legacy format (by virtue of being an ISO standard and also because it is a generic markup system that can be used to design other markup languages). Indeed, textual data available in an SGML application of any kind should be interconvertible into any other SGML-equivalent format.

Link infrastructure is more contentious. It is possible that even the use of a filesystem as an organizing structure for discrete units of information may become obsolete over that time scale. (Some contemporary machines such as Apple's Newton or Be's Be Box already feature data stores based on alternative paradigms.) We can safely assume that resources that contain connections to one another are here to stay, but URLs are not an inevitable component of the Web.

It makes sense to replace URLs in our documents with something that can be translated into any desired cross-reference type; a more abstract system consisting of a target tag and a reference tag. This in turn means writing some software to mediate this mechanism, and if necessary to translate it into current HTML.

URLs are probably on the way out; their demise has been delayed by the phenomenal growth of the web, but they will be replaced by a more general mechanism, the URN, within two or three years. Even if the majority of the web remains operational on the basis of URLs, URN resolvers can be distributed as Java applets.

The question of software is totally up in the air. The temptation just to pick a very-high level language (like Perl, Python, Tcl or Scheme) is strong. In principle there is nothing wrong with this, as long as it is remembered that a language is merely a tool – the product on which it is being used, the documentation, is more important. I personally expect at least one of these VHLLs to exist ten years from now, although there will be radical extensions to the current state of the art. Perl, in particular, is nearly 10 years old and has been widely adopted. The source code to Perl, Python and Tcl is publicly available and written in C or C++; this suggests that it will be available (in some form) for a long time to come. And Scheme has been standardized to a sufficient degree to ensure its continuity. Nevertheless, who today remembers JOVIAL, Coral-60 or Snobol-4? All those languages once had an enthusiastic following. It should therefore be obvious that in planning for software legacy maintenance, a strong dose of pragmatism is required – and above all, fully documented software specifications should be retained with the date that the programs are intended to work on.

Design for an uncertain future

There are several things you can do to design for uncertainty.

Firstly, don't tie yourself to a specific platform. HTTP servers exist for several operating systems; there is a high probability that in 10 years more than half of those platforms will be completely obsolete, and new ones will have emerged. Likewise, the protocols used to transmit information are subject to change. HTTP 1.0 is due to be superseded by the HTTP 1.1 protocol within a two-year time span; preliminary requirements for the HTTP-NG (next generation) are being drafted already. (See `http://www.w3.org/` for details on the current draft standards for HTTP and HTML.) Even TCP/IP is going to be gone by then; plans are already afoot to develop an improved version with support for high-bandwidth links and a wider address space.

It is probably sensible to assume that you will need to move your web application to a new server architecture or protocol before your current operating system becomes obsolete – and to do it again every two or three years. This is based on the assumption that the rate of obsolescence of networking technologies will outstrip the current rate of obsolescence of software, because networking bandwidth (which drives the technology) is rising on a faster exponential curve. The speed with which new operating systems are coming out is dropping – as of early 1995, new OS releases were taking an average of 4–5 years to ship, and innovative microprocessors (as opposed to incrementally improved ones) appeared to be coming out on the same timetable. However, bandwidth appears to be doubling every year.

Because the web is changing so fast, it makes sense to distinguish between the published rendition of your files and the private source. The published version needs to be visible on an HTTP server in whatever format is appropriate (HTML 2.0 today, HTML 3.0 next year). The private source can be in whatever format you like – as long as you can transform it into HTML (or HDL, or any other Web delivery format) in due course. A number of possibilities spring to mind.

Proprietary document formats can be used to store source files, although you are then dependent on the manufacturer sticking around as long as your documents are needed. For example, Microsoft Word format files can be exported to HTML via Microsoft RTF (using RTF-to-HTML, Microsoft HTML Extensions for Word, Microsoft SGML Author or some similar product).

Alternatively, a variety of macro processors can be used to filter a source file, replacing symbolic tags with actual markup information where necessary. In principle, ASCII files are not subject to the vagaries of proprietary software solutions; one text editor is as good as another, and if you know how to write in a macro package, you can probably buy or figure out how to write a program that translates the macro-encoded text into some usable format. However, ASCII files lack semantic content and by the time you add extra markup conventions, they may be as structurally complex as the HTML they represent. Several macro-driven ASCII to HTML processors are available for different platforms; for example, htxp by Man Kam Kwong, available at

```
http://www.mcs.anl.gov/home/kwong/htxp1.html
```

provides a tool for defining macros that can be expanded into HTML by a single-pass processor under UNIX. AutoWeb and Clay Basket, by Dave Weiner, available at

```
http://www.hotwired.com/Staff/userland/
```

do a related job on the Macintosh, taking collections of text files and flowing them into a web (with automatic URLs generated along the way), or taking outlines and turning them into webs. Latex2html takes LaTeX documents (LaTeX is a typesetting macro set based on T_EX) and turns them into HTML webs.

Most importantly, the structural meta-information that governs the relationship between entities in your web needs to be in a protocol-independent format. URLs are going to be rendered obsolete within a fairly short period of time. There is a good reason for this; their brittleness can be a serious problem.

For example, a large Californian software company moved its engineering division to a new building in late 1994. During the move, over 800 workstations were relocated; for administrative reasons, someone in the support department assigned them to a new subdomain. Every URL pointing to a file on any of those machines broke, overnight. This would not have been too bad, except for the fact that company was using web servers behind a firewall, to coordinate the development of its flagship product. Virtually every host in the company's product development arm supported one or more HTTP daemons. Searching out and repairing every URL on those servers that pointed to a moved host turned into a minor nightmare that lasted over a week and took a team of support staff to sort out.

This fuss was a result of web structural information being hard coded. A move from one Internet domain to a subdomain was enough to break the system. If your development source contains hard-coded URLs, these will be a perpetual source of problems as you maintain and upgrade the web.

It is quite reasonable to keep the web source in HTML. However, HTML places fairly stringent limits on the semantic content of documents. It is also prone to gross user input errors; most people take a while to become used to writing HTML, and they make mistakes during the learning process. Because it is impossible to predict the software that will be used to view a web, it is important that HTML files should conform to the accepted HTML standard. (Non-standard extensions provided by the manufacturers of certain products should be treated with extreme caution.) Consequently, if HTML is used to store web documents, it should at least be formally validated for conformance to the SGML DTD in one of these ways:

- by using a conformant editor

- by testing the HTML files using a parser

A conformant editor is one that reads an SGML DTD and uses it to structure all the text input operations. For example, if you type some text in and decide to highlight it, the editor automatically inserts begin and end tags and provides you with a choice limited to the highlighting options specified in the DTD. In fact, the editor constantly checks its input, and ensures that it is producing valid SGML.

An example of a conformant editor is SoftQuad's HoTMetaL Pro. HoTMetaL Pro is a powerful text editor built around an SGML parser and an HTML DTD. (It is a subset of SoftQuad Author/Editor, a full-fledged SGML editor that can handle any valid DTD; HoTMetaL Pro only supports HTML. See http://www.sq.com/ for details.) When inserting text, you can mark it up with any permitted tags – you cannot, however, insert illegal tags. A document prepared with this editor has no choice but to be valid HTML; in principle, any conformant web browser will render it correctly.

The advantage of this sort of editing should be obvious; if you are maintaining a web to which numerous people have access, or a publication site to which several people contribute, it really helps to know that the HTML in the web is certifiably sane. A conformant editor like HoTMetaL Pro goes a long way towards this; in conjunction with a knowbot (knowledge robot) to validate the interdocument cross-references (such as the MOMSpider or EINet's web checker) you can ensure that the web is viable.

However, there are no free conforming editors. And your users may not want to use one specific piece of software to write their HTML.

The alternative to a conforming editor is a static test program: a piece of software that tests the HTML document for conformance and provides an error report if it is not of an acceptable standard.

Two types of static test are available. Firstly, dedicated SGML parsers exist. These programs read a DTD and a file, and check the file to ensure that it conforms to the application described in the DTD. Several of these tools exist in the public domain; notably, ARC SGML (now obsolete), and James Clark's SGMLS and SP parsers. While these tools are not useful as editors, you can feed them the HTML 2.0 or 3.0 DTD and an HTML document and they will validate the document against the DTD, producing an error report. Hal Software provides an interactive forms-based front-end to their SGMLS-based SGML verifier; this is accessible at

```
http://www.halsoft.com/html-val-svc/
```

The main SGML ftp repository at the University of Oslo (ftp://ftp.ifi.uio.no/) contains a large store of publicly available SGML tools and documents. (SGMLS and SP can be retrieved from this repository.)

The second kind of static test program is not an SGML parser. Rather, it is a fairly pragramatic tool designed to spot common coding errors that HTML browsers can't cope with. HTML Lint (by neilb@khoros.unm.edu) scans HTML files and checks them for various common problems. HTML Check, written by Henry Churchyard (churchh@uts.cc.utexas.edu), available via http://uts.cc.utexas.edu/~churchh/, is a similar, possibly more thorough program. Both are available in Perl; HTML Check is also available in awk. Neither program feeds an HTML document through an SGML parser, therefore neither can be considered to be totally authoritative – but between them they spot numerous problems. Not all web browsers incorporate SGML parsers; indeed, some of them are downright eccentric in their handling of tags. Consequently, the more tests you throw at a web the better.

Foreseeing the unforeseeable

Finally, there are the totally unpredictable brickbats that fate sometimes hurls. It is possible to say with some confidence that URLs will be obsolete in a year or two, or that some other feature may be deprecated, or that this or that is a sensible way of protecting your documents from the attrition of time – but sometimes something happens that is so preposterous that it beggars belief and defies prediction.

Such an event happened on 29 December 1994; as of the time of writing, the situation is not yet resolved. It is recounted here as a cautionary tale.

In 1987, CompuServe, the large online information provider, developed a format for transmitting graphics files. The GIF file format (graphic interchange file) was designed to help owners of modems download pictures.

Unfortunately, CompuServe was not aware that the compression algorithm they used in the GIF 89a format (LZW, or Lev–Zimpel–Welch compression), was covered by an obscure patent granted in 1985. The patent was owned by Unisys (formerly Sperry), in the United States. It covered a variety of data compression applications, including the V42.bis encoding commonly used with modems in the early 1990s; consequently, the patent holder's rights were maintained. (IBM also had a patent covering LZW, although the issue of which company had priority was obscure.) However, CompuServe was unaware of the patent infringement – and so was Unisys.

The GIF file was used extensively on the Internet. It was, after all, designed for data communications. The competing standards were the X windows bitmap format (XBM) and JPEG. XBM had no built-in compression, and therefore gave rise to huge, ungainly files. JPEG is a public standard from the Joint Photographic Engineering Group; it has excellent compression facilities,

The GIF file format

GIF has several features that make it desirable on the web.

Firstly, it compresses the image bitmap. (Images take one or more bits to encode each pixel; if you double the horizontal and vertical size of the image you square the number of bits it takes to encode an image. But many pixels are identical to their neighbours; so by using data compression to reduce the redundancy in the bitmap, considerable savings can be achieved.)

Secondly, it provides the ability to tag the image with text or some other information, stored in such a way that it does not interfere with the image or become separated from it during the download process.

Thirdly, the GIF can be interlaced. Interlacing means that rather than scanning the bitmap from top to bottom, scan lines from various positions in the raster are encoded, and the gaps are then filled in by subsequent scan lines; thus, the outline of the picture appears first, acquiring fine detail as the picture is downloaded.

Fourthly, GIF was convenient; storing 8-bit colour images (256 possible colours), it has sufficient colour to be useful while not carrying so much information that the files became unwieldy.

can store 24-bit colour images, can provide 'lossy' compression (that sacrifices information content but gains a massive size improvement), and is slow to decode. JPEG therefore was seen as something of a Rolls-Royce of compression standards, while XBM was unpopular due to its size. Consequently, HTML 2.0 recognizes two standard IMG types: GIF and XBM. Most HTML browsers can handle JPEG images, but many of them require an external viewer – they cannot display inline JPEGs.

Enter the Unisys lawyers. In mid-1994, Unisys discovered the massive patent infringement going on in the online world. They demanded their pound of flesh from CompuServe: a 1.5% retroactive royalty on all software capable of handling GIF images. This was subsequently scaled back to apply only to programs intended 'mainly for use with CompuServe online services' that could create GIF images – the applicable patent covered only LZW compression, not LZW decompression. CompuServe negotiated a deal whereby after six months they'd begin enforcing the patent on Unisys's behalf. This came to light on 29 December 1994, in the form of a confusing, oddly worded press release from CompuServe.

A large chunk of the world wide web developer community were furious. At this time, GIF was a major infrastructure component of the world wide web. To discover that such a keystone was covered by an obscure patent, eight years after the fact, was most disquieting.

Luckily, three different resolutions presented themselves. Firstly, CompuServe (and Unisys) responded to public pressure by back-pedalling, insisting that royalties on the use of GIF technology would be levied only on new, commercial, GIF creation software for use with CompuServe – not on the net at large. Secondly, the most common browser in use during 1995 (Netscape) supported JPEG images, a public standard with built-in compression; concerned individuals could in principle convert all their GIF files to JPEG, change the filenames in their URLs, and carry on working. Thirdly, an effort is underway to define an unencumbered, public-domain graphics format (the Portable Network Graphics file, PNG) that can be used in future web tools.

The central message should be clear: expect the unexpected.

A URN-like system for the near future

So much for future-proofing the web.

We've seen the desirability of using URNs as opposed to fragile URLs to link documents. The main reason why URLs are fragile is that they render documents dependent on the filesystem in which they are stored – if the filesystem structure is changed, the links are broken.

However, it is possible to devise web structures that are much more resilient than usual, even though URLs are still used to describe the connection between documents. The key is to reduce the dependency of URLs (which are, after all, purely a means of retrieving information resources) on the actual file layout on your system.

Included in the following are two Perl programs that are designed to replace the URLs in a web with a robust, URN-like mechanism for symbolic referencing. If you want to use this mechanism you will need to write or rewrite your files to make use of it – but once implemented, it allows you to move files around or rename them without breaking the fundamental relationships between them.

The key to this system is fairly simple. URLs refer to a file explicitly, by name. What if we could replace the filename with some other information, related to the file's content? Then, the URL wouldn't break if we changed the filename – the information used to retrieve the file would by related to the file's context in the web, not its position in the filesystem.

HTML files do include internal identification information. There is the <TITLE> tag in the header. Then, there are the optional tags; notably <META>. This tag is used to incorporate meta-information explicitly into the header of an HTML file. For example:

```
<META NAME="LocalInfo"
CONTENT="Local_information_goes_here">
```

This tag defines the attribute LocalInfo, and assigns the designated contents to it. The <META> tag isn't generally used as part of HTML 2.0, but it does provide a handy way to add descriptive content to files. For example, a suitable CGI script can be written that adds such tags to outgoing (requested) documents.

The `<META>` tag is not the only way to embed information in a file. You can use HTML comments: `<!-- comment text looks like this -->`.

Technically speaking, it is probably better to embed meta-information in a `<META>` tag than in a comment. Comments are not defined as elements within the structure of a document; they may be discarded by some processors (such as SGML parsers or validating editors). The `<META>` tag, in contrast, is an official feature of the HTML 2.0 language specification (at level 1 conformance). Thus, it ties the meta-information to the document at a specific place.

Let's suppose that we are about to design a web that needs to be reconfigured frequently. For example, it may be moved to a different HTTP server, or it may be expanded drastically and partitioned into subdirectories. Because hard links will almost certainly break when subjected to such treatment, we can tackle the problem as follows:

1 Every document in the web is 'branded' with a META tag. The META tag looks something like this:

```
<HTML>
<HEAD>
<TITLE>Sample file</TITLE>
<META NAME="symbol" CONTENT="symbolic_name">
</HEAD>
</HTML>
```

(The attribute `symbol` is associated with the string `symbolic_name`.)

2 We follow an unusual convention when writing URLs to documents in the web. Instead of writing a URL that points to a file, we write a URL that calls a CGI script, passing the symbol value for that file as a query. For example:

```
<A HREF="http://localhost/cgi-bin/finder?symbolic_name">
Sample file</A>
```

It is then the job of the script `finder` to locate the file containing `symbolic_name` and return it in response to a query.

So far this looks reasonably flexible. We have moved the task of keeping track of files out of the URLs, into a CGI script. But how does the script know where to look? A simple linear scan through all the files in a web can take a long time. So it makes sense to add an additional stage:

3 Every time we reorganize our web (adding, deleting or moving files) we run a separate program. This program recursively reads all the HTML files in the directories occupied by the web, scans for the `<META>` tags and extracts the symbols. These are then stored in a database, structured so that a lookup of a given symbol can be used to retrieve the file it was found in.

193

This mechanism does the job of the URN system, albeit locally (rather than in a distributed manner). Files that use the tag system and refer to each other using symbolic identifiers rather than filenames are isolated from the underlying filesystem by an additional abstraction, the lookup table.

Note that it is possible for one file to contain several symbolic reference tags, but each reference can only be contained by one file. Otherwise we face problems in uniquely identifying the target of a reference.

Note also that using this mechanism doesn't preclude the use of local anchors within documents. Instead of referring to `document.html#part_one` URLs simply point to `symbol#part_one`. It is the job of the finder script to parse its input, splitting the symbolic identifier from the rest of the query, replacing the symbolic identifier with a hard filename, and returning the appropriate URL to the HTTP server by means of the CGI interface. The interface permits a CGI script to return some commands to the server: notably, the `Location:` command. For example, a CGI script that returns:

```
Location: somefile.html
```

causes the browser to redirect the query to the HTML file *somefile.html.*

Suppose, then, that we have a file called */stuff/sample.html:*

```
<HTML>
<HEAD>
<TITLE>Sample file</TITLE>
<!-- now for a META tag that sets the value of attribute
"symbol" to "sample" -->
<META NAME="symbol" CONTENT="sample">
</HEAD>
<BODY>
<A NAME="#title"><H1>Here is some text</H1></A>
<!-- Text goes here ... -->
<A NAME="#more_text"></H2>Here is some more text</H2></A>
<!-- More text goes here ... -->
</BODY>
</HTML>
```

The file is tagged, so that the attribute `symbol` has the value `sample`. It contains two local anchors: `title` and `more_text` (each linked to a heading).

Suppose we now write another file. To refer to the first, we use URLs that look like this:

```
<A HREF="/cgi-bin/finder?sample#more_text>
Here is some more text</A>
```

This URL sends a query to **finder**, passing it the value `sample#more_text`. The finder has to split this up: `sample` is used to determine that the file is called */stuff/sample.html,* while `#more_text` is used to determine the (optional) anchor within *sample.html* to point to. The finder then assembles this information and returns to the HTTP server:

```
Location: /stuff/sample.html#more_text
```

The server then replaces the CGI-script output with the contents found at that URL.

Implementation details

The magic takes place in two scripts. First, the symbol table builder, *symtab.pl*. This program scans a directory hierarchy, looking for HTML files. Each time it finds such a file it places the file's name on a stack. Once it has read all the directories it can find, it begins opening the HTML files. It searches for lines matching:

```
<META NAME="symbol" CONTENT="something">
```

When it finds one, it extracts something and writes it into a database file as a key. (The key's value is the name of the file it was found in.)

The database actually consists of an associative array declaration appended to the program *scan.pl*, rather than a separate DBM file. This is because the database is relatively small (it is unlikely to grow above about 50 kb, unless over a thousand files are added to the web), and keeping it in the same file as the search program reduces the amount of file I/O the program must carry out. We write the database out to the finder script in the form of a predefined array; when the script first runs it loads this array and uses it as an index of symbols and their associated files..

Note that Program 7.1 is designed to be fairly platform-independent. Note also that it does not handle symbolic links at all. (If you don't know what symbolic links are, this probably won't be an issue for you. If you need to handle symbolic links, you will need to add a test to ensure that, when you add a filename to the stack, it is not already present in it – in other words, that your program has not got stuck in a loop.)

Program 7.1 *symtab.pl* – build a symbol table.

```perl
#!/usr/bin/perl
#
# Build HTML symbol table from comments containing META: tags
#

$serverroot = "docs";          # home of CGI scripts
$cgi_root = "/cgi-bin";        # where this script lives
$tmp_root = "/cgi-bin";        # where to put temporary files
                               # - must be on same filesystem
                               # as /cgi-bin
```

```
$scr_base = "finder";                    # basename of search script
$findscript = "$cgi_root/$scr_base";     # pathname of search script
$tmpfile = "$tmp_root/$$.tmp";           # a random temporary filename;
                                         # $$ is perl for "my process ID"
$thisdir = `pwd`;                        # where am I running?
umask(22);                               # set file creation mask
$perms = 0755;                           # set file creation permissions


sub basename {                           # take a pathname and return the
    local ($a) = @_;                     # final component
    @stuff = split("/",$a);              # split pathname on "/"
    $a = @stuff[$#stuff];                # find last chunk
    return $a;
}

sub glob {

    # usage: @files = &glob(directory,pattern);
    # returns all filenames in directory that match pattern
    # see Chapter 6 for details
    #
    local ($dir) = @_[$[];
    local ($patt) = @_[$[+1] ;
    if (( -e $dir ) && ( -d $dir)) {
        opendir (DIR, $dir) || warn "could not open $dir\n";
        @files = readdir (DIR);
        closedir (DIR);
        eval (@globhits = grep(/$patt/,@files));
        return @globhits;
    } else {
        die "$dir nonexistent\n";
        return;
    }
}

# ------------------------------------------- main program
#
# We are going to descend recursively all the directories below
# this one, looking for HTML files. When we find them, we'll read
# them and look for META tags.
#
# This is essentially similar to the search script in Chapter 6, except
# that the search starts from the current directory ($thisdir)
#
print "Now in $thisdir\n" ;

$path = $thisdir;
```

```
$pattrn = '^[^.]*';                           # exclude dot files
chop $path;
chop $pattrn;

push(@dirstack, $path);
#
# Note: we are about to reuse $path in another context!
#
# --------------- recursively walk the directories below our starting point

while ($#dirstack >= $[ ) {
    $path = pop(@dirstack);
    @result = &glob($path,$pattrn);           # get files in $path
    foreach $file (@result) {                 # for each file ...
        $path =~ s/(^.*)\/$/$1/;
        if ( -d "$path/$file") {              # if $file is a directory
            $location = "$path\/$file";       # remember it for later
            push (@dirstack, $location);
            $visited++;
        }
    }
    @htmlfiles = &glob($path,'(^.*\.[Hh][Tt][Mm][Ll])|(^.*\.HTM)');
    foreach $target (@htmlfiles) {            # for each HTML file
        if (! -l $target) {                   # ignore symlinks
            push(@targetfiles,"${path}${dirsep}${target}");
        }                                     # add HTML files to list
    }
}

print "\n\nFound $#targetfiles matching files in $visited directories\n\n";

#
# We now have a list of all the target HTML files in our tree.
#
# We now need to search each file for a line containing
# <META NAME="symbol" CONTENT="foo">
# where <foo> is a symbol to use as an Xref target.
#
# symbolic Xref targets are stored in an associative array, bound to the end
# of the search script.
#
# note; a one-to-many relationship is implicit, insofar as one file may
# contain more than one Xref symbols but one Xref symbol may not point
# to more than one file.

# Open search script and copy it as far as sub defdata(), then start array:
#

open (INP, "<$findscript") ||
    die "Fatal error: could not read from $findscript\n";
```

```perl
    open (SCR, ">$tmpfile") ||
        die "Fatal error: could not write to $tmpfile\n";
    foreach (<INP>) {
        last if ($_ =~ /sub defdata {/);
        print SCR ;
    }
    print SCR "sub defdata {\n";
    print SCR "\t%data= (\n";


    # now we walk through the files, extracting META information and appending
    # them to SCR
    #
    foreach $path (@targetfiles) {                    # for each HTML file
        open (CURRENT, "<$path") || die "ERROR: Cannot open $path\n";
        @lines = <CURRENT>;                           # read in the file
        close CURRENT;
        open (CURRENT, ">$path") || die "ERROR: Cannot open $path\n";
        foreach $line (@lines) {                      # search for tags
            if ($line =~ /(<meta.*NAME\=\"symbol\".*CONTENT\=\")(\S+)\".*>/i) {
                $xref = $2 ;                          # get the CONTENT bit
                $npath = $path;                       # get the path
                print SCR "\t\"$xref\",\"$npath\",\n";
            }                                         # print them in defdata()
            print CURRENT $line;
        }
        close CURRENT;
    }

    print SCR "\t);\n\treturn %data;\n};\n";          # close defdata()
    close SCR;

    if (-s "${findscript}.old") {                     # now get rid of old
        unlink("${findscript}.old") ||                # copies of files that
            die "Could no unlink $findscript.old\n"; # might be around
    }
    link($findscript,"${findscript}.old") ||          # keep copy of find
        die "Could not relink $findscript to $findscript.old\n";
    unlink($findscript) ||
        die "Could not unlink $findscript\n";
    link($tmpfile,$findscript) ||                     # link temp file to
        die "Could not link $tmpfile to $findscript\n";# find
    unlink($tmpfile) ||
        die "Could not unlink $tmpfile\n";            # get rid of temp file
    if (chmod ($perms, $findscript) != 1) {
        die "Could not set permissions on $findscript to $perms\n";
    }

    exit 0;
```

Program 7.2 is the search script that works with the *symtab.pl* symbol table generator. **finder** (aka *find.pl*) simply looks up an entry in a predefined associative array and returns an appropriate URL. Because it is a simple query, rather than a full-scale POST type request, we can assume that it is processing a GET method.

Program 7.2 *finder.pl* – retrieve files using table generated by *symtab*.

```perl
#!/usr/local/bin/perl
#find.pl    retrieve a file using the table generated
#     by symtab.pl
#
#
#
# first get the query
#
if ($ENV{'REQUEST_METHOD'} eq "GET") {
    $request = $ENV{'QUERY_STRING'};
} elsif ($ENV{'REQUEST_METHOD'} eq "POST") {
    die "Content-type: text/html\n\n<HTML>\n<H1>Fatal Error</H1> \
 Could not get query\n</HTML>\n";
}
$cgiroot = "/cgi-bin/";       # where this CGI script lives
$script = "finder.pl";        # my own name
$serverroot = "/docs";        # where indexed files are located
#
# sanity check; return an error if the query is empty
#
if (length($request) == 0) {
    print "Content-type: text/html\n\n";
    print "<HTML><HEAD><TITLE>Error</TITLE></HEAD><BODY>\n";
    print "<B>No</B> query was detected. Did you send a request?\n";
    print "</BODY></HTML>\n";
    exit 1;
}

#
# now parse the query
# first, unpack the arguments by converting them into a useful format
# second, check for an optional anchor and set the flag $extratag if one
# exists
#

$request =~ s/\+/ /g;
$request =~ s/%(..)/pack("c",hex($1))/ge;
if ($request =~ /.*#.*/) {
    ($request,$anchor) = split(/#/,$request);
```

```
        $extratag = "TRUE";
} else {
        $extratag = "FALSE";
}

#
# now initialize% symtabto contain the associative array declared in defdata()
# below
#
%symtab = &defdata();

# look for the requested symbol name in %symtab

if (!defined($symtab{$request})) {
    print "Content-type: text/html\n\n";
    print "<HTML><HEAD><TITLE>Error</TITLE></HEAD><BODY>\n";
    print "Requested symbolic identifier does not have a file\n";
    print "</BODY></HTML>\n";
    exit 1;
}

# if we got this far, the symbol has a filename associated with it

$target = $symtab{$request};

#
# now print an appropriate response that directs the server to
# return either the URL contained in $target, or the URL followed
# by an optional anchor
#

if ($extratag eq "FALSE") {
    print "Location: $target\n\n";
} else {
    print "Location: $target#$anchor\n\n";
}

exit 0;

# the following subroutine, defdata(), is created when symtab.pl creates a
# copy of this file. It does nothing except declare the contents of the
# array %data, which are symbol/filename pairs.
#
#
sub defdata {
    %data= (
    "home","/home/local/etc/httpd/cgi-bin/es/home.html",
    );
    return %data;
};
```

These scripts work, and have certain advantages and disadvantages.

Advantages

- Our HTML files are no longer identified by hard-coded pathnames, but by symbols.

- The mechanism for retrieving a file is flexible; if a file needs to be moved, all URLs pointing to it can be effectively updated by re-executing **symtab**.

Disadvantages

- Because it issues a `Location:` directive rather than returning a file, the script causes the web server and client to engage in an extra transaction (fetching the file designated by the `Location:` command).

- A script has to be executed every time a file is retrieved. (On the other hand, if the script is executed frequently it will probably remain in the server's buffer cache, reducing the disk access overheads.)

- This system is not the only way of retrieving the indexed files: it is still possible to create a URL pointing to one of them. To provide robust access to files, this system needs to be developed so that files cannot be obtained in any other way. One method to do this is to:

  - Place the files being indexed in */cgi-bin*. Web servers are generally configured so that they cannot return to a client any file in or below the CGI directory.
  - Modify the **finder** script so that instead of issuing a `Location:` response, it actually opens the file and passes it to the server, to return to the client.

As of the time of writing, a somewhat extended version of this mechanism is in use to provide a controlled-access system for a newspaper; the *Evening Standard* online edition, at `http://www.standard.co.uk/`. The *ES* system includes additional services such as access control and tracking, search interfaces and security features.

As an aside, this system works and provides a web with a degree of portability and reconfigurability, while retaining the capacity to embed links in text. However, this is not the only approach to web portability. A web of documents which contains no links, but is bound together by index pages, is substantially easier to reconfigure than one in which links are interspersed in the document contents; and the situation is likely to stay that way, even after URNs come into general use.

Avoiding links entirely: an embedded web browser

Putting links in HTML documents makes them less portable and future-proof. Here I'm going to demonstrate a totally different approach to making a collection of web documents robust, by removing *all* links from the documents and providing an external organizing framework. The quid pro quo of such a system is that the organizing framework is highly dependent on the current platform; but in many cases it's easier to rewrite a file retrieval program than to rejig all the links in a large web.

In general, a web contains two kinds of URL; those that are used for navigating through the local web, and those that point to other sites – references, citations or pointers to interesting related material.

You can pull the internal navigation links out of a web fairly easily; just create an outline table of contents with links to each document. Your readers have to use their browser's 'back' button before they can go on to the next file, but the structure of the web is fairly consistent and the links are extremely easy to maintain. The external pointers are a bit harder. One method, though, is to replace them with pointers to 'references' files, files containing nothing but links to other sites. Then you can maintain these as a separate issue.

However, there are more sophisticated ways of organizing things. I'm going to break one of the rules I set up earlier, and talk about a proprietary, browser-specific feature: Netscape 2.0's <FRAMESET> and <FRAME> tags.

Framesets

A 'frame' is a separate subdivision of a browser window. You specify a URL to load into a frame and it occupies that part of the browser window.

A 'frameset' is a set of frames, and/or more framesets. Framesets control how much of the browser window a child frame occupies. A frameset replaces the <BODY>...</BODY> portion of a standard HTML document.

For example:

```
<HEAD><TITLE>Frame Example</TITLE>
<FRAMESET COLS="40%, 60%">
   <FRAME SRC="index.html" SCROLLING="YES" NAME="lframe" >
   <FRAME SRC="document1.html" SCROLLING="YES" NAME="rframe">
</FRAMESET>
```

This sets up a frameset in the current browser window. It is split vertically into columns, one of them occupying 40% of the width of the window and the other occupying the remaining 60%.

Within the frameset there are two frames. Both of them are scrollable. One of them (named `lframe`) sources in the HTML file *index.html*. The other (named `rframe`, the one occupying the right 60% of the frameset window) sources in the file *document1.html*.

In addition to scaling frames to a percentage width, you can scale them to an absolute number of pixels, or use an asterisk, *, to say 'take all the available space'. And in addition to specifying columns, you can specify rows of frames. For example:

```
<FRAMESET ROWS="40,*,40\>
    <FRAME SRC="strapline.html" SCROLLING="NO" NAME="top">
    <FRAMESET COLS="40%, 60%">
        <FRAME SRC="index.html" SCROLLING="YES" NAME= "lframe" >
        <FRAME SRC="document1.html" SCROLLING="YES" NAME="rframe" >
        </FRAMESET>
        <FRAME SRC="bottom_row.html" SCROLLING="NO" NAME="bottom">
</FRAMESET>
```

The ability to name frames deserves some explanation. Netscape 2.0 adds a TARGET attribute to the HREF tag, so that you can specify a target window for a document to appear in. Thus, you can click on a link in one window, and the file it points to will appear in a nominated target window or frame. For example, *index.html* could contain a link like this:

```
<A HREF="document2.html" TARGET="rframe">Document 2</A>
```

If you click on this link, rather than appearing in **lframe**, *document2.html* appears in **rframe**, while *index.html* stays in **lframe**. Thus, you can use *index.html* to hold a list of URLs pointing to documents, and the right-hand frame to display them as they are selected – in effect, providing a permanent document table of contents in the left-hand half of the Netscape window.

The frameset syntax is of course totally alien to all other browsers. However, Netscape recognizes a special tag that permits backward compatibility: <NOFRAME>. For example:

```
<HEAD><TITLE>Frame Example</TITLE>
<FRAMESET COLS="40%, 60%">
    <FRAME SRC="index.html" SCROLLING="YES" NAME="lframe" >
    <FRAME SRC="document1.html" SCROLLING="YES" NAME="rframe">
    <NOFRAME>
    If you can see this text, you do not have Netscape 2.
</FRAMESET>
```

Text between <NOFRAME> and </FRAMESET> is invisible as far as a frame-capable browser is concerned, but because frameset-unaware browsers ignore the frame tags it shows up fine. So a browser such as NCSA Mosaic 2.5 will show a page containing:

```
If you can see this text, you do not have Netscape 2.
```

As an aside, although the frame syntax is definitely not part of the HTML standards yet, Netscape have submitted them to the World Wide Web Organization standard process as a proposed extension. They strike me as being a fairly sensible addition; not only because of their usefulness, but also because they don't automatically break earlier browsers.

Dynamic outlining

You can use a left frame to hold a document's table of contents, and have the links in it load files into the right frame. The top and bottom frames are useful for captioning, or even for client-side imagemaps, another feature of Netscape 2.0.

But how much more useful would it be if the table of contents were dynamic – if it changed to reflect the user's location in the web, and if you could update it automatically by simply dropping a document into a set of directories? The web would then be no more and no less than the arrangement of files in subdirectories on the server, and you could extend or change it as easily as moving a file from one directory to another.

Here's an interesting program that does just that. It's a CGI script that generates and fills a frameset, showing a graphical view of a document repository (Figure 7.3). Its mode of action is modelled on the Macintosh Finder's outline view, or the Windows File Manager. It is actually a prototype, a small program modelling some of the workings of a much larger project which is far too large to present here; but it is useful in its own right as a Netscape-specific web browser.

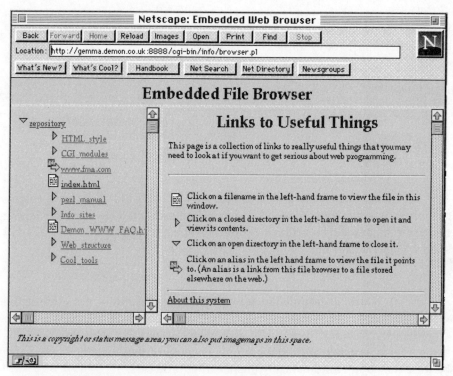

Figure 7.3 Example output from the file browser.

The first time you point your web browser at the program, it prints a small HTML page containing the FRAMESET tag, and some associated frames that split the screen into four areas: a top and bottom row (where you can put control buttons, imagemaps, copyright declarations or anything else that takes your fancy); a left frame (for showing the file hierarchy); and a right frame (for viewing files in).

As you can imagine, things are a bit more complex than that. Each frame must source in a file from somewhere, and in fact they source in the output of the CGI script itself – when it runs, it works out (from the HTTP request) that it is running inside a subframe, rather than the top-level frameset, and modifies its output accordingly.

Inside the left frame, the script works out which directories are 'expanded' for viewing, which files are actual target HTML files and which are 'aliases' (described below), and which are 'condensed' directories, the contents of which are currently invisible. It then prints out a hierarchical outline of the directories it can see, into the left frame (the table of contents) (Figure 7.4).

- If you click on a file icon in the left frame, it is displayed in the right-hand frame. The browser is aware of MIME types; if you click on a non-HTML

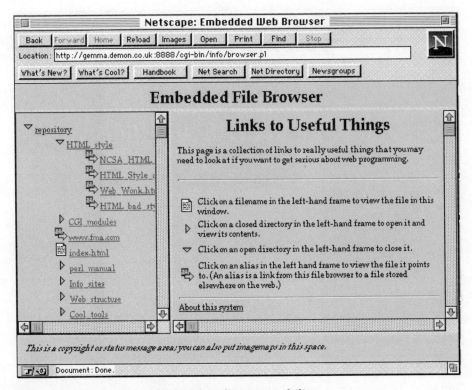

Figure 7.4 File browser showing outlining capability.

file it issues an appropriate content/type directive and sends the file to your browser, which can then deal with it accordingly.

- If you click on a 'compressed' or closed directory, it opens to reveal its contents (the script redraws the left frame).

- If you click on an 'expanded' directory, it closes again (as the script redraws the frame).

'Aliases' are a special feature of this browser; a mechanism for handling links to other sites. In a nutshell, Netscape 2.0 recognizes client-pull directives (as described in Chapter 3). An alias is a small HTML file consisting of a header with a client-pull command in it. The browser recognizes files containing client-pull directives and gives them a different icon, to indicate an off-site link. If you click on one, the file loads into the right-hand frame, then pulls the target URL in after it – neatly encapsulating a foreign reference within the framework of the browser.

For example, in the screen shot of Figure 7.5, the mouse pointer is positioned immediately over the alias pointing to the web style manual displayed in the right frame.

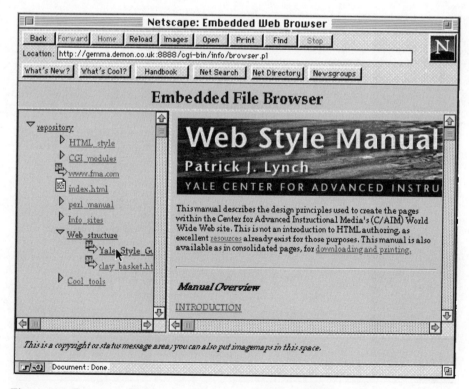

Figure 7.5 Browser showing results of clicking on an alias file.

A note about aliases. The dynamic browser checks all HTML files for HTTP-EQUIV directives; if it finds one, it assumes the file is an alias, as such directives have no place in such a minimally linked web as the one this browser is intended to work with. The browser also examines files with names starting with *www*, in case you have created stub files named after frequently visited web servers. The browser does not look for files with names that are valid URLs, because unfortunately the URL syntax makes for illegal (or embarrassing) filenames on just about every operating system.

To create a web for use with this browser, just create a directory and dump a load of unstructured HTML files into it. It helps if they have no internal links, and it helps to separate the components into subdirectories, for example one subdirectory per chapter or appendix for a book, but the browser can cope anyway if you don't do this. You can also create aliases, by replacing the URL in this example and saving it under an appropriate name ending in *.html* or beginning with *www*.

```
<HTML>
<HEAD>
<TITLE>fma Ltd</TITLE>
<META HTTP-EQUIV="Refresh"
CONTENT="0; URL=http://www.fma.com/">
</HEAD>
</HEAD>
<BODY link="#CC0000" alink="#FF3300" vlink="#000055">
If you can see this, your browser doesn't support client pull.
</BODY>
</HTML>
```

To use this browser, you need access to a web server that supports CGI scripts and Perl 4 or better. (Although it was written in Perl 5, it can work under the earlier version described in this book.) The server should be fairly robust; the browser makes heavy use of scripts. You also need an audience equipped with Netscape 2.0, or a browser that recognizes the FRAMESET syntax. (To this end, the file browser checks for the HTTP_USER_AGENT environment variable and sends a polite rejection note to users who don't have the right web browser.)

You also need a directory containing some icons – small GIF files; *condensed.gif* and *expanded.gif* are the arrows beside directory names, *file.gif* is the standard icon for a document and *alias.gif* is the icon for an alias file. (In these screen shots, I used an icon resource from within Netscape 2.0 itself for the aliases, in order to maintain a consistent look and feel for the browser; in practice, it is prudent not to use someone else's icons without first obtaining permission.)

Program 7.3 *browser.pl* – file browser for unstructured webs.

```perl
#!/bin/perl
#
#
#
# server configuration array follows. This is an associative array that contains
# configuration parameters for the program.
#

%server = (
    "srv_base"        , "/usr/local/etc/apache",    # server home dir
    "html_base"       , "docs",                     # name of docs dir
    "icon_base"       , "/info/icons",              # icon directory
    "cgi_base"        , "cgi-bin/info",             # name of CGI dir
    "conf_base"       , "conf",                     # where config files go
    "MIME"            , "mime.types",               # MIME types list
    "myname"          , &basename($0),              # this programs name
    "startdir"        , "info/repository",          # the top level directory
                                                    # to show in the browser
    "targetfile"      , "index.html",               # the default file to view
    "default_state"   , "frameset",                 # starting state
    "host"            , "$ENV{SERVER_NAME}:$ENV{SERVER_PORT}",
    "condensed_ico"   , "condensed.gif",
    "expanded_ico"    , "expanded.gif",
    "file_ico"        , "file.gif",
    "alias_ico"       , "alias.gif",
    "toolbar_ico"     , "top_buttons.gif",
    "newsbar_ico"     , "bottom_buttons.gif"
);

# first ensure that only Netscape 2 (or close) browsers can run this
# script. If not using Netscape 2, redirect the browser to a boringly
# normal HTML index file.

if ($ENV{'HTTP_USER_AGENT'} !~ /Mozilla\/2/) {
        print "Location: /info/index2.html\n\n";
        exit 0;
}
&ReadParse(*inputs);

# We expect to be invoked with METHOD=GET, and three parameters:
# "dir" a listing of open directories to include in the file browser
# "file" a target filename to display in the right-hand frame
# "state" an indicator: is the program being invoked to draw a
# containing frameset, or to draw the contents of a frame within the
# frameset. (The usual execution procedure is initially to draw a
```

```
# frameset, with frames that invoke the program in "Frame" state.)
#
# FIRST, ensure that there are sane default values for each of these  parameters

if (defined ($inputs{'dir'})) {
        $tdir = $inputs{'dir'};
} else {
        $tdir = "0-" . $server{'startdir'};
}
if (defined ($inputs{'file'})) {
        $tfile = $inputs{'file'};
} else {
        $tfile = $server{'startdir'} . "/" . $server{'targetfile'};
}
if (defined ($inputs{'state'})) {
        $tstate = $inputs{'state'};
} else {
        $tstate = $server{'default_state'};
}
#
# SECOND, depending on what state we're in, do different things:
#
# "frameset" print an enclosing frameset, sourcing in the program
#                 output in the other modes
# "lframe"   draw a "left" frame, that is, a file browser
# "rframe"   draw a "right" frame, that is, the target file
# "header"   print a header message (non-scrolling)
# "footer"   print a footer message (non-scrolling)
#
if ($tstate eq "frameset") {
    &print_set($tdir, $tfile, $tstate, *server);
}
if ($tstate eq "lframe") {
    &print_frame($tdir, $tfile, $tstate, *server);
}
if ($tstate eq "rframe") {
    &print_file($tfile, *server);
}
if ($tstate eq "header") {
    &print_hdr(*server);
}
if ($tstate eq "footer") {
    &print_trailer(*server);
}
if ($tstate eq "dump") {
    &envdump(*server);
}
```

```
    exit 0;
    #
    #----------- end of main program
    #

sub print_set {
    # print a frameset, sourcing in lframe and rframe state-constrained
    # versions of this program

    local ($directory, $targetfile, $mystate, *srv) = @_;
    local ($lurl,$rurl,$turl,$burl);

    # define a URL that points back to this script

    $lurl   = $rurl = $turl = $burl =
        "http://$srv{host}/$srv{cgi_base}/" .
        "$srv{myname}?dir=$directory&file=$targetfile";

    $lurl .= "&state=lframe"; # invocation to create a left-frame
    $rurl .= "&state=rframe"; # invocation to create a right-name
    $turl .= "&state=header"; # invocation to print header
    $burl .= "&state=footer"; # invocation to print footer
    #
    # Now print the frameset, along with URLs pointing back to
    # this script, with appropriate parameters
    #
    print "Content-type: text/html\n\n";
    print "<HEAD><TITLE>Embedded Web Browser</TITLE>\n";
    print "<BASE TARGET=\"fbrowser\">\n";
    print "<FRAMESET ROWS=\"10%,*,10%\">\n";
        print "<FRAME SRC=\"$turl\" SCROLLING=\"NO\" NAME=\"top\">\n";
        print "<FRAMESET COLS=\"35%, 65%\">\n";
            print "<FRAME SRC=\"$lurl\" SCROLLING=\"YES\" NAME=\"lframe\">\n";
            print "<FRAME SRC=\"$rurl\" SCROLLING=\"YES\" NAME=\"rframe\">\n";
        print "</FRAMESET>\n";
        print "<FRAME SRC=\"$burl\" SCROLLING=\"NO\" NAME=\"bottom\">\n";
    print "</FRAMESET>\n";
    return 0;
}
sub print_frame {
    #
    # This is a big subroutine; it prints a hierarchical outline of
    # a directory tree, including URLs that point back to the browser
    # and "flip" the state of open or closed directories
    #
    local ($dir, $oldfile, $state, *srv) = @_;
    local ($tuple, $lvl, $item, $maxlevel, $dname, @stack, @inputdirs);
    local ($href) = "http://$srv{host}/$srv{cgi_base}/$srv{myname}";
```

```
local ($icons) = "$srv{icon_base}";
local ($maxlevel) = 0;
# NB: the "dir=" parameter is a _list_ of directories that are open.
# Each directory name is preceded by a digit, and a hyphen; this is
# a measure of its 'depth' below the starting directory. For example
# 5-perl_scripts means that the directory perl_scripts is open, five
# levels down in the directory hierarchy.
local (@inputdirs) = split(/:/,$dir);
local ($root) = "$srv{srv_base}/$srv{html_base}/$srv{startdir}";
local ($outpage);

# first print a header
$outpage = "Content-type: text/html\n\n";
$outpage .= "<HEAD><TITLE>Embedded Web Browser</TITLE>\n";
$outpage .= "</HEAD>\n";
$outpage .= "<BODY>"; # BGCOLOR=\"#FFFFFF\" TEXT=\"#000000\"";
# $outpage .= "VLINK=\"#000000\" ALINK=\"#0000FF\" LINK=\"#FF0000\">";


# next, for each listed open directory, maintain a record of its name,
# including the level at which it exists below the starting directory.
foreach $tuple (@inputdirs) {
        ($level,$dname) = split(/-/,$tuple);
        if ($level > $maxlevel) {
                $maxlevel = $level;
        }
        $opendirs[$level] .= "$dname:";
}
# @opendirs contains a series of strings. For a given directory level,
# $opendirs[$level] consists of a colon-separated list of directories
# which are 'open' (i.e., their contents are visible).
#
# Now we recursively traverse all the directories and files below the
# starting directory. We do not enter directories which are not 'open',
# but give them a 'condensed' icon and a URL that invokes the script
# with their name added to the 'dirs' argument (list of open directories).
# That way, clicking on a directory opens it.
#
# We enter directories which are 'open' and index their files and sub-
# directories. We give open directories an 'open' icon, and a URL that
# invokes the script _without_ their name appearing in the 'dirs' list
# (thus clicking on an open directory closes it).
#
# Because this is an intensive recursive process, we improvise our own
# stack -- an array of unprocessed files or dirs. Whenever we find a new
# item it goes on the stack; whenever we finish an item, we take
# the next one off the stack. When the stack is empty, we have finished.
```

```
#
# Note: we build our output in the variable $outpage, then print it
#
push(@stack, "0:$root");
$thisdir = $root;
$level = 0;
$outpage .= "<DL>\n";                          # we use HTML Definition Lists to
                                               # format directory
                                               # listings, starting/closing a
                                               # DL when we enter/leave
until ($#stack < 0) {                          # a directory.
    undef ($title_text, @title_text);
    $item = pop(@stack);                       # get next open directory
    ($lvl,$file) = split(/:/, $item);          # parse its name and level
    if ($lvl < $level) {                       # if it's 'higher' than the
        $outpage .= "</DL>\n";                 # last, close off a def list
        $level = $lvl;                         # and track the current depth
    }
    if ( -f "$file") {                         # we're processing a file
                                               # first, process aliases
                                               # an alias is an HTML file, or
                                               # a filename beginning 'WWW'
        if (&basename($file) =~ /(^www\.)|(\.html$)/) {
            open (TMP, "<$file") || die "Aargh!\n";
            $file =~ s/$srv{'srv_base'}\///;
            $file =~ s/$srv{'html_base'}\///;
            @tmp = (<TMP>);
            close TMP;
            # check for HTTP-EQUIV client pull directives, which
            # distinguish aliases from other files
            if (grep(/HTTP-EQUIV="Refresh"/i, @tmp) > 0) {
                    $myicon = $icons . "/" . $srv{'alias_ico'};
                } else {
                    $myicon = $icons . "/" . $srv{'file_ico'};
                }
            } else {
                $myicon = $icons . "/" . $srv{'file_ico'};
            }
            # that's all there is to aliases! A different icon ...
            $url = "<A HREF=\"$href?" .
                dir=$dir&file=$file&state=rframe\" TARGET=\"rframe\">";
            $outpage .= "<NOBR><DT>$url" .
                        "<IMG SRC=\"$myicon\" BORDER=\"0\"></A> ";
            $outpage .= "$url" . &basename($file) . "</A></NOBR>\n";
        next;
    }
```

```
if ( -d "$file") {
    # we're dealing with directories
    $baseitem = &basename($file);
    if ($opendirs[$lvl] =~ /$baseitem/) {
        # this directory is open
        $output = $dir;
        if ($lvl != 0) {
            # you're not allowed to close the root directory
            # if dir is open, remove it from the 'dir=' parameter list
            # in the URL, so that if it is clicked on, the dir
            # becomes closed
            $output =~ s/$lvl-$baseitem//;
            $output =~ s/::/:/;
            $output =~ s/^:([^:]*)/$1/;
        }
        $url="<AHREF=\"$href?dir=$output&file=$oldfile&state=1frame\">";
        $outpage .= "<DT><NOBR>$url";
        $outpage .= "<IMG SRC=\"$icons/$srv{expanded_ico}\"";
        $outpage .= "BORDER=\"0\"></A> $url";
        # NB: both the icon and the filename are separate URLs
        if (&basename($file) eq $srv{startdir}) {
            $outpage .= "<B>http://" . $srv{host} . "/" ;
            $outpage .= $srv{startdir} . "/</B></A>";
            $outpage .= "<IMG SRC=\"$icons/$srv{expanded_ico}";
            $outpage .= "\" BORDER=\"0\"></NOBR>\n";
        } else {
            $outpage .= &basename($file) . "</A></NOBR>\n";
        }
        # Now we look for all files in this directory and add them to
        # the stack
        @files = &glob("$file", '^[^.]{1,2}.*');
        $level = $lvl+1;
        foreach $newfile (@files) {
            # push the file onto the stacK
            push(@stack, "$level:$file/$newfile");
        }
        $outpage .= "<DL>\n";
        next;
    } else {
        # process a closed directory
        # adding its name and level to the 'dir=' parameter of its URL
        # so that clicking on it, opens it. NB: we don't look in closed dirs
        $output =$dir;
        $output.= ":$lvl-$baseitem";
        $outpage .= "<A NAME=\"$baseitem\"></A>\n" unless
```

```
                                ($baseitem eq $srv{'startdir'});
            $url="<A HREF=\"$href?dir=$output&file=$oldfile&state=lframe\"> ";
            $outpage .= "<DT><NOBR>$url<IMG SRC=\"";
            $outpage .= "$icons/$srv{condensed_ico}\" ";
            $outpage .= "BORDER=\"0\"></A>";
            $outpage .= "$url". &basename($file) . "</A></NOBR>\n";
        }
      }
    }
    print $outpage;
    return 0;
}

sub print_file {
    # binary-print a target file, getting MIME type info correct
    local ($target, *srv)       = @_;
    local ($mimefile)           ="$srv{srv_base}/$srv{conf_base}/$srv{MIME}";
    local ($chbase)             = "http://$srv{host}/";
    local ($content_type)       = &nearest_mime($mimefile,$target);
    # nearest_mime() determines the mime type of a file from its suffix
    if (&basename($target) =~ /(^www\.)/i) {
        # the file can only be an alias, and we know aliases are HTML
        $content_type = "text/html";
    }
    local ($buffer, @htmlfile);

    $target = "$srv{srv_base}/$srv{html_base}/" . $target;
    open (CURRENT,"<$target") || die "Content-type: ",
        "text/html\n\nERROR\n",
        "Could not open $serverroot$target\n";
    # this is the target file we're going to send down to the browser
    local ($dev,$ino,$mode,$nlink,$uid,$gid,$rdev,$size,$atime,
        $mtime, $ctime,$blksize,$blocks) = stat(CURRENT);
    # print an appropriate content-type string, using the file's mime type
    print STDOUT "Content-type: $content_type\n";
    print "Content-length: $size\n\n";
    if ($content_type ne "text/html") {
        binmode CURRENT;
        sysread(CURRENT,$buffer,$size);
        print STDOUT $buffer;
        close CURRENT;
    } else {
        @htmlfile = (<CURRENT>);
        close CURRENT;
        if (grep(/<base>/i, @htmlfile) == 0) {
            grep(s/(<\/head>)/<BASE HREF=\"$chbase\">$1/i, @htmlfile);
```

```
            } else {
                grep(s/(<BASE .+>)/<BASE HREF=\"$chbase\">/i, @htmlfile);
            }
            foreach (@htmlfile) {
                print STDOUT;
            }
        }
    return 0;
}

sub nearest_mime {
    # inputs: MIME types table (as per httpd), target filename
    # outputs: mime type
    #
    local ($mimefile, $file) = @_ ;
    local ($line, $mime, $item, $target_ext);
    local (@suffix, %extension);

    # open MIME types file
    open (MIME, "<$mimefile") || die "Content-type: text/html\n\n",
        "<H1>Error</H1>\n",
        "Could not open $mimefile!<P>\n";
    foreach $line (<MIME>) {
        next if ($line =~ /^\s*\#/);
        $line =~ s/\s+/ /g;
        ($mime, @suffix) = split(/\s/,$line);

        foreach $item (@suffix) {
            $extension{$item} = $mime;
        }
    }
    close MIME;

    $target_ext = $file;
    $target_ext =~ s/(.*)\.(.+)$/$2/;

    if (defined ($extension{$target_ext})) {
        return ($extension{$target_ext});
    } else {
        return ("text/plain");
    }
}

sub print_hdr {
    #
    # print an appropriate header block for the topmost frame
    # this could equally well be a client-side imagemap to control the
    # browser's additional functions
```

```perl
    #
    local (*srv) = @_;
    local ($gsize) = "WIDTH=\"443\" HEIGHT=\"25\"";
    # print a header
    print "Content-type: text/html\n\n";
    print "<HEAD><TITLE>fma Ltd DynaFrame Tool</TITLE></HEAD>\n";
    print "<BODY VLINK=\"#000000\" ALINK=\"#0000FF\" LINK=\"#FF0000\">";
    print "<CENTER><H1>Embedded File Browser</H1></CENTER></BODY>\n";
    return 0;
}

sub print_trailer {
    #
    # print an appropriate footer block in the bottom frame
    # this could equally well be a client-side imagemap to control the
    # browser's additional functions
    #
    local (*srv) = @_;
    local ($href) = "http://$srv{host}/$srv{cgi_base}/$srv{myname}";
    local ($gsize) = "WIDTH=\"442\" HEIGHT=\"25\"";
    # print a standard footer
    print "Content-type: text/html\n\n";
    print "<HEAD><TITLE>Footer</TITLE></HEAD><BODY>",
        "<I>This is a copyright or status message area; ",
        "you can also put imagemaps in this space.",
        "</I>",
        "</BODY>\n";
    return;
}

sub envdump {
    # diagnostic routine:
    # dump the CGI scrip environment, formatted as an HTML table
    print "Content-type: text/html\n\n";
    print "<BODY BGCOLOR=\"#FFFFFF\" TEXT=\"#000000\"";
    print "VLINK=\"#000000\" ALINK=\"#0000FF\" LINK=\"#FF0000\">";
    print "<H1>Environment on server</H1>\n";
    print "<TABLE BORDER=\"4\">\n";
    print "<TR><TD><B>Variable</B><TD><B>Value</B>\n";
    foreach (keys (%ENV)) {
        if ($_ =~ /PATH/) {
            $ENV{$_} =~ s/:/<BR>/g;
        }
        if ($_ =~ /HTTP_ACCEPT/) {
            $ENV{$_} =~ s/,/<BR>/g;
        }
        print "<TR><TD>$_<TD>$ENV{$_}\n";
```

216

```
    }
    if ($ENV{'REQUEST_METHOD'} eq "POST") {
        $stdin = <STDIN>;
        print "<TR><TD COLSPAN=\"2\"><B>Uploaded file follows</B> ";
        print "(raw MIME data)\n";
        print "<TR><TD COLSPAN=\"2\">$stdin\n";
    }
    print "</TABLE>\n</BODY>\n";
    return;
}

sub glob {
    # usage: @files = &glob(directory,pattern);
    # returns all filenames in directory that match pattern
    #
    local ($dir) = @_[$[];
    local ($patt) = @_[$[+1] ;
    if (( -e $dir ) && ( -d $dir)) {
        # $dir is a real directory
        opendir (DIR, $dir) || warn "could not open $dir\n";
        @files = readdir (DIR);
        closedir (DIR);
        # eval (@globhits = grep(/$patt/,@files));
        @globhits = grep(/$patt/,@files);
        return @globhits;
    } else {
        # directory is bogus!
        die "$dir nonexistent\n";
        return;
    }
}

sub ReadParse {
    # get the CGI query - based on a much-copied routine by S. Brenner
    local (*in) = @_ ;
    local ($i, $key, $val);
    # Read in text
    if ($ENV{'REQUEST_METHOD'} eq "GET") {
        $in = $ENV{'QUERY_STRING'};
    } elsif ($ENV{'REQUEST_METHOD'} eq "POST") {
        read(STDIN,$in,$ENV{'CONTENT_LENGTH'});
    }
    @in = split(/&/,$in);
    foreach $i (0 .. $#in) {
        # Convert plus's to spaces
        $in[$i] =~ s/\+/ /g;

        # Split into key and value.
```

```
            ($key, $val) = split(/=/,$in[$i],2); # splits on the first =.

            # Convert %XX from hex numbers to alphanumeric
            $key =~ s/%(..)/pack("c",hex($1))/ge;
            $val =~ s/%(..)/pack("c",hex($1))/ge;

            # Associate key and value
            $in{$key} .= "\0" if (defined($in{$key})); # \0 is the multiple
            separator
            $in{$key} .= $val;

      }

      return 1; # just for fun
}

sub basename {
      # given a pathname, return the file name part with no preceding
      directories
      local ($a) = @_;
      $a =~ s/.*\///g; # note s flag
      $a;
}
```

8

KNOWLEDGE AGENTS AND WEB SEARCH ENGINES

● ● ● ●

In the previous chapters, we looked at techniques for organizing a web and making it accessible. However, most such webs are connected to the world wide web – the collection of webs that intermesh over the Internet to provide the world's largest information repository. The world wide web, in the absence of a URN-based schema with per-object records like URCs, has no overall organization. Therefore, making effective use of all that information mandates the use of different techniques, aimed more at discovering information than at structuring it.

In this chapter we'll take a look at some mechanisms for searching and scanning the world wide web, and examine how they fit in with a local web. Robots (or spiders as they are sometimes known) can be very useful indeed, but there are deep pitfalls associated with their indiscriminate usage. Finally, we'll examine some of the requirements of a working robot, and see where to go to get hold of one.

Defining the problem

The web has grown fast since it first appeared on the Internet at large in late 1992–early 1993. As of the mid-1995, it accounted for approximately 15% of Internet traffic. It is now probably the largest single information source in the world; estimates in late 1994 indicated that if it continued to grow at its then rate of 1% compound growth per day, the bandwidth requirements of the web would exceed the total bandwidth consumed by voice communications mechanisms by late 1996.

The size of the web poses some problems. For example, it is not possible to search the web exhaustively, or to locate information rapidly using non-automated tools such as Mosaic, without a degree of insight into the web's organization. And the structure of the web aggravates the problem in four ways:

- Hyperlinks are unidirectional. (It is not possible, given a file, to determine how many other files on the web contain pointers to that file, without searching the entire world wide web.)

- Link information is freely interleaved in document content. (To identify the links that depend on a given resource, you have to read the entire resource; there is no way of determining the link structure of a section of the web without searching the entire content of every document stored in it.)

- There is no resource registration mechanism, to permit documents to be identified by function. (Once the URN/URC mechanism is adopted, it will be possible to obtain information about a document by retrieving its URC, which may contain meta-information describing the document's purpose or content; but at present, all HTML files are created equal – it is necessary to read the file to determine its content, unless it is assumed that its title is an accurate description.)

- Information stored in the web is not partitioned on the basis of content, from the top down. (Though there are some systems that attempt to do so, none of them is an integral part of the web itself, and none of them is exhaustive.) In a catalogue system such as a library, information about a given field is co-located with other books about that field, which are in turn shelved near to similar disciplines. But on the web, there is no overall content-oriented organizational structure, except that which is assembled by the authors of individual sites or by web-searching robots.

This makes finding information about a given topic in the web a real problem. It may even be the prime problem facing the future growth of the web; how to make sense of it as an information resource, on the largest possible scale.

The evolution of web-searching tools

The original mechanism for allowing users to find resources on the web was a regular HTML page, maintained from 1992 to 1994 by NCSA, listing 'what's new' items. Mail documenting new servers and services was sent to the NCSA 'what's new' pages, and updates were regularly added. The pages were searchable (for text), and provided a cumulative, human-readable index to new sites.

This system worked well when the web was in its infancy, but the explosive growth of Internet services rendered the system obsolete in early 1994. Today, although GNN still maintains the 'what's new' pages, it can take over an hour just to skim-read a single day's listings. To anyone other than a dedicated reader, the 'what's new' listings are only of real use with the aid of a search tool. They are further handicapped by the fact that they contain only sites that have been officially announced to the maintainers, and that they do not track changes in the web or actual content (as opposed to announced content).

Even before the 'what's new' pages had ceased to be the focus of web resource discovery, new tools were being developed to automate web indexing. Two general techniques have emerged; active resource discovery by search robot and resource categorization (by hierarchical or free text index).

Perhaps the best known spider on the web today is Lycos:

```
http:// www.lycos.com/
```

Lycos consists of a web-exploring robot that retrieves HTML documents from the web, and an indexer (Pursuit) that extracts relevant information from the documents and builds a free-text index to them. By querying the index for keywords, it is possible to determine the URLs of files that match those keywords. As of mid-1995, Lycos/Pursuit had visited and indexed over four million URLs in over one million documents on the web.

Possibly the most useful hierarchical resource index today is Yahoo:

```
http://www.yahoo.com/
```

Yahoo is a hierarchical hotlist; information is broken down by subject area, so that (for example) to reach the section of Yahoo containing pointers to HTML documentation, you select first 'Computers' (from the top-level table of contents), then 'World Wide Web' (from the 'Computers' menu), then 'HTML' (from the 'World Wide Web' menu). Yahoo differs from most earlier hotlist systems in that it is user-extensible; users can submit URLs to index via a form, and the Yahoo curators can verify the target URL and then add it to the hierarchy. Thus, Yahoo grows when people add useful sites to it. Other examples of collaborative web indices include GENVL:

```
http://www.cs.colorado.edu/homes/mcbryan/public_html/bb/
summary.html
```

and the CUI W3 catalogue:

```
http://cui_www.unige.ch/W3catalog/README.html
```

A major problem with both Yahoo and Lycos is that, although they are very useful search tools, they tend to be overloaded. Because there are few global indices to the web, any index that appears is swamped by access requests. Furthermore, a collaborative system like Yahoo is even more vulnerable – the more people who know of it, the better it becomes (as users add links); but the better it becomes, the more users it attracts, and the more bandwidth they consume. As of the present day, both Lycos and Yahoo have been adversely affected by their own popularity, to the point where they are both now conducting commercial fund-raising activities in order to purchase the bandwidth necessary to keep operating.

The apparent paradox here is that because there are no web indices, if an index is created, it is overwhelmed by demand. A secondary problem is that active web exploration robots consume bandwidth in bulk. (See 'Web indexing systems' below for more information on this.) There are a number of possible solutions to this problem; these are discussed in 'Harvest – the next generation', p. 232.

Web indexing systems

Web indices typically consist of a database that has been hooked up to a robot. The robot recursively scans through the entire web and indexes everything it comes across. (Alternatively, it parses the HTML it finds and indexes data tagged as being title or heading text.) Such indices are far larger than the hand-compiled ones, but contain a fair amount of junk. A search of such a database can be very productive, but it depends largely on the ability of the user to focus on some appropriate search terms. The web does not come with a controlled vocabulary, and such search systems do not usually provide an online the-saurus or dictionary, like commercial online search systems (such as Medline).

In general, the usefulness of a web index depends on the amount of information it stores about each indexed document. A free-text index that indexes every word in a web page stores more useful information about that document than one that stores only its title and subject, because the title of a document does not always summarize it effectively. A structure-sensitive index that segregates the words in a document on the basis of their enclosing tags is even more valuable – it permits users to search for information in titles, or high-level headings, or in citation tags.

Another technique used by web indexers is to analyse the URLs contained in a given document. Files containing lots of URLs are likely to be quite useful, as tables of contents to local webs; large files containing few URLs are also likely to be useful as documents discussing something or other in detail.

Robots and spiders

A robot (or spider) is a knowledge robot – an autonomous program running on a networked computer that searches for, and acts upon, information found in the Internet. Robots can sit on a single node and probe the net, or can in principle wander from server to server (as a worm). (No worm-type robots currently exist, but when Java-based browsers become common they may proliferate, subject to security and trust considerations.) Examples of currently existing robots are archie servers, some directory servers, the SIFT usenet filtration tool, the web meta-indexes, and the Lycos/Pursuit spider/index system.

A distinction needs to be drawn between first-generation and second-generation robots. Most of the first generation of robots were simple tools that traversed the web and retrieved raw data with no post-processing (except possibly URL extraction, so that the robot could derive secondary sources from it). Very often, these robots provided no output beyond a list of URLs visited and some basic statistics.

First-generation robots serve one useful purpose; they can detect broken URLs. This is a fairly important issue. Imagine that you have to administer a server to which dozens of people contribute files. How can you verify that all the URLs in all those files are correct? You could probably 'walk' the web using a browser, but it wouldn't be very fast. And how could you check that all the external references, to other webs on other servers, are also valid? This is a job best carried out by a robot. For example, MOMSpider (described below) was designed with just this task in mind. A combination of a robot and an HTML parser/validator (such as Henry Churchyard's HTML Check) is actually a very useful tool for webmasters responsible for a large server with many users.

Recently, more sophisticated robots have emerged. A second-generation robot is a tool that uses some kind of knowledge analysis system to provide access to the information extracted from the Internet. Information about each document is stored, along with the URL of the document; then the URLs in the document are extracted and the files referenced by them are visited in turn.

Some robots support multiple internetworking protocols like ftp or Gopher, allowing them to retrieve documents from a variety of servers; others are limited to just HTTP (or ftp, in the case of archie servers).

There are also a variety of information-sharing systems based on robots. Some, like Harvest (from `http://harvest.cs.arizona.edu/`) are designed to interface to multiple information-gathering robots, each specialized to handle a single protocol, feeding into a database held on the same site. Harvest servers can distribute queries, so that if the local server is unable to answer it the other Harvest servers on the net can be consulted.

There is a world wide web Wanderers, Spiders and Robots home page (hosted at `http://www.nexor.co.uk/`); this describes some of the robots on the web. There is also a mailing list for robot designers: subscription email should be sent to `robots-request@nexor.co.uk`. (Note that this list is not intended for user support – only designers and those interested in the technology of robots need apply.)

Design considerations and robots

The basic design of a robot is fairly simple. It is a small program that sends out an HTTP HEAD or GET request for a document. (Typically, a HEAD request is issued first, to determine whether a file exists, then a GET request is used to pull the file in if it is a suitable candidate for searching.) When it receives the document, it analyses it and saves some descriptive information in a local database. It then extracts the URLs from the file and repeats the request/strip process for each document it finds. Operating recursively, the robot digs down into the web because virtually every document it finds will add another URL to its list of places to go.

The world wide web is cyclic; it can contain loops. (That is, it is possible to navigate from A to B to C, only to discover a link on C that goes back to A.) Consequently, all robots need a way of figuring out whether they've been somewhere already and are stuck in a loop. They also need to track failed file requests, so that servers that are impossible to contact can be avoided.

Then there is the question of how to traverse the web: one site at a time, or as many sites as possible, in parallel.

The main constraint on any robot is the bandwidth it consumes. A robot can rapidly bring a server to its knees by requesting every single document stored on the server in rapid succession, monopolizing the server's entire CPU and disk I/O resources (over a high-speed network) or the server's entire network bandwidth (over a slow network). It therefore makes sense to leave a reasonable interval between requests directed to a given server. One way of keeping the robot busy without overloading any one server is to give it a round-robin queue of servers to visit, and a list of URLs to retrieve for each server. The robot can then request a document from each server in turn; any URLs found are either added to a new server's list, or appended to the list associated with an existing server.

For any given server, the question to answer then becomes one of whether to probe depth first, or breadth first. These are two ways of traversing a web; they are analogous to the old-fashioned tricks for escaping from an ornamental maze. The difference between the two methods is subtle, but the consequences of selecting one as opposed to the other are striking. (For an introduction to graph theory, see Sedgewick (1988) or any other introductory text on algorithms.)

Depth-first or breadth-first searches

To conduct a breadth-first traversal of a web, you start from a designated node and work outwards. Each time you reach a new node, you check it for URLs. You add them to the top of a list of nodes to visit, then when you finish your current node you take a new node off the bottom of the list. The effect is that you visit each node on the top level of your list before you go down to the next level, sweeping slowly deeper into the web and covering a wide but shallower range of nodes. As servers are added, the search fans out across the web as a whole. This strategy is therefore most efficient for a single robot, attempting to cover the broadest possible number of servers on the web while causing minimum disruption.

> To conduct a depth-first traversal of a network like the world wide web, you start from a designated node and work outwards. Each time you reach a new node, you check it for URLs. As soon as you find a URL you recursively follow it (storing the node you just left on a stack). When you run out of links you pop the top item off the stack, and visit the first URL on your list. The effect is that you travel as far from your starting point as you can get, then double back, always probing deeper into the web. A depth-first search restricted to the local server is the most efficient mechanism for indexing a local site, but is more likely to overload remote servers if used across the web (because it will make repeated requests directed to a target server, as it seeks down through that server's web).

It should be noted that depth-first traversal tends to 'flood' servers. This is because most servers organize their webspace as a hierarchical tree with occasional cross-references and URLs pointing to other sites. It is therefore common to encounter 'chain' documents where each item points to the next, or where they are all indexed from a common table of contents. A depth-first search will retrieve every file in such a document before tracking on to the next item in the search list – and if the server that hosts such a document is at the wrong end of a 14.4 kb leased line or modem connection this will annoy the webmaster intensely. Nevertheless, depth-first traversal is a good retrieval strategy for servers that are organized hierarchically – which means most of them, in working practice.

An appropriate compromise is therefore to run a depth-first search system for local indexing and link validation purposes, while using breadth-first exploration for remote access to other sides.

It is invariably necessary to place constraints on web traversal. Because the web is almost infinitely deep, any web walker needs not only to be able to bail out of loops, but also to be able to see how far it has gone into the web (how many 'layers' down it has probed), and where its current location is in relation to its starting point. This permits the robot to monitor its progress and determine whether it is sensible to continue.

It is necessary for a robot to keep track of the hosts it has visited, including the results from a given visit, so that 'bad' sites can be avoided in future. It is also necessary for robots to keep track of the time a given site was last visited (to avoid overloading it by too-frequent accesses), and for the robot to checkpoint its progress regularly. A long robot run can last for days or weeks; during that time, it is likely that the system hosting the robot will need to be rebooted, or that the robot itself will encounter a situation leading to errors. There is a lot of bad HTML on the web, and robots need bulletproof URL parsers in order to cope with malformed references. A robot that falls victim to a malformed URL may stall, unless provisions are made in its design for it to handle such errors effectively. Robots also need to know how to handle CGI scripts gracefully – typically by ignoring them, or by flagging them for later inspection.

Given the hierarchical nature of the web, and the URL naming schema, working out where the robot is at any given time is a non-trivial activity. The web resembles the prospero virtual filesystem in some ways; this complexity is imposed on top of the usual problems of parsing directory paths and unwinding the directory stack on encountering the '..' operator embedded in a relative URL. Robots need to be able to build an absolute URL from the combination of the URL of the current document being analysed and a partial URL embedded in that document.

Robots also need some way of communicating what they've found. A web validation robot can simply print out the URLs it parses, and their state when it visits them; in this way errors (like broken links) can be reported. A knowledge-gathering robot, however, needs to retrieve entire documents in order to analyse and index them. Because file storage space may be constrained locally, the retrieval and indexing may not always be practical – a smart robot makes use of the Content-length HTTP header to decide whether or not to retrieve a large file. Indexing generally tends to impose a big load on local file storage space and bandwidth; robots are notoriously greedy network hogs. In fact, it is a bad idea to point a robot at someone else's web server unless you know exactly what you're doing and are either building a public database (and thus conducting a service that benefits the common good of all web users), or checking links (with a <HEAD> request rather than by pulling in the entire body of every file on the server).

All web administrators and users of robots really ought to know about the draft robot exclusion protocol. This standard, available in an implemented Perl library from:

```
http://fuzine.mt.cs.cmu.edu/mlm/rnw.html
```

and in a draft document by Martin Kjoster, from:

```
http://web.nexor.co.uk/
```

defines a protocol by which web site maintainers can exclude civilized robots. The robot, on first encountering a new site, checks for a file called *robots.txt* in the root directory. If this file exists, it contains directives about which files a given robot (or group of robots) can or cannot look at. Unfortunately not all web sites have *robots.txt* files, but its importance cannot be exaggerated.

The protocol for dealing with the *robots.txt* file is as follows:

1 If you have not visited a server (called *www.host.domain*) before in the current session, attempt to retrieve the file:

```
http://www.host.domain/robots.txt
```

2 If the attempt fails, the server has no *robots.txt* file.

3 If the attempt succeeds, read the file and obey it (as described below).

4 If you have visited the server earlier in this session, and it had a *robots.txt* file, then you should obey it.

The file contains records separated by optional blank lines; comment lines are introduced by a hash sign, #. The records consist of one or more `User-agent:` `<agent>` lines (specifying a user agent to which the directive applies), followed by one or more `Disallow:` `<resource>` lines (specifying a resource to which access is disallowed). The wildcard, *, is recognized. For example:

```
User-agent: FooSpider
Disallow: /local/maps/*
# FooSpider gets confused when it sees a map

User-agent: Crawler
Disallow: *
# Crawler is badly behaved, so it is not allowed to read
# anything on this site!

User-agent: *
Disallow: /local/maps/bigmap
Disallow: /cgi-bin/*
# applies to any agent not specified above
# tells them to keep out of the cgi-scripts and one
# particular map
```

The draft protocol for handling *robots.txt* is stored at:

http://www.nexor.co.uk/users/mak/doc/robots/norobots.html

Sample Perl code implementing the protocol is stored in:

http://www.nexor.co.uk/users/mak/doc/robots/norobots.pl

Support for the *robots.txt* exclusion file is built into libwww-perl (described later).

Mapping the web

As noted earlier, a robot that can't remember where it has been is likely to wander into some odd traps – loops in the web being the most obvious. (Suppose two researchers in a given obscure field both maintain web sites containing items of interest to them. They know of and respect each other's work. What is the likelihood that they will *not* have pointers to each other's pages?)

A robot that walks the web using a depth-first or breadth-first strategy needs a data structure that represents the web. While it can walk the web by recursively calling a function that takes an absolute URL and visits it, this puts the burden of keeping track of the call stack on the programming system used; this is not a good idea. It's more efficient to use a non-recursive algorithm that makes use of a queue (for breadth-first traversal) or a push-down stack (for depth-first traversal). Both data structures can be modelled in Perl using an array and either the `push()`/`pop()` functions or `push()`/`shift()` (`push` and `pop` add and remove elements from the front of an array; `shift` removes elements from the end of an array). In either case, the stack or queue represents a historical log of your tree-walking exercise; each item in the data structure is a point on your search path through the web.

Note, however, that a list (such as a stack or queue) consumes local system memory and needs to be regularly checkpointed against a database generated by the robot. It therefore makes sense to use the list only for 'current' items, and to offload sites visited a long time ago (or sites that will not be visited for a long time) into disk-based database files.

If you've got a stack or a heap, or a database table, you have a lookup table containing a list of all the nodes you've got left to visit (and that you know about). Unless you're particularly sloppy, you've also got a list of all the nodes you've already visited, and some indication of what you found there . If you are at a node, and the node crops up again later in your list, you know that there's some risk of recursion. If you've already been there, you are in a loop. So to avoid recursion, whenever the robot arrives at a new node it should scan the list for the node's name; if it finds it, prune the list and go on to the next node.

The pruning strategy determines how the robot handles complex cyclic graphs. In principle, the following options are available:

Delete prior entity The robot removes the URL from the search list and adds it at the end. This ensures that it will be the next/last item to visit, and effectively ensures that the visit will take place from the deepest point of the traversal map.

Delete this entity The robot ignores the current URL; it bails out and goes on to the next URL. This ensures that the entity will be visited from the highest pointer to it in the traversal map.

These correspond loosely to depth-first and breadth-first strategies for visiting multiple-referenced nodes.

One thing to bear in mind is that the web does not consist simply of documents; it can contain anything that can be expressed in the name space available for URIs. Certain areas of the URI name space confuse robots; the most obvious are query forms, virtual web pages and image maps. Different strategies must be used to deal with these; pruning is insufficient, as the space may contain an enormous number of possible URLs. For this reason, most robots stick to text and HTML documents, and ignore image maps, graphics and CGI scripts.

Optimizing web exploration

The basic considerations listed above make several basic assumptions. Notable among these are that bandwidth is not a limiting factor (that is, all document retrievals are equivalent), that all documents are intelligible to a simple grab-and-parse routine and that the robot is exploring real files rather than a virtual information space mediated via something like a Z39.50 gateway (WAIS or similar) or a query form on a large database.

In real life, most of these are false assumptions at one time or another. Specific optimizations are necessary to deal with them.

Bandwidth constraints

Firstly, the web is not a homogeneous medium which serves documents in real time. The web is constrained primarily by bandwidth, not server performance, except in those isolated pockets where web server and client are connected by high-bandwidth local links. Because the rate of document delivery is limited by transfer speeds over the Internet, the speed with which a server can be searched is limited by the slowest network link between it and the client conducting the search. Because most commercial and non-backbone academic sites connect via the slowest networking option capable of supporting their essential traffic, the additional burden of world wide web communications tends to result in less than optimum performance: the web – or, more accurately, the tasks people use it for – is a network resource hog.

A web robot that repeatedly accesses a given server is going to be very unpopular with site administrators. Indeed, experience shows that a single robot with no delay between subsequent retrievals can bring a 64 kb leased-line feed to its knees. To avoid this problem, two options are available; the use of a suitable robot exclusion protocol, and a smart algorithm that avoids retrieving documents from the same site at the same time.

(Of course this kind of search strategy isn't so useful at spreading the load if documents are retrieved by spawning a subprocess, but that's another matter. The point remains; in general, robots should be written with consideration for the bandwidth limitations of the server sites they may be visiting, and should take pains not to flood servers with requests.)

Virtual spaces

Certain types of document can confuse robots. Notably, although robots are good at dealing with graphs of passive documents, they are appallingly bad at dealing with search spaces. Search spaces include imagemaps (where clicking on a section of an image returns the coordinates to a server, which then sends an appropriate document), query-based forms (which act as front-ends to a database) and dynamic web pages (generated on-the-fly by a server-side application, so that the content of a given URL may vary uniquely depending on when and where it is accessed).

There is no obvious solution to the problem of query spaces. Most simple robots avoid them by discarding URLs that have a question mark, ?, in them, and by ignoring forms. A system that can probe a query space can be envisaged, but it would need much more complex document parsing – indeed, it would have to parse the semantic structure of a query, and formulate well-formed queries, in order to explore a database effectively. As an aside, it is worth noting that the ratio of information content to apparent size of a query form or virtual page may massively exceed that of a 'normal' passive document. For example, a URL might be the gateway onto an Oracle database containing many tens of megabytes of data. There is no obvious way of discovering this without actually trying to exhaust the query space by composing permutations of all possible queries. New techniques are needed to explore these resources.

Inverted-text indexing tools

Conventional inverted-text databases work by scanning a file as it is added to the database. For each word, a pointer to the word's position in the file is stored in the index. So the index consists of a set of words, each of which has an associated set of pointers to a {file,offset} pair. When a query is received, each item in the query is scanned for through the index. A set of pointers is retrieved for each query item, and the search engine then sorts the query sets into order on the basis of proximity; if all the sets contain pointers to one document, then the odds are that this document is a suitable target.

This tends to create a large index. The mean length of an English-language word is 5.6 bytes (based on an informal sampling of about 6 Mb of self-generated text over the past few years). A document is unlikely to be more than 1 Mb long, therefore a 10-bit pointer is sufficient to identify a given word offset in any document. A database is unlikely to contain more than 1 million files; therefore another 10-bit index will suffice to identify any file. The problem this results in is that 20 bits (3 bytes) are required to identify a unique string of average length 45 bytes – so the index will be of the order of 50% of the file size.

There has been pressure to develop smaller, faster indexing technologies. One of the more promising avenues of exploration is glimpse, (available from `http://glimpse.cs.arizona.edu/`), a free-text indexing system that creates a very small index. It does this by storing pointers to the block offset within a file at which each word is found, rather than to the precise location of the word. When you look up a word using glimpse, it first determines the block the word is present in, then does a rapid linear search through the block to retrieve the word context information; this means that glimpse can get by with much smaller pointers (10 bits, and a 1 kb block size, to index a megabyte of text, for example).

Another is Pursuit, the back-end database of the Lycos engine. Pursuit extracts keywords from web documents and stores them in an index, discarding most of the text. In this way, the Lycos–Pursuit combination has become one of the broadest, most comprehensive databases on the web; with over 1.3 million files indexed (as of late 1995), it is an extremely rich research tool.

Using a robot

In general, the use of robots on the world wide web at large should be discouraged. A robot can consume vast amounts of bandwidth. Unless you plan to make its research findings publicly available, you probably shouldn't run such a tool. However, there are three reasons why you might want to do so.

Firstly, you might want to run a local, depth-first robot in order to test link coherency in your documents. Such a robot mostly confines itself to your own server; it starts at the top and works down, checking that URLs to local documents are valid, and compiling a list of URLs to documents on other servers. It then issues a series of HEAD requests to those neighbouring servers, just to ensure that the links exist. This imposes a fairly light load on the Web and has a major benefit insofar as it lets you confirm that your site doesn't contain annoying dangling references.

Secondly, you might want to create a web index for some specialized purpose. It is common practice for companies with Internet access to maintain a firewall between their own private computers and the net at large. Such a firewall filters out TCP/IP packets for the 'wrong' (disabled) services, and redirects others to servers on one specific (public) machine. So a company might have a single web server visible to the outside world, but several hundred secret web servers behind its firewall, containing company-confidential project information. (This situation exists in many large companies, especially software companies in the UNIX field: a single public web server is visible to the outside world, but there are many servers behind the firewall that nobody outside the company ever gets to see.) If you work for such a company you might well want to set up a local web indexing service (similar to Lycos–Pursuit) that will give your co-workers better access to resources on their private network.

It is worth noting that the bandwidth situation within a company is likely to be much more hospitable to a robot than the Internet connection itself – companies tend to have LANs running at T1 or higher speeds, connected to the Internet via a relatively slow gateway. So the problem of robots being bandwidth hogs is primarily a long-range issue (although robots can still harm local servers by overloading them with file requests if no restriction is placed on the frequency of queries).

Thirdly, you might want to provide services to the world at large by running a Harvest site.

Harvest – the next generation

A next-generation robot should address the problems of indexing the web by adopting a distributed approach to information gathering, storage and retrieval.

The job of indexing the entire web is too big for any one site to conduct. If a single site attempted to build such an index and make it publicly available, it would be swamped by the flood of users, therefore any such index should be available from many local points of presence on the Internet.

An index of the entire web is also impractical. Free-text systems like WAIS typically build an index of the order of the same size as the document set being indexed; even space-efficient systems such as glimpse build an index of the order of 10% of the size of the document set being indexed. An index 10% of the size of every document on every machine connected to the world wide web would be unmanageably huge (running into the terabyte range, over a thousand gigabytes).

Therefore, a more sensible approach is to build lots of local indices, and to provide a query interface to them that distributes queries to remote servers and forwards responses back to the users.

The Harvest system promises to make such a distributed web indexing service practical. Harvest consists of a set of software tools that interoperate to provide a distributed web resource index. Harvest can be found at:

```
http://harvest.cs.arizona.edu/
```

Harvest consists of a number of discrete subsystems that communicate data between each other, primarily in the form of descriptive information about web resources, and queries requesting information or files.

Gatherers collect and index information about local web resources. Gatherers are local robots that index a site or specified sites, feeding the files they discover to a system called Essence. Essence is an information identifier; it works out what kind of file it is handling, and passes it to an analyser (called a summarizer) that is format specific. The summarizer processes the files and returns its results to the gatherer in a format called SOIF (Summary Object Interchange Format). Finally, these are made available to a program called a broker. A broker incrementally indexes SOIF information, and communicates with other Harvest brokers to ensure that information is not redundantly stored. Each broker interacts with a local cache of harvest information. Information and queries are communicated between brokers via a replicator process, and the entire Harvest system is tracked from the top by the Harvest Server Registry (which contains information about every broker, replicator, gatherer and cache in the network). Systems running Harvest are expected to make their contents accessible via a local HTTP server.

In use, the Harvest broker provides a form-based query interface that lets users input queries to the system. The object cache can be used as an HTTP proxy server or as an HTTP accelerator to speed user HTTP requests; it is claimed to be an order of magnitude faster than other HTTP-based proxies and cache systems. The replicator is invisible to users, but distributes the local harvest broker's database among other servers dynamically, to minimize the load on the system.

Harvest represents one successful approach to the problems of indexing the world wide web. Unlike the centralized web indexing systems, Harvest's distributed model means that no one server, standing alone, is likely to be hammered by access requests from all over the Internet. Meanwhile, queries to one server can be answered using the combined resources of every system in the Harvest network.

To obtain and run Harvest, you need to have a UNIX-based web server and various pieces of ancillary software; the installation and setup details are available from:

```
http://glimpse.cs.arizona.edu:1994/
```

A newsgroup exists for the discussion of Harvest configuration and related issues (`comp.infosystems.harvest`) and is your first port of call if you encounter problems. Generally speaking, the number of components required to set up a Harvest installation and the amount of work required make it a non-trivial proposition, although precompiled binaries are available for a number of systems (including SPARCstations running SunOS 4.1.3, and HP-UX workstations). A Harvest server makes a very useful adjunct to a LAN with two or more web servers on it, and running a public Harvest server is a good service to offer to the Internet at large.

Harvest is not the only possible model for a distributed system. Some systems based on client-side executable programs transmitted across the web (worms) have been suggested. Worms, programs that travel from machine to machine and replicate, have a very bad name on the Internet (since Robert T. Morris Jr. released one in 1988 that replicated out of control for days and crashed many machines). Worms are, however, potentially useful information-gathering tools if they can be controlled. Suitable criteria for such control are: that the manager of a system should be able to prevent worms from entering the system, and veto their use of resources that are required for other purposes; that worms should not be able to access confidential information; and that the benefits to the owners of the system they run on should outweigh their costs. Right now, no general accepted basis for worm usage exists on the Internet. However, this may change as systems like Java, Frontier and Safe Tcl gain acceptance.

Verifying the local link structure: MOMSpider

Probably the best way to go about checking or maintaining a local link structure is to obtain and install an existing web maintenance checker. One such robot which is available and effective is the MOMSpider, or Multi-Owner Maintenance Spider.

MOMSpider is written in Perl (version 4.035 or better is required), and depends on an external package called libwww-perl (version 0.40 or better is required). You can obtain MOMSpider from

```
http://www.ics.uci.edu/WebSoft/MOMspider/
```

and you can obtain libwww-perl from

```
http://www.ics.uci.edu/WebSoft/libwww-perl/
```

(Note that MOMSpider and libwww-perl assume that they are running on top of a UNIX Perl installation. A MacPerl port of libwww-perl is available, but MOMSpider has not yet been ported to it.)

Libwww-perl implements a common core of HTTP code in Perl as a library that can be used by other programs; several examples are included. It includes full support for HTTP 1.0 requests, proxies, the robot exclusion protocol and local host requests. It also includes libraries of routines for handling HTML files, MIME content types and for parsing URLs. If you plan to do any robot work of your own, libwww-perl is an absolutely vital starting point that will save you lots of pain reinventing the wheel.

To get MOMSpider up and running is a fairly straightforward process. If you have a UNIX system with Perl pre-installed, you simply obtain libwww.perl and install its files (using a Makefile to distribute them to the appropriate directories), then obtain MOMSpider and edit its configuration files. Full documentation is included with each package.

MOMSpider is designed to traverse periodically a set of webs (listed by owner, server site or document tree). It checks each web for changes which may require the owner's attention, and builds an index document that lists the connections of the web in a form that can itself be traversed as hypertext. To start with, the MOMSpider reads a configuration file. This contains task instructions; each task describes a web structure in such a way that it can be integrated into the traversal. A task instruction describes the mechanism used to traverse the web, a name for it (for future reference), the entrypoint at which to begin searching, and a location in which to place its output file. Optionally, MOMSpider can send email messages containing warnings to the owner of the web in event that certain conditions are identified.

The main goal of the MOMSpider is to find four conditions:

- moved documents (referenced objects have redirected URLs);

- broken links (referenced objects cannot be found);

- new documents (a recent modification date is found);

- expiring documents (a document containing an expiration date that is close to the current date).

When files matching these conditions are found, they are recorded in the log-file; optionally, their owner is notified via email.

Wherever possible, the MOMspider sends HEAD requests rather than GET requests. Consequently, information about document age, ownership or expiry needs to be stored in the header section. The META element is used for this, for example:

```
<META header name="Expires" value="Mon, 29 Feb 2000 00:00:00 GMT">
```

This adds a document meta-information variable called Expires with a value consisting of the indicated date. Obviously, such information is not currently widely available; however, if you intend to use MOMSpider for local web maintenance it might be sensible to write a short utility to 'brand' existing documents with their owner's name.

Running an index server

Writing a robot in Perl using libwww-perl is not too difficult; working out how to index a web constructively is another matter. Some quick rules of thumb can be used:

1 Any word which is in the target of a cross-reference may be worth searching on.

2 Any word in a header element is also worth looking for.

3 The title field of a document header can contain valuable information.

Free-text indexing of an entire web is, however, somewhat more difficult. It implies that each retrieved document should be sent to an indexing engine, which should correlate the keywords in the document against its URL. (Because a URL is a rather bulky, inefficient pointer, it is more likely that some efficient way of internally storing document pointers will be used, for example, adding URLs to a database and indicating that a given keyword was found in the document by storing a pointer to the URL's database entry.)

A simple robot

A (very abbreviated) skeleton for a robot is likely to look like this:

```perl
#!/usr/bin/perl

require <www.pl>;                # core package for lib-www.perl

#
# Support code
#
sub get {
    # Do application-specific checks in here, then get the requested
    # URL. This routine should typically check for boundary conditions
    # (such as wandering away from the local web, or getting trapped
    # in a query space or a loop back to a previously visited document).
    # If the knowbot is deployed on the web at large it should check for
    # a /robots.txt file on the server being visited, and should control
    # the load it imposes on the visited servers by calling sleep()
    # between successive visits to the same site.
    #
    # This routine probably looks like this:

    local($timeout) = 30;
    local($method) = "GET";
    if (@_) {
        $url = @_[$[];
    } else {
        $url = "http://www.fma.com/index.html";
    }

    $header{'User-Agent'} = "WebRobot using MOMSpider/1.0 $www'Library";
    #
    # use libwww-perl to get the file
    #
    $respcode = &www'lrequest($method, $url, *header, *body, $timeout);

    if ($respcode !~ /200/) {
        # do some error recovery here
    }
    return $body # $body contains the body of the document that was requested
}

sub index {
    # Add the contents of the HTTP request's body to the index. This will
    # probably entail extracting header, title and URL information and
    # storing them as keys in a .dbm file, the value being the URL of the file
    # they were found in. (Ideally, the value should be a pointer to the
    # URL, which should be stored in another database.)
}
```

```
sub url_parse {
    # Takes the contents of the HTTP request and a reference to the stack
    # as arguments. Parses out all <A> ... </A> tags, extracts the values
    # associated with HREF=... assignments, and checks to see if they are
    # acceptable references to follow. Uses the value of $url (the current
    # document) to assemble relative URLs into absolute URLs. A sensible
    # knowbot will ignore exotic references (such as forms, mailto and WAIS), and
    # will quickly check to ensure that the URL does not already appear on the
    # stack. The parameter '*stack' that is passed into &url_parse() in the
    # main program body ensures that references to '@parse' in &url_parse()
    # refer to the variable @parse defined in the main symbol table.
    # All valid URLs are then pushed onto the stack.

}

sub wait {
    # wait until an acceptable length of time has passed since the last
    # request to the given site, so we don't overload the server. This is
    # inefficient; if we were searching the Web, rather than just one
    # server, we would use a more complex mechanism to select the URL to
    # use, taking into account the least recently visited server.
    #
    # minimally ...
    sleep 60;
    return;
}

#
# Main program ----------------------------------------------------------------
#

$start_point = "some URL";      # this is the URL from which to traverse
                                # the web
push(@stack,$start_point);      # @stack is an array of URLs to visit, stored
                                # as a pushdown stack

while ($#stack > $[ ) {         # repeat, while there's something on the stack
    $url = pop(@target);        # take item off top of stack (for depth-first
                                # traversal)
    &wait($url);                # wait until it is safe to visit the site
    $response = &get($url);     # $response contains the HTTP response
    &index($url,$response);     # the response is indexed
&url_parse($url, $response,*stack);
                                # push any URLs in $response onto the stack
}                               # end of core loop

exit 0;
```

The important bits of this robot are right at the bottom.

The robot is based on a simple stack. While the stack contains URLs, the robot takes the first one off the stack and retrieves the document it refers to. It then processes the document in some way and extracts URLs from it; these are then added to the stack, then the process repeats.

Of course, it uses libwww-perl to do all the heavy lifting. The subroutines need to call the (rather more complex) libwww library routines. (Otherwise it would be much bigger, or much buggier – neither of which are desirable.)

Several points should be noted.

1 This robot is visibly designed for depth-first traversal. A breadth-first traverser should use a queue, rather than a stack; an array is still suitable, but instead of URLs being popped off it in the main traversal loop, they should be unshift()ed from the head of the list.

2 A robot that follows this skeleton is not going to go very far. Additional code is needed to initialize the local databases needed to keep track of where it has been, a database of sites for which *norobots.txt* files have been retrieved, and the database of queries that have been carried out. Boundary conditions need to be determined in the get() subroutine, at the latest; these could include excessive time, excessive server load, distance (in traversal hops) from the starting point, the Internet domain in which the traversal is constrained, and so on. It would also be sensible to limit the robot to the local server, by disallowing all URLs that point to other sites (or by tagging them so that only a HEAD request is issued, to verify their existence).

3 No checks are present in this code to control the resources being consumed, except for a crude wait() function. A robot eats bandwidth; it also consumes disk space (for the information being retrieved) and time (for the retrieval process). Resources are consumed on the target server as well as on the robot's home system. Some form of load-balancing system is useful if a robot is to visit more than one site. As of December 1994, the database constructed by Lycos–Pursuit at Carnegie Melon University contained entries for 1.3 million URLs. It is unlikely that anything less than a powerful UNIX workstation, several gigabytes of disk space and a T1 or better connection to a network backbone, are suitable for serious exploration of the web at large. Exploration of a local web will consume smaller, but still formidable, resources.

4 This robot does virtually nothing of any use – yet. It would be sensible to use it to verify the link structure of a web, reporting bad URLs, and to validate the HTML in the local web. For example, the url_parse() function could be extended to invoke an SGML parser and HTML DTD, or a less formal HTML scanner such as Henry Churchyard's HTML Check.

However, given a useful task (such as recursively applying some HTML validation checks to a local site, or mapping the usage of web resources by local users) such a special-purpose robot can be invaluable to a site administrator.

In summary, it is worth knowing about robots; if used wisely they can enable an administrator who looks after a company-wide web to explore and index several servers, and they allow several research projects to keep an eye on the web at large. However, the construction and deployment of a robot is not a trivial undertaking and you should never deploy one on the Internet at large without first familiarizing yourself with the hazards of such projects and the standard etiquette for making robot-based requests from a server. Better systems for discovering Internet resources exist; these are decentralized robot-driven tools (such as Harvest), collaborative human-mediated hotlist systems (such as Yahoo), or human-driven web explorers (such as the browser outlined above).

## 9

SERVERS, SECURITY, COMMERCE AND COPYRIGHT

● ● ● ●

In the preceding chapters, we've looked at abstract techniques for making webs work on any environment. We've also looked at the basics of HTTP 1.0 and HTML 2.0, plus the Perl 4 programming language. However, there comes a point in any engineering project when it's necessary to get down to work and bend metal. Constructing and running a web is a type of software engineering project, and the abstract metal to be bent is the HTTP server. In this chapter we'll take a look at some servers and browsers, and at anything else that comes to hand. We'll also glance at security issues and the proposed mechanisms for exchanging secure data over the web (a matter of crucial importance for financial transactions).

Servers

There are two ways of getting a server: you can rent space on a commercial one or run your own.

Renting space commercially makes a lot of sense if you are just getting into the game, or if it isn't particularly profitable yet. Indeed, it's probably sensible to say that you *should* rent space on someone else's server; it's a lot cheaper than buying one, and if you really need your own it should become evident before you've spent too much money. (Doing it the other way round can be a very expensive mistake to make.)

The main watchwords when renting server space are: shop around, and pick the one with the highest bandwidth and largest quantity of space available for your money (subject to concerns about support, reliability and so on). A cheap account on a machine with a 64K line is probably less use than a more expensive account on a 1.5 Mb line; however, you won't be the only user on the machine, so the available bandwidth is divided between the different subscribers. A machine on a 64K line that has only 5 users is of more use than one on a 1.5 Mb line that has 500 users.

Bandwidth

You will need a high-bandwidth Internet connection, preferably better than 64 kbit/s, if you intend to do serious publishing on the Internet. T1 or ISDN connections are most suitable for serious servers anticipating more than five users to access the site simultaneously. It is also sensible to obtain your feed from an IP connectivity provider who offers a similar or greater amount of bandwidth to other areas of the Internet, and who has fallback links in case their main network connection suffers an outage.

The costs of a high-bandwidth connection may seem extravagant, and you could be forgiven for wondering why a 64K line is inadequate, given that it can transfer 8 kb per second (for a total throughput of up to 690 megabytes in a 24 hour period).

Firstly, the load imposed by a web server is not evenly distributed throughout the day. World wide web traffic varies with time, weather conditions and whether or not a public holiday is in effect. (One large commercial site in Europe regularly experiences a 300% rise in traffic on Friday afternoons after 3 p.m., and can track dips in access rates that occur when there is an unexpected sunny spell; office workers surf the net before going home at the end of a week, and home users go and sunbathe instead when the weather's fine.) Consequently, peak demand periods can see throughput rise by an order of magnitude relative to quiet patches, and it is during periods of peak demand that most users will see your site.

Secondly, even a single user can impose a fair load on a 64K line. For example, consider an HTML page 5 kb long, that sources in three GIF files, each 10 kb in size. Suppose a user accesses this page using Netscape. Netscape initially loads the HTML file, then opens up to four simultaneous connections for the inlined images. Thus, a single user can grab three sockets and attempt to transfer 30 kb at the same time when accessing this page. This is equivalent to the total capacity of the 64 k line for a period of some four seconds. If users are accessing your site at the rate of more than 15 per minute, they are going to experience some performance degradation as the 64K line saturates. Access rates of the order of 15 per minute are not extraordinary; the large European commercial site referred to above has an average access rate of 12 million hits per month (or 7 hits per *second*), and in 1994 the site hosting the official Olympics home page was battered by 2 million accesses in a single 24 hour period (23 hits per second on average).

Running a server

Before you can set up an HTTP server, you need a server machine to run it on. The server needs to be connected to a network – either a local LAN, if you intend to use the HTTP server for a private project, or the Internet, if you intend to publish using your server. (Both these types of connection fall outside the scope of this book, as they are effectively open-ended issues.) In general, it should be noted that you can never have too much bandwidth.

The host system needs to support a TCP/IP stack of some description. In general, you can run an HTTP daemon on any multitasking operating system with a TCP/IP stack; in practice, it is best to use a system that provides pre-emptive multitasking, or multithreading, and services equivalent to a UNIX environment. (Both Macintosh and Windows servers are available, but versions of Windows other than Windows NT, and versions of MacOS prior to System 7.1 Pro provide neither threading nor pre-emptive multitasking.)

It's also useful for the server to be very good indeed at handling large numbers of files. A filesystem optimized for serving large numbers of files, possibly with software support for RAID (Redundant Arrays of Inexpensive Disks – where the data is distributed in parallel across disks, to speed access), helps a lot, as does a large disk cache (an area of memory used to stored frequently accessed disk data for rapid retrieval against future requests).

The preferred server environments appear to be UNIX and UNIX variants (such as Linux and NetBSD), and Macintosh, VMS or Windows NT, then other exotica. (For example, there is a server for IBM mainframes running MVS; this is a useful tool for providing access to legacy data.)

If you have money to spend and require the ability to handle commercial transactions, you will need several things from your server. Notably:

- reliable, high throughput

- forms support and gateways

- access control mechanisms

- authentication and encryption

- support

Throughput

A commercial server that can't cope with a high volume of queries is a server that is not suitable for doing business. Although you might not anticipate a huge load, various factors can cause a steep rise in the visit rate. For example, a mention in the GNN 'what's new' page (see http://www.gnn.com/) may be taken as an advertisement of your existence. Alternatively, a mention in one of the many 'Web page of the week' entries can boost the number of visitors to your server by over an order of magnitude within a matter of hours.

In terms of performance, bear in mind that external factors will probably weigh heavily, whatever software you choose.

The biggest bottleneck of all is the bandwidth of your network connection; a WebStar server running on a Macintosh Classic II over a T1 line will probably outperform any HTTP daemon you care to name running on a SparcServer over a 64K leased line.

The next bottleneck is process handling. In general, server daemons require multitasking; when a request comes in, a child process is spawned to service the request, while the parent process continues to listen for requests. A heavily used server may succumb to a full process table if dying server processes are not reallocated properly or if requests come in too fast – such that the number of pending requests exceeds the maximum number of processes. For this reason, multithreaded applications may be preferable; the unit of execution that services a request is a thread within the main application, which does not normally expend the overheads of child process creation when it recieves a query. Alternatively, a non-forking server may be used; some servers (notably Netscape Commerce Servers) fork a collection of 'peer' server processes at startup, and allocate incoming connections to whichever process is free at the time. This reduces the process creation overheads on a heavily laden system and avoids problems such as the process table filling up.

In a nutshell: non-forking or multithreaded servers are faster and more efficient if you expect to service a lot of requests. These include WebStar (multithreaded), NCSA HTTPD 1.4 (but *not* 1.3 or earlier), Netscape commerce server, Plexus, late versions of Apache and many others. They do *not* include early versions of Apache, CERN HTTPD 3.0 (and earlier), and quite a few others.

Finally, the operating system itself may prove an obstacle. A computer which is slow at context switching, or which supports numerous other applications, may prevent the HTTP server from operating at maximum throughput.

A good rule of thumb is that users are likely to become unhappy if they don't see something on screen within 10 seconds of pressing the button. If you're willing to invest the time and effort to set up a commercial server, it pays to use the libwww-perl software to write a script that repeatedly accesses your server, to get some idea of how it behaves under stress – and do this *before* you put data on it or make it publicly available. Indeed, before you commission a server, you need to sit down and work out several things:

- how many queries you expect it to receive

- how much bandwidth you can afford to buy

- how much disk space it will need

- how fast it needs to find and serve files in order to keep up with the anticipated demand

Multiply all your answers by at least a factor of five, because experience shows that all such estimates are conservative – the web defies experience. *Then* you can start testing it to see if it's up to the job.

Forms support and gateways

Needless to say, the easier it is for you to write extensions and form-handling scripts, the better things will be. (However this feature is now so standard that you are unlikely to run across a server that does not provide it.) Moreover, it is usually the case that access to external programs is available via the scripting interface; this may be critical to you if, for example, you are establishing the server to provide access to some information resource such as an Oracle database (using a web-to-database gateway like the Perl DBI interface – see http://www.hermetica.com/).

Access control mechanisms

You will probably want to be able to deny access to some categories of user. The most obvious drain on resources are spiders, and a */robots.txt* file can be installed on any server. However, most servers provide a variety of tools for filtering out unwanted visitors. Access control mechanisms based on the following criteria represent a bare minimum:

- IP number, domain, hostname, from which HTTP request originated

- user ID (enclosed in HTTP request)

- directory to which request is directed

- usage of symbolic links (or Macintosh Aliases)

- HTACCESS protocol (to check user identity)

For example, if you are providing web access to your mission-critical database, you want to prevent users from requesting access to documents that they are not authorized to see – or from using the web server to poke around your computer at will. And you certainly want to be sure that hackers from elsewhere in the net are not reading your proprietary information. Being able to control access to directories and usage of symbolic links controls the first problem; authentication and query origin coverage address the second issue.

Authentication and encryption

If you want to serve sensitive commercial information, or if you need to send or receive data such as credit card numbers, you probably want to use a server that supports authentication and possibly encryption. Authentication is the process of using cryptographic techniques to verify that the client or server you are dealing with really is who they purport to be. Encryption is the process of scrambling a message in such a way that it cannot be decoded without access to a 'key' piece of data, which is available only to the person who encrypted the data and its designated recipient.

Security and cryptography, as applied to the web, are discussed in 'Security', below, along with an explanation of the HTACCESS authentication mechanism.

Support

If you are working in an environment where time is critical, or if you feel uncertain about how to go about compiling and testing one of the public domain web servers, you may want to buy a commercial server. The commercial servers are not necessarily faster or more robust than the public domain ones, but they have a major advantage: they are supported by a vendor who can be held responsible for bugs and who should be able to help dig you out of any problems you encounter.

Several companies are already selling web servers. In general, the commercial offerings are sold on the strength of encryption systems and the availability of support. This field is bound to mushroom over the next few months, so anything printed here is liable to be obsolete; the best reference is the World Wide Web Organization web site, http://www.w3.org/. Of particular interest at this point is the availability of Netscape's server technology (described below).

The first world wide web servers were developed at CERN (along with the world wide web standard); they supported HTTP 0.9. The current CERN server, version 3.0, supports HTTP 1.0 and runs on a variety of UNIX platforms (available from http://www.w3.org/), but is no longer supported by CERN. It provides support for SOCKS firewall software (enabling you to run the server from behind a firewall, allowing conditional access to outside users while blocking out unwanted intruders), and can be configured as a proxy server. It runs on just about every flavour of UNIX, including Linux, and VMS; precompiled versions are available for these platforms.

The CERN HTTPD did not originally support encryption or security features. However, a fair amount of research has gone into providing secure HTTP facilities. The CERN server supports the HTACCESS protocol for handling user authorizations. A particularly notable development is SHEN; the

Secure Hypertext ENvironment. SHEN runs as a component of a modified CERN HTTPD, using RSA data encryption to encode the contents of an HTTP request. Documents explaining SHEN can be found at `http://www.w3.org/`. (Note, however, that SHEN is not the only proposed security system for the web.)

The other main UNIX server comes from NCSA, the National Center for Supercomputer Applications. NCSA HTTPD 1.4 (available via `http://hoohoo.ncsa.uiuc.edu/`) supports HTTP 1.0. Earlier, the NCSA HTTPD was the first server to introduce CGI scripts. (The team who developed NCSA Mosaic and NCSA HTTPD left in 1994 to form Netscape Communications Corporation, whose client and server products can be viewed as linear developments of the original NCSA tools.) Like the CERN server it is available for a variety of platforms and supports HTACCESS.

The NCSA server has spawned a more recent child – Apache. Apache (available from `http://www.apache.org/apache/`) is based on the NCSA HTTPD source code, but is intended to extend the server into new areas. Its development is being funded by a number of companies who require stable, high-throughput web servers suitable for commercial operations, but who do not want to use Netscape's systems; Apache is available as freeware and is used by several heavy-duty public systems. It provides all the facilities of NCSA HTTPD, and adds the ability to set up multihosted web servers, that is, to have several separate Internet addresses mapped to different areas on the server, so that a single Apache system can appear to the outside world to be several different web sites running on different computers. A non-forking version of Apache is under development (to offer better performance when handling large numbers of requests).

Netscape Communications Corporation sells a commercial server with support for encryption; their products are designed specifically for commercial information providers who intend to sell products and who therefore require a degree of security. The technology used, SSL, is layered below the application level but above the TCP/IP connection level; it was invented by NCC, and has not yet become a formal standard, but specifications and reference code have been released to the Internet community. Netscape commerce servers are easy to install and configure, offer good security facilities and are non-forking; however, unlike the other servers mentioned above, they are not free.

A large number of other servers are available for UNIX, some of them are commercial, some are free and most of them have some particular advantages. For example, Plexus 3.0, written entirely in Perl, is easy to extend and customize for specific jobs. OpenMarket supports encrypted transactions for online sales. But none of these programs has more than a small segment of the user base, and space is too short here to discuss them in depth. For links to most of them, see

`http://www.yahoo.com/text/world_wide_web/servers/`

There is one heavyweight server for the Macintosh system; WebStar (formerly MacHTTP). WebStar is a multithreaded PowerPC native application; the issue of forking versus non-forking servers does not arise on MacOS. WebStar can execute CGI scripts in AppleScript, MacPerl, Frontier or any other Macintosh scripting language, and can interoperate with Macintosh applications via AppleScript and AppleEvents. WebStar is also the only non-UNIX-based server to support SSL. It has one further advantage over UNIX servers: its security system is realm based rather than access permission based, and there is no privileged administrator account. You can compromise a Macintosh if you can get at its keyboard, but as an Internet server it is fairly secure. (WebStar is available from StarNine: see http://www.starnine.com/).

Power Macintosh systems running WebStar servers compare well on price-performance ratio with Sun and Silicon Graphics workstations running UNIX-hosted HTTP servers; allegedly one UK-based Web newspaper suffered a major systems failure and managed to keep going by pressing their production department's Quadra into service as a server in place of their HyperSparc.

A fairly robust high-throughput HTTP server is available for Windows NT; called Emwacs, it is available from http://www.emwacs.ed.ac.uk/. Other Windows HTTP servers include win-http and WebSite. Again, they offer broadly equivalent facilities on a different operating system platform. However, Windows (except possibly for Windows NT) is not a popular server platform owing to problems with multitasking and throughput.

It is probably fair to say that the CERN and NCSA servers are the commonest in use (as of mid-1995). However, Apache and the Netscape Commerce Servers have appeared in the meantime. A general list of web servers can be found below the World Wide Web Organization's home page, at http://www.w3.org/ ; this lists the servers on a per-platform and per-vendor basis, with a brief rundown of their features and URLs pointing to their home pages.

Security

Security is a slippery subject. What exactly does it mean, and to whom? What is a security threat? And how do you secure a web server on the Internet? Given that the whole idea of a web server is to provide publicly accessible information, how does this fit in with the idea of preventing unwanted people from gaining access to it?

HTACCESS

In general, it is fair to say that most information currently passed over the web is not secured, and does not need to be secured. However, information with commercial value needs to be protected against the possibility that the wrong people will request it and be given access. It is also necessary to prevent unauthorized people from snooping on a transaction. For example, NCSA Mosaic (and most web clients) support a form of access control called HTACCESS. HTACCESS can restrict access to files and directories on the server to client applications that present a valid authorization of some kind. Authorizations are granted on the basis of username, user's group and usually a confirmatory password; `http://hoohoo.ncsa.uiuc.edu/` contains a detailed tutorial.

However, the HTACCESS authorization mechanism is insecure. Information is passed from the client to the server in a GET request – in plaintext, within a TCP/IP packet. Moreover, password data is merely uuencoded, which is not a cryptographically secure technique. A wily hacker can in principle monitor all packets crossing a network, running a program designed to look for name/password combinations, and uudecode any passwords it finds. Although this might sound a bit far-fetched, and although the vast majority of actual hacking incidents are inside jobs, incidents like this have happened in the past. (Although the media are full of hackers being arrested after penetrating defence department computers on the Internet, far more damage can be done by a company's disgruntled employee, who – within a few minutes of being given their marching orders – can damage the system. Again, the person best positioned to fiddle a company's electronic accounts is the accounts clerk. Before looking for external security threats, computer system administrators are well advised to consider internal ones.)

If you are not conveying vital or secret information over the net, HTACCESS is probably very useful. Indeed, most 'secure' sites today use it.

HTACCESS is configured in the web server setup – using the NCSA HTTPD, look in *srm.conf* for a line containing **AccessFilename**. This specifies a filename, usually *.htaccess*. If a file of this name exists in a directory on the server, the HTTP daemon checks it and ensures that the appropriate access permissions are available before serving any files from the directory.

A *.htaccess* file typically contains something like this:

```
AuthUserFile /security/.htpasswd
AuthGroupFile /dev/null
AuthName access to environment dumper script
AuthType Basic

<Limit GET POST>
require user charlie
</Limit>
```

This means that access to the files in this directory using GET or POST is restricted (limited). You need to have the named permission, 'access to environment dumper script'. You can get this by entering a valid password for user *charlie*, which is checked against the encrypted password stored in the authorized user file */security/.htpasswd*. (There's no authorized group file;

/dev/null is a UNIX-ish term indicating a null file.) If you don't have this permission, which is passed in your HTTP request, you can't get the file.

The authorization type specified is Basic. No other authorization types are available in standard HTACCESS, though in principle this could be replaced by some encryption mechanism supported by the server – that's why the AuthType line exists at all.

Note that it's important the /passwordfile is somewhere outside the current directory. If the bad guys get access permission to this directory under one name, they could swipe your complete list of passwords and use them to hack access under other names (by running a password file cracking program such as **crack**).

Note: There is a hidden gotcha in NCSA HTTPD. The source code for HTACCESS insists that the pathname to the */password* file is an absolute pathname, relative to the server root directory – it won't accept a relative pathname from the directory of the *.htaccess* file. Moreover, if you get it wrong, the HTTP server won't tell you why – it will simply say 'access denied' until you get the pathname right.

Most web browsers are smart enough to display a password entry dialogue when they encounter an HTACCESS-protected directory. If you've got the password and username, you enter them in the box and they're sent to the server as part of your request.

The server encrypts the password and compares it to the (encrypted) copy of the password it has access to, /passwordfile. If they're identical, it knows that you are authorized to look at the contents of the directory.

Here's what the simple environment dump program from Chapter 5 sees in its environment before you make an HTACCESS-authenticated request:

```
SERVER_SOFTWARE        Apache/0.6.4b
GATEWAY_INTERFACE      CGI/1.1
DOCUMENT_ROOT          /usr/local/etc/apache/docs
REMOTE_ADDR            158.152.nn.nn
SERVER_PROTOCOL        HTTP/1.0
REQUEST_METHOD         GET
REMOTE_HOST            antipope.demon.co.uk
QUERY_STRING
HTTP_USER_AGENT        Mozilla/2.0b1(Macintosh; I; 68K)
PATH                   /bin
                       /usr/bin
                       /usr/etc
                       /usr/ucb
```

```
HTTP_CONNECTION         Keep-Alive
HTTP_ACCEPT             image/gif
                        image/x-bitmap
                        image/jpeg
                        image/pjpeg
                        */*
SCRIPT_NAME             /cgi-bin/capture.pl
SERVER_NAME             xxx.demon.co.uk
SERVER_PORT             80
HTTP_HOST               xxx:80
SERVER_ADMIN            charlie@antipope.demon.co.uk
```

And here's the extra stuff that appears in your environment after you've entered the username and password:

```
REMOTE_USER             charlie
AUTH_TYPE               Basic
```

The password file contains line consisting of a name, a colon and a string of apparent gibberish. This is an encrypted version of the password. You create passwords using a program called **htpasswd**, that comes as part of the NCSA server suite. Type:

```
htpasswd -c /passwordfile username
```

htpasswd prepares to add an entry for the user username in the file */password-file*. It prompts you to type in a password, which isn't printed on the screen as you type; it then asks you to type it again (for comparative purposes) then saves the new password entry.

This is somewhat inconvenient at times, especially if you need to let users change their own passwords or subscribe to your service. Because HTACCESS is not secure (in the cryptographic sense) it is not so much a useful tool for preventing security breaches, as a convenient way of monitoring who is accessing your site and when; the HTACCESS authorizations show up in the server logfiles, and include the name of the authenticated user.

Here is a short Perl script that does the same job as htpasswd, except that it doesn't conceal the password as you type it:

```perl
#!/bin/perl

if ($ARGV[0] !~ /-c/) {
    print "Error: wrong usage\n";
    &usage;
    exit 0;
}
```

```perl
$pwfile   = $ARGV[1];
$username = $ARGV[2];

if ( -e $pwfile) {
    open (PWFILE, "<$pwfile") || die "Could not read $pwfile!\n";
    @pwords = <PWFILE>;
    close PWFILE;
    $res = grep(/$username/, @pwords);
} else {
    $res = 0;
}
if ($res == 0) {
    open (PWFILE, ">>$pwfile") || die "Could not open $pwfile!\n";

    print "Enter password: ";
    $pwd1 = <STDIN>;
    print "Re-enter password: ";
    $pwd2 = <STDIN>;

    if ($pwd1 ne $pwd2) {
        print "Error: passwords do not match\n";
        &usage;
        exit 1;
    }

    if ($pwd1 =~ /\n/) {
        chop $pwd1;
    }

    # Encrypt the user's password

    # First, generate the salt

    srand;
    $salt = rand(65535);
    $saltc[0] = $salt & 077;
    $saltc[1] = ($salt >> 6) & 077;

    for ($i = 0; $i < 2; $i++) {
        $c = $saltc[$i] + ord('.');
        $c += 7 if ($c > ord('9'));
        $c += 6 if ($c > ord('Z'));
        $saltc[$i] = $c;
    }

    $pass=(crypt($pwd1,$salt));

    # Open the .htpasswd file for appending and add new user

    print PWFILE "$username:$pass\n";

    close(PWFILE);
```

```
    } else {
        print "Error: user already exists in password file!\n";
        print "You'll have to delete their entry manually, then retry.\n";
        &usage;
        exit 1;
    }

sub usage {
    return 0;
    print "htpasswd.pl\n";
    print "Usage:\n";
    print "htpasswd -c password_filename username\n";
    print "\nThis program is a simple clone of htpasswd.\n";
}
```

You can gut the code in this simple example and turn it into a component of a CGI script that adds usernames and passwords to a password file. The other half of the coin is a script that adds the user to the *.htpasswd* file. This entails:

● reading the *.htpasswd* file into a Perl array

● finding the section listing required authorizations

● inserting a line of the form `require` *username*

● writing the *.htpasswd* file back out again

The advantage of using a user-registration script like this is that you get additional information about who is using your site (if your users are honest); when users log on and register, their authorizations are added to the HTTP headers supplied when they access your site, so you can see who is doing what. See, for example:

`http://www.wired.com/` or `http://www.newscientist.com/`

The disadvantage of using HTACCESS: seeing that official-looking password entry dialogue box in your browser can lull you into a false sense of security. As the precise implementation of such a registration script varies considerably with the application, no full example is given here.

What is cryptography?

Cryptography is the science of convoluting messages in such a way that they can be retrieved by an authorized recipient, but not by a third party. In general, encryption techniques rely on applying a mathematical transformation to a message (the plaintext), to generate an output (the cyphertext) that appears to be random. Some 'key' data is convoluted with the plaintext by the encryption program; without the correct key, the decryption program, when applied to the cyphertext, will be unable to retrieve the message.

For example, a modern equivalent of Caesar's letter substitution cypher goes like this:

> Use a number between 1 and 127 as the key. For each letter in the plaintext, take its position in the ASCII collating sequence. Add the key to the number of the letter; if the result is greater than 127, subtract 127. The resulting number is the ASCII letter to use in the cyphertext. To decrypt the message, subtract the key from the value of the cyphertext character; if the result is negative, add 127.

There are only 127 possible keys to this cypher, so a computer with a dictionary can rapidly scan the entire key space. Furthermore, the same key is used for each letter in the message, so as soon as it is found the entire message becomes readable.

It is possible to encrypt a message using a different key for every character. A mechanism of this sort, using a non-repeating random key (a Vernam cypher, or 'one-time pad') is provably uncrackable (if the keys are truly random) because there is no repeating pattern to follow; you can break the cypher for one character, but it provides no clue to the cypher for the next character, and no information to tell you that you have succeeded. The problem with using a one-time pad is that it loses its value if it is reused, so it's necessary to carry a huge pad of keys around wherever you expect to receive a message. And in real use, cyphers are most vulnerable at the point where keys are exchanged. If a listener can get a copy of the keys, all communications using them are compromised. The ideal cypher is one which allows you to encrypt a message to someone without knowing the key which enables you to decode it.

During the 1970s a number of (non-defence employed) scientists became interested in the field. One mathematician, Whitfield Diffie, worked out that it was possible to produce an encryption algorithm that uses two keys. The two keys have the property that a message encrypted with one key can only be decrypted using the other. Therefore, in use, the owner of a pair of keys publishes one key (the public key), and keeps the other private (the private key). Anyone with the public key can then encrypt a message that only they can decrypt.

The result is that two parties can exchange encrypted messages even if they had not previously planned to do so. Each party publishes its public key, keeping its private key confidential. Party A takes its plaintext message, encrypts it with its private key, then decrypts it with B's public key. Party A then sends the (thoroughly scrambled) message to party B. Party B encrypts the message with its own private key (reversing the second transformation A put the message through), then decrypts it with A's public key (reversing the first transformation).

The result is that neither A nor B (Alice and Bob, as they're traditionally known in cryptography circles) need disclose their private key, in order to set up a secure communications channel. However, it is not possible to decrypt the message without knowing at least one private key. So if the encryption algorithm has a large number of possible keys, it is impossible to break a public key transmission without access to privileged information.

Breaking a cypher requires several bits of information. A knowledge of the algorithm is vital; trying to decrypt a public key message as if it's a substitution cypher is not going to work. A knowledge of the key helps; failing that, some guesses at 'commonly used' or insecure keys can go a long way. Keys are a potential weak point. Like passwords, they are frequently chosen by the system's users; and also like passwords, they are frequently chosen naively. One famous paper co-authored by Robert T. Morris (later to become the NSA's chief scientist) demonstrated that around 30% of all passwords on a large UNIX system where the users were naive about their choice of password could be guessed using a chosen plaintext attack. (A chosen plaintext attack is one where the algorithm is known, and an attempt is made to deduce the key by encrypting various plaintexts likely to occur in a message and comparing them with a sample encrypted message. If a match is found, then the key can be applied to the entire message; this is particularly useful because many messages contain fairly long strings of repeating text that can be chosen as targets.)

The main commercial cryptosystem approved for commercial use is the DES (Data Encryption Standard) system. The NSA approved this in the 1970s, and it is now known to be vulnerable to chosen plaintext attacks mounted using custom-engineered hardware. DES uses a 56-bit key, which led to some controversy over allegations that NSA had approved only it because they knew they could crack it, and it is not a public-key cryptosystem.

More recently, the RSA (Rivest–Shamir–Adelman) cryptosystem has come into use. RSA is a public-key system and is considered sensitive by NSA and is subject to NIST export controls, even though the algorithm has been published and RSA programs are available virtually everywhere in the world. RSA have patented the algorithm in the United States, and PKP Inc. license users. Zimmerman's PGP provides a secure hybrid RSA/IDEA/MD5 cryptosystem, and is becoming a de facto standard for encrypted email on the Internet.

For further details, see Schneier (1994).

Cryptographic systems on the web

In general, the best way to minimize the risk of data on the Internet being intercepted is to encrypt it. Encryption can be applied at several levels:

Application level

The applications that communicate over the network are encryption-aware. For example, a standard exists for Privacy Enhanced Mail (PEM) using the MIME message protocol; it requires the mail agents to be aware of encrypted data types, and either to decode and encode messages, or to pass the plaintext of any messages through an encryption engine before transmitting or after receiving them.

Data level

The applications are unaware of encryption, but the contents of messages sent by them are nevertheless encrypted. The data is encrypted before being passed to the network stack by the transmitting application; at the receiving end it is decrypted before being passed to the receiving application. (This might be the case in an email system where, for example, PGP is used to encrypt a message which is then sent as if it is cleartext by the mailer; the recipient then has to run PGP to decrypt whatever was sent.)

Protocol level

The applications that use the network are unaware of encryption – but the network itself is encrypted, using some encryption technique that scrambles the contents of packets.

Two main commercial proposals for encrypted HTTP have surfaced. The first is the Secure Sockets Layer (SSL), from Netscape Communications Corporation (http://home.mcom.com/). In an SSL transaction, a TCP/IP socket is established and the two systems negotiate a secure transaction (using each other's public key to encrypt data that only the other system can decrypt). HTTP requests are then encrypted, punted across from the client to the server, decrypted and acted upon. This is an example of a protocol-level encryption method.

A major problem with SSL is its key length. The security of any public key cryptosystem is related to its key length – but nearly exponentially, a 64-bit key is something like 2^{24} times as secure as a 40-bit key (16.7 million times).

The version of SSL approved for US domestic use has a 128-bit key, which is adequate for most current purposes. But the export-approved version is limited to a 40-bit key. In mid-1995, scientists using a network of 120 workstations succeeded in breaking a 40-bit SSL-encrypted message in 9 hours. This may sound unimpressive, but given the thousandfold improvement in performance in computing that takes place every decade, it implies that in ten years' time a single workstation will be able to crack SSL messages at the rate of one an hour. Given that most people don't change their credit card accounts that often, it is not inconceivable that very patient criminals are saving up TCP/IP packets for a rainy day. 128-bit SSL messages are unlikely to give way for a while to come; but this should be taken as a warning – encryption doesn't buy you a safe to keep your data in, it buys you a time lock.

(Additionally, in October 1995 some enterprising programmers discovered a hole in Netscape 1.1's security algorithm which enabled them, in the worst case, to crack SSL packets in *30 seconds* on a single workstation. However, it should be emphasized that this bug has since been fixed, and Netscape Communications Corporation is apparently taking a tougher line on cryptographic security in their new releases.)

The second proposal is SHTTP, Secure-HTTP, from EIT (Enterprise Integration Technologies: `http://www.eit.com/`). SHTTP adds encryption to the HTTP protocol; the TCP/IP packets may be unencrypted, but the data contained in them has been encoded by the applications at either end of the socket. (Basically, SHTTP adds encryption options to the HTTP request, using the MIME/PEM mechanisms.) This is an example of an application-level encryption method.

A third non-commercial proposal exists. This mechanism is supported by the NCSA HTTP daemon and NCSA Mosaic 2.2 (and up), and was designed by Rob McCool of NCSA; see:

```
http://hoohoo.ncsa.uiuc.edu/~robm/sg.html
```

for more information. Both pieces of software invoke the external PGP or RIPEM encryption engines on files that are to be passed in an encrypted form. The actual method is a variant on GET that adds extra `Authorization:` and `Content-type:` lines to the request (to specify the user whose public key should be used to decode the request, and the encryption method to use). The response is encrypted, using the same content-type and public key as the request. This is effectively a data-level encryption mechanism; neither the protocol nor the underlying network is aware of the encryption, which is built in as a local extension to the software.

In principle, because these methods all work at different levels there is no reason why they cannot be combined. All of them have been proposed to the World Wide Web Organization or the Internet Engineering Task Force (IETF) as proposed draft standards for encrypted transfer of information over the Internet. All of them are supported by one or more browsers and servers. And the standards for each of them are public, because even the ones originating with commercial bodies were drafted with full awareness that the HTTP standard for security can only succeed if everyone adopts it.

As of the time of writing, it looks as if SSL has a lead – if only because it is built into the popular Netscape browser, and servers that support it are

Example PEM transaction in NCSA HTTPD

```
GET / HTTP/1.0
Authorization: PEM entity="charlie@antipope.demon.co.uk"
Content-type: application/x-www-pem-request
--- BEGIN PRIVACY-ENHANCED MESSAGE ---
this is the encrypted HTTP request
--- END PRIVACY-ENHANCED MESSAGE ---
Server:
HTTP/1.0 200 OK
Content-type: application/x-www-pem-reply
--- BEGIN PRIVACY-ENHANCED MESSAGE ---
this is the encrypted HTTP response
--- END PRIVACY-ENHANCED MESSAGE ---
```

already being used by various commercial outfits (including Mastercard). However, by the time you hold this book in your hands, the situation may have changed completely.

Encryption is a politically sensitive issue (the United States has strong controls over exports of any encryption technology, no matter how trivial), and this has affected the application of authentication and security to the web. For example, the Apache web server included hooks for external encryption programs (as for NCSA HTTPD) up to release 0.63 – at which point the security services in the United States warned the Apache group that it would be in violation of the ITAR regulations if it left crypto hooks in software that was available for export. (Patches to reinstate the encryption hooks in Apache are developed in Europe, where the legislative framework is different.)

Until there is some clarification of the legal position of cryptography, both in domestic and international commerce over the Internet, it is unwise to make any assumptions about the security of the web (or about the most appropriate way to conduct financial transactions over the Internet).

Commerce on the web

The world wide web is already proving itself to be a powerful commercial medium. However, its use is not without pitfalls. Firstly, it is not a centralized broadcasting system (like television or radio). It is not a capital-intensive publishing system; there is no paper and no printing plant involved in producing a book or magazine over the web. Distribution is also a contentious issue. On the one hand, it holds immense promise for information providers to reach out and touch their audiences directly, without any intervening production and distribution chain. The cost of setting up a web publishing operation is low; about a thousand pounds' worth of computer equipment, some free software and an Internet connection. A 64 kb leased line in the United Kingdom costs £1000 to install, then £500 per month; in New York, a 1.5 Mb/s T1 line can be had for $800 a month. Alternatively, space on a web server can be hired by the megabyte. Never before has it been so cheap to reach a mass audience.

On the other hand, the lack of intermediate stages between producers and consumers may be seen as reducing the number of checks on production – mere publication is no longer any kind of guarantee of quality. When you step into a bookshop today, you have an unwritten assurance that everything on the shelves has been accepted as being of publishable quality by numerous people: editors, technical reviewers, marketing and sales experts, distributors and book buyers. This is because it is quite expensive to edit, typeset, print and distribute a book. Web publishing costs are an order of magnitude lower, and the potential audience on the web an order of magnitude larger (or more, depending on the bandwidth your server can accommodate).

There are several aspects to web commerce, each of which could fill a book the size of this one. The web can be used to publish directly existing media, such as books or magazines. Subscription media are especially interesting; HTML 3.0 has features, such as support for text flow around graphics, that make it more suitable for the composition of visually attractive material. The web can also be used to provide sales access to hardcopy books; for example, by hosting chapters or outlines along with an automatic order form.

In fact, the web can be seen as a direct replacement for any hardcopy publication mechanism, subject to one proviso: it is virtually impossible to prevent a user from duplicating what they are reading. In conventional publishing, the author's copyright is effectively enforced by the physical difficulty of duplicating a book or magazine. People don't pirate paperback novels because the photocopying bill would exceed the cost of buying an extra copy. The web comes with no such guarantee.

The web can also be used as an advertising, marketing, and sales tool – but it is in these areas that its innovative features render it most questionable. Conventional advertising technologies are costly, and assume that the reader will passively assimilate the message. A full-page spread in a magazine is there whether you want to see it or not. A television advert produces an unavoidable interruption in the program it is embedded in. Such adverts attempt to sway your judgement by presenting an impression of the product that will make you pay more attention to it when you see it in the flesh.

However, the web consumer is not passive. If you are browsing the web and come to a page consisting entirely of adverts, it is quite easy to ignore it or navigate around it. There is no guarantee that pretty images will be rendered as intended on a reader's browser – the reader may well have switched off image loading in the interests of reading speed. And the underlying assumption that the reader can't act on the advert immediately is also broken, for by adding a form, you can solicit direct feedback or even an order.

Preliminary attempts to use the web for advertising have run across an interesting insight; the web is more like a classified advertisement medium than a broadcast one. People who want to see your product will use the web indices to find you, wherever you are: people who have never heard of you will probably exercise their power to ignore you however loudly you shout. Thus, a workable strategy appears to be to provide some valuable information for free, and to use the public 'reputation' this gains to sell some extra information that extends the service. For example, a magazine might be published on the web, but paying subscribers might gain access to the editorial wire feeds and advance copy not available to the general public.

Some economic estimates of the impact of the web on marketing have already been made; see, for example, the Vanderbilt college web server for computer mediated commerce (`http://colette.ogsm.vanderbilt.edu`), or the large list of electronic commerce resources maintained by Thomas Ho (at `http://biomed.nus.sg/people/commmenu.html`). The economist Arnold Kling has opined that unlike conventional advertising media, the web is an active substitute for sales people; as a consequence, it is far more cost-effective than other advertising mechanisms (if used appropriately). Indeed, it is so useful for information providers that it will tend to reduce the ratio of marketing costs to production costs, radically change the costs of entering a new market (to the extent that such costs are defined by marketing and sales rather than by design), and ultimately allow the consumers to participate in the design of products to an unprecedented degree. Most importantly, the web is not capital-intensive; the efficient economic use of the web depends on marketing and information costs.

Digital shopping

The economic future of the web hinges upon the ability to transfer money. If you can't pay for something, nobody can sell it to you. Unencrypted transfer of credit information over the net is widely considered to be undesirable. It is unsafe because network packets are vulnerable to interception as they cross from one network to another; it is relatively easy to monitor streams of packets destined for a site or sites, and scan them for credit card-like numbers. No real economic growth is likely without either encrypted transactions, or the use of out-of-band financial arrangements.

Out-of-band arrangements make commerce on the net possible without encryption. In a nutshell, if you wish to establish an account with somebody selling goods via the Internet, you fax, telephone or mail them your credit and address details. Once the account is set up, you can buy goods to your heart's content, but they will only be invoiced and delivered as specified in the account setup. Thus, to actually compromise the transaction, a hacker would not only have to intercept your TCP/IP packets, but would also have to tap your phone and intercept your mail at the same time. The downside of this mechanism is that it is inconvenient; every vendor needs a separate account, you can't do everything through the same medium, and it's generally inelegant.

To put together such a system you need to:

- Set up a telephone line where user credit card account details can be registered. (This includes registering as a credit merchant with the main credit card companies.)

- Construct a web site.

The web site is largely open to the public, but contains an area which includes:

- An inventory of your items for sale (preferably in the form of a database that can be updated regularly, rather than as separate HTML files).

- A contact form, to let people mail you questions.

- A registration form, to request a new account.

- A 'shopping cart' mechanism.

The registration form takes a new customer's details and forwards them to you. How you process the information is down to your business.

The inventory database is typically accessed via a search form and a CGI script. The script passes queries entered in the search form back to a database (such as mSQL, FoxPro or Oracle), which retrieves all matching items; the script then formats the items as a neat report, along with 'add to shopping card' buttons for each item. Typically, the database stores information such as unit ID number, cost, number in stock, a brief description and any other relevent information; using a form-based front-end to such databases works quite well insofar as it lets the customers carry out database searches with keys restricted to appropriate values, and structures the information they see in a uniform manner.

The 'shopping cart' is a a customer record (probably stored as a data file on the server). Typically, shopping cart systems are integrated in the search system; the search script returns a list of items, and clicking a link next to an item adds it to the customer's record.

On finishing shopping, the customer has an option to send an order. This usually brings up a form containing the shopping cart, along with a subtotal and options to allow the customer to edit it and correct any errors. At that point, the customer can then press an 'Order' button, and send the order in to you, the retailer. From there on in, it's your business how you deal with the order.

There is no law that says that you can't take credit card details at this time, in this way, although it's inadvisable to pass unencrypted credit information over the net; likewise, you don't *have* to use HTACCESS to restrict access to the final order form, but it helps to reduce the risk of fraud.

It's not really possible to provide a general-purpose online shopping system in this book. Different businesses have different requirements: a personnel agency, for example, may use something very similar to a shopping system to provide CVs to client companies, but will look totally different to potential employees. A bookshop will have completely different structural requirements to a car parts vendor, or a wine merchant.

Digital cash

The one overwhelming problem with shopping cart systems like the one described above is that, as described, you still need a human being to set up account details over the phone – or risk taking credit card details via the net.

A more sensible mechanism would be the use of encrypted HTTP to allow you to send your credit details to a vendor electronically, without fear of being tapped. This is convenient insofar as it is equivalent to the telephone/postal credit clearing currently available. The disadvantage all such mechanisms have is that fraud is too easy; to steal goods, all you need is a stolen credit card and a bit of information about its owner. (Needless to say, such information is available for a small fee from any credit information bureau, and some are already on the net.)

Digital cash is an interesting proposition that, if implemented, would overcome these problems. The idea is to produce a digital token equivalent to cash money, that can be transferred from person to person but used only once. Developed by Professor David Chaum, it is under trial (see http://www.digicash.com/ for details; see also *Scientific American* (1994) and Schneier (1994)). Other schemes based on the same general premise exist; for example, Mondex, currently on trial as a general-purpose digital cash system in Swindon, United Kingdom.

If you are a consumer, you normally have an account with a bank. In the case of digital cash, your bank is on the Internet. You ask them to debit your account for, say, 50 dollars, and send you some digital cash tokens. The bank debits your account, and issues some (unique, cryptographically signed) tokens.

Suppose you now want to spend the cash tokens with some retailer. You pass them to the retailer, who forwards them to the bank for deposit. When they arrive at the bank, the bank deposits money into the retailer's account – as long as tokens bearing the same unique digital signature have not already been deposited.

A mechanism is built into the digital cash exchange protocol that ensures the honesty of all participants in the exchange; if either the customer, or the merchant, attempts to cash the token twice, the bank can not only detect this, but can also determine the identity of the fraudster. (The protocol for this process is discussed in detail in Schneier (1994).)

The point about this transaction is that the tokens retain only limited information about where they've been. They are signed by the bank, and partial (encrypted) information about the drawer of the cheque and the merchant who cashes it are added, but no further information about their audit trail is available. In particular, it is not possible to deduce who the drawer was, unless they try to use the same token twice (in which case the bank and the merchant, in collaboration, can work out who is attempting to defraud them). In this way, digital cash ensures anonymity and does away with the requirement for a secure HTTP server. The downside is that digital cash tokens are equivalent to real money; if you lose them, they're gone for good.

Some of the possible consequences of widespread use of digital cash are quite hair-raising. An information worker can in principle be paid anywhere in the world. Today, governments rely on bank transaction information to validate income tax bills. But what if you are paid in anonymous digital cash? What if you keep your cash in a computer in the Cayman Islands? The government will be able to tax you on the basis of physical goods you buy, but your informational needs will be paid for from outside the country, by anonymous means, and your income will not show up in the bank. Such tax evasion schemes are today relatively rare, but just as the net is providing individuals with marketing and information acquisition tools that were formerly the domain of large organizations, digital cash could provide everybody with the means to avoid income taxation effectively. (Of course, this does not mean that governments will fall as their tax base evaporates. It is far more likely that as the trend becomes apparent, the burden of taxation will shift towards sales taxes imposed on the physical necessities of life – food and clothing. The social implications of such changes lie outside the scope of this chapter.)

Copyright

Copyright is (loosely) the right of authors to determine the publication of work that they created. Until relatively recently, the copyright mechanism varied between countries; under the terms of the Berne Convention the rights have become regularized internationally, and a work copyrighted in one signatory country is considered to be copyrighted in all of them. (In the United Kingdom, copyright subsists in a work automatically, unless it is specifically assigned to a third party or it was created for an employer under the terms of an employment contract.)

However, the whole notion of copyright is based on the classical assumption that duplication or production of a work is a costly exercise. Thus, as long as authors had the legal right to demand compensation for any publication of their work, no further protection was needed.

The Web, and the Internet in general, make a mockery of such assumptions. The cost of data storage is tending towards $250 per gigabyte (during 1995); the cost of storing, say, a novel (as HTML) is thus of the order of 25 cents. This is lower than the marginal cost of printing an extra copy in a print run, and far lower than the cost of photocopying an illicit duplicate. Piracy is therefore cheap; the expense lies in the bandwidth required to transmit information, rather than its storage.

But that's not all. If a publication is accessible over the Internet, you don't need to store it locally. All you need is a link to it from another document, that includes it in the current one when it is formatted. (Such links are a part of the HTML 3.0 specification; in effect, the text is sourced in – rather like an inline image. Alternatively, you can break with the standards and use a Netscape 2.0 Frameset.) Password-based authentication is no guarantee that a copy of the work will not be leaked; someone with permission to read the file might accidentally disclose their password. Alternatively, if they find it irritating to keep typing the password they might splice it into a URL in a page of their own, so they can read the document at will – not realizing that everyone else on the Web could be reading over their shoulder.

Then there is the issue of 'fair usage'. Most copyright laws make allowance for quotations from copyrighted works to be used without the payment of a royalty, as long as the usage is for some fair purpose, such as a review. However, this presupposes that the work being quoted is reprinted. What if it simply exists somewhere, on the web? That is, does a URL pointing to it constitute a quotation, which mu st be considered for the 'fair usage' definition, or is the URL simply a piece of another document (such as a footnote referring to the document by name)? What if the URL takes the form of a source directive that sources part of the document into the URL owner's file?

URIs are not explicitly addressed by contemporary copyright law, and are likely to cause a legal headache or two in the near future. For example, suppose I am writing a web page, and want to include some graphics in it. I happen to like a logo used by, say, the Corporate Corporation (whoever they may be), and include an <IMG SRC> tag in my file. The Corporate Corporation asserts copyright control over its logo, and its use, and if I made a copy of it I would be breaking the law. But I am not making a copy of it – only my readers are making a copy of it! Furthermore, they are doing so unintentionally – and while this is technically a violation of the law on their part, it would be a harsh judge indeed who penalized them for it.

As for copying, it is unlikely that any easy way to prevent it will come along. It is possible to fingerprint all downloaded files uniquely, using steganographic techniques. This will not prevent their duplication, but will permit identification of the source of the leak; a partial palliative measure that may deter the worst violations.

Steganography is the art of concealing information by masking it into other, innocuous data. For example, suppose I wish to conceal a text file. I take a colour GIF image, or some other image format that supports a large number of colour bits per pixel, ideally 24-bit colour. (JPEG is unsuitable for this process, because it is a 'lossy' compression technique.) I take each byte of my hidden text, split it into eight bits, and assign each bit to the least significant bit of one pixel. Thus, 8 pixels (in a 24-bit colour image) will contain the information that makes up my single byte. Because 24-bit pixels can represent any one of 16.7 million colour shades, the effect on the colour of the image will be undetectable without the aid of software. However, my 1024×768 pixel image can store 98 kb of concealed information (such as a serial number, copyright declaration and so on). A recipient of this image who does not know which particular bits to extract will be unable to decode this information, or even detect it – but with the aid of appropriate decoding software, the steganographically concealed data can be recovered even after copying.

The only way to defeat steganographic fingerprinting is to inject an element of random noise into the file. While this might be acceptable in some image files, it certainly won't work on other file types such as text. You can steganographically tag HTML by adding space characters or newlines randomly – characters that are discarded during the formatting and viewing process. An insufficiently paranoid thief might well not bother writing a filter to insert extra spaces randomly, thus leaving some particularly well-hidden document meta-information to identify the miscreant who leaked the copyrighted material to the net.

An alternative mechanism can be envisaged, if Java, Safe Tcl, or another 'trustworthy' language for executing software over the net achieves ubiquity. It would be possible to distribute a software agent that communicates with your local server via a cryptographically secure channel and handles the display of information that you want to distribute, in such a way that the decrypted plaintext cannot be saved by the reader. The text could then be charged for on a pay-per-view basis, with the software agent refusing to decrypt it unless digital cash was paid into the owner's account. However, all such systems are bound to incite crackers to attempt to subvert the software – and if nothing else, such schemes are inimical to the whole purpose of the Web (which is to promote the widest possible sharing of information, not its rationing and restriction).

In the future one can envisage copyright-enforcement knowbots roving the web, equipped with steganographic signatures, on a mission to hunt down and identify illicit document copies. But that scenario still lies some time hence. A year ago, I would have pegged it as 'not in this century'. Today, I pause for thought ... maybe in 1996? The exponential growth of the web has telescoped the timescale for many developments in computing, to such an extent that science fiction novels written during the 1980s, predicting a far-future cyberspace, are set to be realized within the next five to ten years.

10

THE FUTURE OF THE WEB

• • • •

In the preceding chapters we've looked at the basic protocols of the world wide web, at the aspects of web design, the anatomy of knowbots, and some issues associated with running a server. In this chapter, I'm going to extrapolate five to ten years into the future and link the current developments into the context of the web's overall development.

There are several technological factors governing the development of the web over the next decade. At the very outset, it's necessary to be clear about one point: technological determinism, the assumption that because something is possible it will happen, is a dangerous trap. For example, hypertext, in the form associated with the world wide web, was first written about by Ted Nelson in the early 1960s. For years, Nelson promoted his Xanadu system as a vision of information sharing. (At one stage, in the late 1980s and early 1990s, with backing from AutoDesk, it looked as if a Xanadu product would reach the market.) Today the Xanadu vision has been co-opted by the world wide web. In some respects, the web is inferior: it suffers from problems such as the conflation of links and content, the unidirectional nature of links, the inability to handle any kind of entity smaller than a file effectively, and a limited range of presentation methods. Nevertheless, the web zoomed into existence almost overnight, while Xanadu remained a speculative adventure for twenty years.

Three underlying trends

The history of technology is littered with bogus predictions of a radiant future that never came to pass. On the other hand, the landscape of computing is dotted with isolated instances of unpredictable success: two guys in a garage who went on to become Hewlett-Packard, or Apple Computers, or Microsoft. It is impossible (indeed, inappropriate) to attempt to predict the winners in the world wide web industry. However, by studying the practical underpinnings of the web it might be possible to get some idea of how they will earn their billions. Here are the three laws that govern the technical base on which the web is built.

Moore's law

In the beginning, there was Moore's law – Gordon Moore, founder and CEO of Intel. Intel, a spin-off of Fairchild Semiconductor, was founded at the end of the 1960s to explore a brave new world: large-scale integrated circuits. Moore placed his money on a simple side-effect of the laws of physics. The resistance of an electrical circuit dictates the amount of power it will consume (and emit as heat) at a given voltage. The resistance is a function of the length of the circuit, and the resistivity of the material the circuit is made of. For a circuit made of a given material, if you reduce its path length, you can reduce its resistance. If you reduce its resistance, you reduce its power consumption. One of the main problems with computing equipment, historically, was cooling; the circuit elements were packed so densely that in the 1940s Vannevar Bush (a pioneer of analogue computing) predicted that computers as powerful as today's PCs could never be made – the entire throughput of the Amazon river would be needed to cool them.

By reducing power consumption, more circuits could be crammed onto a piece of silicon. Smaller meant less power meant more complexity – and the usefulness of a microprocessor is roughly related to its complexity, not to the amount of waste heat it radiates. Indeed, if you halve the minimum length of an electronic component on a chip die, you can more or less square the number of components in the product. More subtly: the speed of a computer is related to the time taken for a clock signal to propagate across its circuitry. Light only travels 30 centimetres in a billionth of a second; at the gigahertz speeds of a modern processor you need to have small circuits. Small circuits can switch faster than large ones – and that, in turn, means more powerful chips.

Moore took this into account and formulated his law, which has dominated the hardware industry ever since. In a nutshell, the synergy between reducing size and power consumption and increasing complexity means that processing power doubles every eighteen months. It has done so for the past twenty five years, and will continue to do so until the size of the circuits becomes so small that quantum effects such as electron tunnelling begin to intrude. (At that point, some ten years hence, we can expect new rules to take over and the nature of microprocessor design will undergo a fundamental change.)

The result is evident in the personal computer industry today. Chip design has become a mammoth enterprise – items like the Intel Pentium series chips or the Motorola/IBM/Apple PowerPC architecture have component counts in the three to six million transistor range, while dynamic RAM chips with up to a billion capacitors are under development. Computer production has become standardized as OEMs buy up large runs of common components and bolt them together at the lowest possible price. Indeed, the PC industry today resembles the car industry more than a leading-edge enterprise.

Gilder's law

Historically, computers have been isolated data processing centres connected only by low-bandwidth links. To believe that a 14.4 kbps modem connection to the outside world is proportionate to the processing power of a 40 Mips workstation (like the one this book was written on) is bizarre.

Moore's law now has a rival in terms of its effect on the future of computing hardware. Economist George Gilder has been studying the telecommunications industry for some years; his take on it is enlightening. During the 1980s, large amounts of money were raised through junk bonds on the US money markets. Much of this capital found its way into the growing cable industry. The forcible dismemberment of the Bell company into a multi-tude of competing 'Baby Bells' opened the US telecoms industry wide; at the same time, the telcos were forbidden by statute from competing in the cable TV industry. Thus, a secondary communications network was installed – one capable of conducting medium-bandwidth data straight to the home. A coax-ial cable TV line can carry up to 100 channels, giving it a bandwidth in the hundred megahertz range. Nevertheless, this infrastructure was not being used for networking – just broadcasting.

During the 1980s and 1990s, demand for network bandwidth grew explo-sively. It will continue to grow. The world wide web, for example, makes heavy use of graphics; only the shortage of bandwidth is preventing it from being used extensively for multimedia data, motion video and sound. As we become more aware of our need for network bandwidth, we demand more. And more is available. Firstly, current twisted-pair telephone wires can carry far more data than a modem or even an ISDN line would suggest. ATM (Asynchronous Transfer Mode) networks can cram 1.5 Mbps down such a line over short distances; all that is necessary is a change of circuitry at the local exchange. ATM is a packet-based protocol optimized for voice communica-tions. The ATM packets are only 53 bytes long, smaller than TCP/IP's standard packet size (of the order of 1500 bytes), and ATM networks are designed to route packets to their destination reliably at a sufficiently high speed to sup-port a conversation. The intelligence to route ATM packets is contained in the telco switches, the big computers that today form the core of any telephone exchange. ATM makes the most efficient use of a cable, by using time-division multiplexing; packets from multiple virtual circuits can be routed along the same cable then filtered and diverted to different destinations on the basis of their headers. The cable, meanwhile, is funnelling a deluge of data along at peak speed – typically two to three gigahertz. Because of this vast surplus of bandwidth, ATM is expected to replace Ethernet (and related packet protocols) as the low-level networking mechanism of choice within ten to fifteen years. Quite simply, an Ethernet (which saturates at 10 Mbps) cannot compete with a medium that can cram 1.5 Mbps down a telephone wire, and up to 3 Gbps down a proper network cable.

However, ATM is by no means the end of the story. Time-division multiplexing relies on the use of fixed frequency pulses, divided up into bits which can be assigned to packets. Optical fibre can support an alternative mechanism, wavelength-division multiplexing; it is transparent to a spectrum of available frequencies of light, each of which can be used to carry information. Estimates suggest that the true bandwidth of a single optical fibre is higher than 2 Tbps – two thousand gigabits per second. As modern cable TV infrastructure brings optical fibre line heads to the kerb, it is possible to consider that the massive bandwidth available with wavelength-division multiplexing will become available for network communications within ten to twenty years.

A corollary of wavelength-division multiplexing is that complex central switches and the ATM networks they support become obsolescent; the bandwidth of a dumb, dark fibre is so huge that simple Ethernet-like protocols (using some equivalent of exponential backoff to handle packet collisions) will take over. The intelligence in the network will diffuse out from the central switches to the peripheral components that are linked to the net by connections between a thousand and a million times as fast as today's T1 lines.

Gilder summarizes these trends in a new law of his own, which parallels Moore's law: available bandwidth will double every twelve months, from now on, right through the early years of the twenty-first century.

Brook's law

The final piece of the jigsaw was first described in public by Fred Brooks, a senior software engineer at IBM, in his classic book *The Mythical Man-Month* (1975). This book describes in detail the software crisis, as experienced by IBM during the development of OS/360, their second major modern operating system. The software crisis has become an ongoing state of emergency; it has existed in one form or another for the past thirty years.

Approximately thirty years ago it became clear that the cost of producing software was escallating relative to the cost of producing new, faster computers. That is, although hardware components were modular, and could in principle increase in power exponentially, software proved hard to maintain; the larger the program, the more effort it took to keep the thing working. Initially, the problem was ascribed to bad programming technique and a lack of formal methodologies for structuring and controlling the organization of source code. Spaghetti programming, in which the logical flow of control was obscured by endless jumps and GOTOs, was identified as one culprit. The cure – modular, structured programming – was prated as a panacea over the next fifteen years; meanwhile, the nascent discipline of software engineering began to coalesce, moving the management of large programming efforts out of the field of art and into the area of an engineering discipline. Powerful operating systems and modern structured languages, coupled with software engineering methodologies, began to improve programmer efficiency. The use of programs as building blocks (typical of operating systems such as UNIX) allowed programmers to work at a new level of abstraction.

However, the underlying problem remained, and if anything it worsened. Source code production is generally not helped by throwing extra programmers at a project halfway through it; it is a function of the native ability of the programmers, coupled with the efficiency of their communications and tools. Structured programming was not a magic bullet; the software never quite succeeded in keeping pace with the dizzyingly accelerating rate of hardware innovation dictated by Moore's law. Thus, the late 1980s saw powerful 80386-based PCs – as powerful as a serious mainframe in the early 1970s – running an operating system as primitive as MS-DOS (described by some disgusted hackers as a glorified boot-loader).

During the 1980s and early 1990s, object-oriented programming gained ground as another possible panacea. However, the severity of the software crisis is indicated by the fact that typical mid-1990s operating system projects are subject to 100% time overruns. Windows Chicago, announced in 1993, mutated into Windows 95 – it finally shipped in autumn of that year. SCO Open Desktop 5.0 (released May 1995) was originally due to ship in 1993. And Apple Computer's Copeland project (due early 1995) slipped into 1996. None of these are isolated failings of an individual company; rather, they reflect the staggering complexity of modern software environments. If one line of source code in a virtual machine is taken as being equivalent to a nut, bolt or piece of bent metal in a physical machine, then on the basis of component counts these software projects are twice as complex as the Space Shuttle. (Having spent nearly four years working on one such huge software project, I am inclined to believe this metaphor.)

Indeed, the burgeoning complexity of a contemporary software project is such that, as the component count increases linearly, the complexity of maintaining it increases geometrically. Brook noticed this, and gave his name to a handful of 'laws' (early descriptive software engineering metrics) that described the phenomenon. Most notably, he discovered that the fastest way to make the delivery date of an overdue software project slip out further was to add programmers to the project. (The experienced engineers spent so much time briefing the newcomers that they became less productive, while the newcomers thrashed about ineffectually, trying to learn the ropes.)

Object orientation is being promoted as the cure-all for the current generation of operating system woes; a new generation of object-oriented systems (Apple's Copeland, Microsoft's Cairo) will replace those old operating blues.

The keystone of this strategy is a standard interface for software objects, to permit chunks of code to connect to and use one another. (Microsoft promotes OLE 2.0; Apple and other companies promote OpenDoc, a superset containing OLE 2.0.) Such objects will be able to intercommunicate over a network, allowing programs on one machine to make use of programs on another machine – a level of binding anticipated in the UNIX and TCP/IP world with RPC, but extending far beyond it in scope.

What they imply about the web

The web is the logical outcome of the collision between Moore's law, Gilder's law and Brook's law. The processors are becoming more powerful exponentially. The bandwidth is increasing even faster, so that within a short period bandwidth will exceed processor resources. Finally, the software resources are totally overwhelmed by this: old systems are bound to be dragged down into obsolescence by the pressure of a hardware and communications environment radically different from the one they were designed for.

Existing operating systems are intended to run on monolithic computers that are connected to the world by tenuous, low-bandwidth connections. Store and forward networks (like UUCP) gave way only slowly to packetized networks (like TCP/IP). TCP/IP itself was designed with the fundamental flaw of a 32-bit address space; while this is due to be fixed by 1997, it might well be too late for a world which, by then, will be wiring up telephones and toasters to the net. Protocols layered on top of TCP/IP (such as HTTP) were written on the initial assumption that relatively few hosts would exist, acting as central data storage repositories, and that their information content would change only slowly. HTTP itself was considered to be a fast, stateless protocol when it was drafted in 1989–90; today it looks long in the tooth, and proposals are under consideration for HTTP 2.0 (an extensible variant) and HTTP-NG, a fast binary protocol proposed as a replacement for HTTP 1.0.

Research by Simon Spero suggests that in a typical transaction HTTP spends more time waiting for data than actually carrying it; the transaction also falls victim to TCP/IP's tendency to carry out a slow start process when initializing a connection, and incurs other overheads by requiring a separate connection for each data object transferred. This has a detrimental effect on performance. His proposed alternative protocol, HTTP-NG, is described in detail in

```
http://info.cern.ch/hypertext/WWW/Protocols/HTTP-NG/http-
ng-arch.html
```

and commented on in

```
http://info.cern.ch/hypertext/WWW/Protocols/HTTP-NG/http-
ng-status.html
```

In a nutshell, HTTP 1.0 starts up a separate connection for every data object. HTTP-NG allows multiple requests to be funnelled across a single connection and serviced asynchronously. The connection is split into layers, with control information going over a control layer; this permits HTTP-NG to multiplex requests. At the same time, an HTTP-NG server should be able to handle HTTP; if by no other method, proxy services should be available (so that an old client that speaks only HTTP 1.0 can send requests to a proxy, which fetches the objects using HTTP-NG).

NTTP-NG will probably intersect with the proposed TCP/IP replacements, which extend the TCP/IP address space for the foreseeable future. At the same time, these protocols will probably sit on top of the new generation of object-oriented operating systems that run on almost unimaginably powerful computers. (A personal digital assistant, not unlike an Apple Newton Messagepad in size and weight, connected to the net by a wireless T1 link and running a web browser, while having only a modest 1 Gb or so of local storage, is quite likely to arrive within five to ten years. Oh, and it should be able to act as a cellular telephone and a television remote control, too.)

However, the software infrastructure of the web is almost irrelevant in comparison with the flood of data coming down the channel of increasing bandwidth. Using fast stateless communications protocols and high-bandwidth line-heads, computers will tend to act as information storage and browsing points at the periphery of the web. Today, the flood of information coming onto the net promises to make it the richest information source in the world. Even though there is relatively little copyright-controlled material there today, it is likely that the availability of the web will transform our current concept of intellectual property. Legislative changes to recognize the new media are likely within one to three years. If per-usage billing becomes available (possibly using digital cash and encrypted objects to store the data) it will be possible to sell information over the web securely, without fear of copying. Indeed, suppose you have an encrypted object that contains a book. Every time you read it, your web browser must send a digital cash token to the copyright owner. It actually falls inside the copyright owner's interests to encourage you to make copies and give them away!

The use of software objects on the web bears some explanation.

Currently the web is used to transport passive data. However, the web constitutes a general communications mechanism that sits on top of the operating layer of the Internet; in effect it is a general-purpose abstraction that can be used to represent any kind of data we can envisage. Today, server-side scripts are used primarily as 'virtual documents'; they are invoked with some parameters, and return a document (which varies depending on the parameters they were invoked with). However, the web transport mechanism can be extended trivially to encompass the distribution of software objects.

In practice, the use of live software on the web is fraught with issues of trust. A program which migrates from computer to computer, operating wherever it comes to rest, is termed a worm; the Internet has had a very nasty experience with one worm in particular, and is leery about them in general. In 1988, Robert T. Morris Jr. unleashed a worm on the Internet. It targetted a back door in the sendmail binary used on SunOS and used other techniques – mostly debugging hooks which had not been removed from distribution software – to migrate to other BSD UNIX systems. If the worm had fulfilled its design goal, it would have constituted little more than a fascinating experiment. Unfortunately the worm contained a bug. It was intended to check for its own presence on a computer, and fail to run if a copy was already present. In practice, the worm persistently reinfected computer after computer, bringing them to their knees. Indeed, the great Internet worm of 2 November 1988 nearly broke the net. (Arguably, it caused more cumulative downtime than a medium-sized nuclear war. The incident is documented in Stoll (1990), and in a technical paper: RFC 1135, 'The Helminthiasis of the Internet' available from:

```
http://info.internet.isi.edu/in-notes/rfc/files/rfc1135.txt
```

The RTM worm was an experiment that backfired. Future developments involving worms will almost certainly be far better controlled. Worms can actually be extremely useful. For example, a knowbot or spider can be used to probe the web from a central point, but it imposes a heavy load on one processor, and causes a local network 'hot-spot'. A distributed worm could be used to carry out a search; each time the worm arrived at a new, unvisited host, it would spawn a process to go searching for the wanted information, then look for new hosts. (Presumably it would do a better job of not reinfecting already-visited systems than RTM's worm.) However, worms use local processor resources; they are, by definition, alien entities and not to be trusted with access to the system's resources. A worm is potentially much more devastating than a computer virus, because worms spread actively – viruses are merely borne from machine to machine by accident.

No standard protocol yet exists for trusted worms on the web. Such a protocol would have to be extremely heavy on the authentication side (to prevent hackers from using worms as, for example, password-gathering tools). It would also probably require digital cash tokens of some kind. For example, worms might be expected to pay for commercial information before returning it to their owners. Some fairly exotic speculations have been made about the possibility of worms embodying bidding rules, such that they can go forth and bid for services on behalf of their owners. However, such tools still lie a little way off. The most noteworthy point is that Java is designed to support worm-like programs (originating on other computers), providing access control mechanisms to prevent them soaking up local resources, and keeping the guest programs from doing anything disastrous to the local hardware.

Another use of the web that has not escaped notice is that, with the forms facilities provided by HTML 2.0, HTML provides a useful platform for writing remote graphical user interfaces. (That is, the web can provide a front-end for programs running on another computer.) The W3Kit developed by:

```
http://www.geom.umn.edu/docs/W3Kit/W3Kit.html
```

is designed to allow HTML to be used as a GUI by programs written in Objective-C, running on UNIX systems. Information defining the state of Objective-C data structures is embedded in the HTML pages in the form of comments or hidden fields (supported by some extensions to the basic form mechanism). The user makes some change to the state of the HTML form, using the graphical widgets embedded in it; the GET or POST request then sends the modified form (including the Objective-C meta-information) back to a server. The server interprets the objects and executes the program they embody. The program gives rise to a new HTML file, containing more shrink-wrapped objects ... in this way, the GUI contains the state information required by the program, which is executed on the server's host.

Fundamentally, the development of the web as a GUI for networked, distributed processes, and as a platform for worms and parallel processes, will mark a watershed in the evolution of digital communications. In the 1980s, Sun Microsystems sold their UNIX workstations with the famous slogan 'The network is the computer'. The web, when fully unleashed, will become the operating system; a totally scalable architecture that provides for information retrieval, GUI, and process distribution across the infinitely large, infinitely scalable parallel processing network of the Internet. Sun is still following this vision with its promotion of Java as a lightweight programming language designed to suit migratory network applications that rove from computer to computer. One of the functions of Java is to provide 'active' GUI facilities in web pages – small programs which, when executed, provide a user interface to some server-side program – but, more to the point, Java's biggest effect is to distribute the web, evening up some of the balance in load between clients and servers, while at the same time making it possible to build smaller, more elegant browsers.

It has been suggested that Java may provide the next platform for the web itself: inexpensive 'JavaBooks' – computers consisting of little more than a terminal, a modem and a Java interpreter – could download the browser code they need as the user needs it, leaving the heavy back-end work on servers running database systems such as Oracle and large applications written in (of course) Java. Other versions of this idea take it even further. Java is a small system, by design; likewise, both ROM chips and modem chips are cheap. The logical end-point of the philosophy of turning the client system into a kind of souped-up mainframe terminal for the Internet is the idea of a plug-in 'Internet cartridge' for a powerful contemporary games console (such as a Sega Saturn) which, containing the modem, IP software and Java interpreter, would actually turn a games system into a read-only Internet host.

The web effectively turns the Internet into a single giant computing resource. It is quite possible that, once the bandwidth explosion runs its course, operating systems as we know them today will be displaced by smaller, faster, less self-contained systems.

An operating system for a web-aware world would probably not need a self-contained GUI, let alone something as complex as the X Window system; rather, web rendering would be built into its display interface (using Display Postscript, and a very low-level HDL or SGML–DSSSL interpreter combination). Networking hooks would also be built in at an extremely low level. The filesystem of the operating system would be accessible only via an HTTP server, with a client effectively replacing the GUI. Additional software support (for example, language interpreters or software tools) would be available as plug-in objects (communicating using OpenDoc or Java or a next-generation object protocol), and the whole thing would run with the help of a software license manager and digital cash reserve manager that would govern access to facilities and services on a pay-per-use basis. (I might as well bite the bullet and call it a Bank Manager.) For example, when sending out remote agents to find some web resource, an agent-creation manager would connect to the display and help users define their requirements. It would then present these to the Bank Manager and negotiate the transfer of digital cash tokens. The agents, possibly written in Java, would then be distributed to neighbouring computers via the filesystem server – which would see other web servers as mere extensions of its own personal file space.

Using the web, you would be able to operate a computer directly on the other side of the world; you could find information anywhere on the Internet; and you could run processes that required vastly more processing power than was available on your own computer by sending out worms armed with the digital cash to pay for the resources they consumed. In this vision, the web would eat the network and the network would dine on the computer, becoming the be-all and end-all of the computing environment. Furthermore, the web would become a lynch-pin in the structure of commerce; virtually all informational transactions would be mediated through it, either by human users searching for useful stuff, or by AI agents equipped with digital cash and search criteria. But there is more to the web than that ...

Entering cyberspace by the back door

In earlier chapters we discussed the plethora of languages used for representing information and meta-information in the web. One of these languages bears further discussion at this stage: VRML, Virtual Reality Modelling Language.

At a Birds of a Feather session held at the spring 1994 World Wide Web conference, Tim Berners-Lee and Dave Raggett discussed possible virtual reality interfaces to the world wide web with interested web developers. Shortly thereafter, the WWW-VRML mailing list was established. To everybody's surprise, the response was staggering; over a thousand people subscribed within weeks. A draft standard for VRML emerged in 1995, and the first VR web browsers are currently available (in early form) from Sun Microsystems and Silicon Graphics; Netscape have announced their intention of supporting VRML in a future release.

VRML is inevitable, important and quite interesting. In the beginning, the Internet came about as a simple distributed data storage mechanism linking computers and allowing them to share information. However, the complex and inaccessible nature of the storage methods made it hard to use; the world wide web was the first successful attempt to impose a general retrieval mechanism on top of the Internet as a whole. However, data on the net is still stored in a rather abstract manner. Entities have names and addresses; you can't see what an entity is just by looking at it, and there is little in the way of memorability about a URL. Human beings don't locate information by memorizing text strings; we tend to work by storing collections of impressions – smell, sound, touch and sight – and associating them with information. A Virtual Reality (VR) environment that tags data with 'visible' attributes, such that entities appear to exist in a space that you can see into, represents the next logical step forward.

Not only that: the web can make VR systems easier to engineer. VR systems attempt to create a model of reality, which is then rendered into a graphical image that the user can see. Using input devices (be they a mouse or a dataglove) the user can change their notional position within the model, and the model is then re-rendered to display the changed perspective. High-end VR systems use twin displays mounted in a helmet to give true three-dimensional visual effects; they track body movements, so that if you turn round, your view of the virtual world swings round with you. At high rendering rates (over 24 frames per second), the virtual world stops jerking around and gives an awesome, rather frightening impression of solidity and motion.

It takes a lot of computing power to generate a VR image. The human eye can handle an input on the order of 100 Mbit/s of data; estimates of the rendering power needed by a graphics processor to create a truly believable virtual environment in real time are of the order of 100 million Gouraud-shaded polygons per second. (See Foley *et al.* (1990), for further details.) However, in a true multi-user VR (such as one based on the Internet) the processing power takes a back seat to the complexity of objects stored in the virtual world. An image of, say, a chair, must be derived from a three-dimensional model of a chair existing in some coordinate space and transformed (using four-dimensional homogeneous matrix transforms) into some specific location in the three-space of the VR. The images that need to be rendered can be restricted to those in line-of-sight, as far as the user is concerned; however, the complexity of a real interactive VR may be huge.

Processors with a few tens of thousands of Mips can provide a decent rendering rate for the user's viewpoint model. This level of performance will be reached by personal computers in the under-$3000 range before the end of the century. But the information necessary to create a multi-user model of reality may be much larger than the information needed to create the viewpoint. The overriding idea of VRML is that the web provides a beautiful platform for distributing objects that can be used to define entities in a shared VR. For example, you might be using a VR simulation of a room with a chair, a painting and a door in it. The painting might be an image file somewhere on the Internet; the chair might be represented by a CAD model at some design bureau; and the door might be a generic piece of 'clip reality' (as opposed to 'clip art') stored on your local computer. In rendering the room, your VR engine would use the web to retrieve definitions for the appropriate objects. Moreover, if you open the door and step outside you might well find yourself in a collection of objects (another room, for example) which are hosted on another computer in the web. No problem: your own system fetches the entities and incorporates them into its model of your location in the universe.

VRML takes a very abstract view of the world. Basically, it is a declarative, object-oriented language for specifying worlds. Objects defined in VRML contain nodes. (A node is some Internet resource: image files, geometry data, transformation rules and so on.) Nodes are connected in a scene graph; the scene graph is a hierarchical structure that describes the relationship between nodes. (Compare this with the document/meta-information split in HTML.) VRML is self-extending; it is possible to define new types of node from within a VRML program. At the time of writing, a draft specification for VRML could be found at:

```
http://vrml.wired.com/
```

and:

```
http://www.eit.com/vrml/
```

By using distributed, standardized objects, it becomes possible to construct a consensual VR with a relatively low investment in design effort. And by so doing, it becomes possible to reify information that has hitherto been difficult to visualize. It also becomes possible to build maps of the information universe that operate at a very high level of abstraction. During the Roman and early mediaeval period (prior to the invention of printing) it was commonplace for educated men to learn various mnemonic techniques that helped them commit to memory long documents. Most such methods worked by the user associating the item or fact with a specific location in some building with which they were intimately familiar; their map of the building would later serve as a map of the contents of their memory. This trick might sound bizarre, but you can test it quite easily. Pick a building or apartment you lived in for over a year, in the relatively recent past. Pick a room in the building, and start listing the contents on paper. (You might be surprised by how much you can remember in this way, by associating the physical location with the associated information.) A VR system helps us rediscover this trick, changing the process of locating information from one of remembering an abstract identification string to one of visual and somatic memory. To deal with the gigantic quantities of information that exist in the human environment, we (arguably) need better interface metaphors, to make the retrieval process more 'natural'. An expansion into cyberspace, via the back door of the world wide web, is on the cards in between one and three years' time, with popular uptake following some time later.

It should come as no surprise to learn that as this book goes to press, some of the big news concerns a VRML browser (from Dimension X, http:// www.dimensionx.com/) written – of course – in Java.

The web as communications engine

In addition to all these mind-bending possibilities, the web can act as an interactive medium for communications. At the time of writing, a draft standard for forms-based file upload to HTTP servers is under discussion. This will permit clients with a conformant forms interface to actively upload a file from their own system to the server. The issue of sending data to a server deserves some consideration; implicit in it is the concept of interactivity and collaboration. Experiments directed at using the web as a basis for collaborative hypertext writing have already begun; in some, the goal is to use the web as a replacement for Usenet news, while in others the object is to use a web server as a replacement for older centralized configuration management programs (such as version control tools like SCCS and RCS).

The possibilities of using the web for two-way communication have not been explored fully. HTTP-NG, with its asynchronous, multiplexed communications could well be extended to support the exchange of real-time video or voice data over fast, ATM-switched networks. To assign a URN to a human being would not be anything new – an almost identical process is used today by the Internet DNS which maps email addresses (such as charlie@antipope. demon.co.uk) to a route through the network of evanescent TCP/IP connections that will reach me. By extension, a personal web-computer (as described in the earlier parts of this chapter) might well provide a handy target for connection attempts from anywhere in the net, allowing a personal digital assistant to act not only as a gateway onto the informational riches of every library in the world, but also as a telephone, voice mail system, collaborative authoring tool and general-purpose everything. (If some recent suggestions about the eventual outcome of domestic connections to the Internet are correct, it might even one day be able to make the tea – certainly there are already coffee pots and cola machines on the Internet!)

The key to the web is to remember that it is a meta-information structure; it maps a URL mechanism onto a variety of sources. Thus, it is effectively infinitely extensible. As George Gilder predicted in the 1980s, the network will in due course eat the computer. And the great simplifying abstraction of the web will, in due course, eat the network.

Finally, one word of caution.

In some industries, the timescale for change is measured in decades; for example, a new aeroplane may be in production for thirty years. In others – cars, for example – the vehicle may be around for about seven years. In computing, a machine is old three years after it is manufactured; and in software it is hopelessly obsolete something between eighteen and thirty-six months later.

The web, however, is a different animal. Right now, the period from novelty to obsolescence is measured in months; an old product is one that is nine months old, and an ancient greybeard in the field has but three years' experience.

So my final word is this: don't be surprised if your wildest speculation comes true next month. And wherever possible, try to keep an open mind. The web is a constantly surprising wave to surf; and we're in for plenty more surprise breakers along the way.

REFERENCES

• • • •

Brooks, F. P. (1975), *The Mythical Man-Month*. Reading MA: Addison-Wesley

Foley, J. D., van Dam, A., Feiner, S. K. and Huges, J. F. (1990). *Computer Graphics: Principles and Practice*. 2nd edn. Reading MA: Addison-Wesley

Schneier, B. (1995). *Applied Cryptography*. 2nd edn New York: Wiley

Schwartz, (1992). *Learning Perl*. Sebastopol CA: O'Reilly

Sedgewick, R. (1988). *Algorithms*. 2nd edn. Reading MA: Addison-Wesley

Stein, L. D. (1996) *How to Set Up and Maintain a World Wide Web Site: The Guide for Information Providers*. Reading MA: Addison-Wesley

Stoll, C. (1990). *The Cuckoo's Egg*. London: The Bodley Head

Wall and Schwartz, 91990). *Programming Perl*. Sebastopol CA; O'Reilly

INDEX

● ● ● ●

web *cont.*
   navigating 157–9
   non-homogeneity 229
   optimizing robot traversal 229
   outlining 169
   portability 177–9
   pruning loops in 228
   robots on 189, 222–3
   simple design 153–6
   size 3, 219–20
   source format 188
   timescale 278
   traversal methods 224
WebForce 170

WebStar 123
well-known ports 53
white space 15
Windows, colour dithering 167
World Wide Web Organization *see* W3O
worm 233, 272
WYSIWYG 10, 18

X 101
Xanadu 3, 7, 265

Yahoo 173, 221

Z39.50 82, 171, 229